The Breast

The Breast

A Cultural and Political History

ANJA ZIMMERMANN

Translated by Nicola Barfoot

polity

Originally published in German as *Brust. Geschichte eines politischen Körperteils* © 2023 Verlag Klaus Wagenbach, Berlin.

This English translation © Polity Press, 2026.

The translation of this book was supported by a grant from the Goethe-Institut.

Polity Press
65 Bridge Street
Cambridge CB2 1UR, UK

Polity Press
111 River Street
Hoboken, NJ 07030, USA

ISBN-13: 978-1-5095-6782-9 – hardback

A catalogue record for this book is available from the British Library.

Library of Congress Control Number: 2025949939

Typeset in 11 on 14pt Warnock Pro
by Fakenham Prepress Solutions, Fakenham, Norfolk NR21 8NL
Printed and bound by CPI Group (UK) Ltd, Croydon

The publisher has used its best endeavours to ensure that the URLs for external websites referred to in this book are correct and active at the time of going to press. However, the publisher has no responsibility for the websites and can make no guarantee that a site will remain live or that the content is or will remain appropriate.

Every effort has been made to trace all copyright holders, but if any have been overlooked the publisher will be pleased to include any necessary credits in any subsequent reprint or edition.

For further information on Polity, visit our website:
politybooks.com

Contents

Figures

Acknowledgements

I want to thank the people who provided the impetus for this project, setting me on the trail of a body part that is interesting simply because of its striking, simultaneous visibility and invisibility in Western cultures. My editor at Wagenbach, Annette Wassermann, had an interest in breasts and, thankfully, a multitude of ideas about how this infinite topic could be turned into a finite book. I'd like to thank Susanne Schüssler for seeing a place for breasts in the catalogue of the Klaus Wagenbach publishing house. I also want to thank Corinna Gathmann for her patient support arranging the text and the illustrations. The participants in my seminar on political elements in art at the University of Oldenburg provided helpful input when it came to the work of artists with a political understanding of their body (and breasts). Martin Cremer's offer to translate Latin quotations where necessary reassured me. Elvira Mienert supplied me with the perfect breast-related memes. And right at the end Iris Carstensen helped me with her customary generosity. Thanks also to Christine Valentin for her help revising the bibliography. The book's remaining shortcomings are all my own.

Thanks to the good will of several artists, I was able to include various illustrations in the German or English editions that would otherwise have been unavailable. For the German edition: huge thanks to Annie Sprinkle for her *Bosom Ballet*. I'm very fortunate to have been able to show Şükran Moral's work. And for the English edition: I'm delighted that Evgenia Tsanana gave me permission to print one of her wonderful photos from her series on breasts. A big thank you to all three! My last thank you – and this has nothing to do with the actual order of importance – goes to Ida and Ulli for comments on 2023, proofreading in Wisconsin, *malectus* – and everything else.

THE POLITICS OF THE BREAST
An introduction

Breasts became a political issue in the summer of 2021 in Berlin. A hot day in June, nearly 35 degrees Celsius. A woman went to the park with her six-year-old son, a male friend and his little daughter. The park had a splash pad, where the children could jump through water jets and cool off. The two adults both took off their shirts and sunbathed topless. It wasn't long, though, before security guards told the woman to cover her breasts. This wasn't a nudist area, after all! The woman refused, the guards called the police, and the pair left the park with two traumatized children.

But the woman who had been forbidden to expose her upper body wasn't prepared to accept this unequal treatment and sued for damages. Her claim was dismissed at the first instance, the court finding no evidence of discrimination. Her legal action wasn't altogether fruitless, however: it led to a change in the park regulations. In future, all users of the splash pad area would be allowed to go topless. And Berlin is everywhere, or at least when it comes to bare breasts. In the US, for example, two Free the Nipple activists, Brittiany Hoagland and Samantha Six, had successfully sued the city of Fort Collins, Colorado, in February 2019, because the city's 'indecency code' allowed men to show their nipples in public but not females over the age of ten.[1] And in November 2023, the state of Oklahoma revised its differing policies on breast visibility, removing restrictions on female toplessness.[2] Or at least this was what I read on the website of the Oklahoma Intercollegiate Legislature, when looking for examples from the English-speaking world for the English-language edition of this book. New laws on the breast in the US? This struck me as quite plausible, given the recent drive for 'freedom' in breast-related matters in Europe. In my enthusiasm, I overlooked the fact that this website was a project by a group of students, a 'student mock government that replicates all three branches of the state government of Oklahoma', and that the laws of Oklahoma had not in fact been changed at all.

The example of the website that presents as yet unachieved political change as if it were already reality shows at least two things. Firstly, Berlin is not everywhere after all. A journey from Berlin to Oklahoma turns the breasts – and indeed the body – into something different, since politics and justice have a significant impact on the way bodies with breasts move, dress and present themselves. Secondly, however, the students' online activism shows that the sentiment behind the slogan 'boobs have no gender' has resonated worldwide. In other words, even if there are major local and national differences in the efficacy of such campaigns, Free the Nipple protests are inter-national because they relate to comparable restrictions. In any case, the German protest group 'Gleiche Brust für alle' (Equal breasts for everyone) illustrated its online campaign with an English-language cartoon highlighting the arbitrary nature of attitudes to breasts (figure 1).

In this image, two small indications of gender – hairstyle and lipstick – are enough to render one pair of breasts offensive. Yet the body parts in question look completely identical. The cartoon thus raises questions. Why is the torso on the left obscene, but not the one on the right? Why do the breasts on the left constitute a bosom, while the ones on the right do not?

This book sets out to show that, while this classification may be arbitrary, that doesn't mean it is totally haphazard or could easily be changed. The power of breasts is huge, but constantly underestimated. Yet there have been so many court cases about breasts in recent decades that it would be naïve to deny their (socio)political potency.[3] In 2004, an American TV station narrowly avoided a $550,000 fine after pop singer Janet Jackson's breast was briefly exposed during the Super Bowl broadcast. At the end of Jackson's performance with

Figure 1 Cartoon used for the internet campaigns #GleicheBrustfürAlle and #EqualBodyRights.

Justin Timberlake, just after Timberlake had finished the line 'I'm gonna have you naked by the end of this song', he tugged Jackson's top, exposing her whole breast for the briefest of moments. The event was later dubbed 'Nipplegate', after the Watergate scandal that cost Nixon his presidency. It highlighted the explosive political force of the female nipple – linguistically at least. The court cases have not always involved bans on breast exposure, however. In 2016 a 'burkini ban' in France caused a stir. The ban, later rescinded, authorized security patrols on beaches to force Muslim women to remove their burkinis.

Breasts, in other words, are by no means 'private parts'. On the contrary, they're a subject of great public interest. The breast has been the vehicle for some of the central cultural and political conflicts within Western societies, now and in the past. These are about the difference between the sexes and the allocation of power. Yet the power of the breast does not lie in any 'natural' force, but in attributions that make it a symbol of femininity, naturalness, motherliness or sexuality – either all at once or mutually exclusively. As cultural studies research on the history of the body has emphasized, body parts exist 'only in the given cultural classification and in the (imaginary) reference to a whole'.[4] And this 'whole' extends into all areas of society, leading to repeated conflicts. Some have been fought out in court and influenced legislation. In others, the breasts have been continually reinvented and disputed, in texts, images, items of clothing, exhibitions, photos, altarpieces, happenings and more. Seventeenth-century theologians, for example, wrote impassioned pamphlets demonizing the décolleté for kindling 'evil lusts' – despite the fact that medieval Christian theology certainly hadn't been averse to breasts. Even the tablets that Moses received direct from the hand of God on Mount Sinai were referred to as 'breasts', from which the 'milk' of spiritual sustenance was expressed (*quasi lac de uberibus duarum tabularum expressum*).[5] The theological gaze – by turns glorifying and denigrating the breast – was succeeded by the Enlightenment gaze, which turned from God towards nature and led the bosom into new social realms. And finally, more than a hundred years later, there was the battle over (or rather against) the corset, one of the fights fought by women's rights campaigners. The American feminists of the 1960s went down in history as bra burners. Since 2008, activists from Femen, a group founded in Ukraine, have drawn attention to their political concerns by baring their breasts in public, usually leading to their immediate arrest. When Bill Cosby faced charges of rape in April 2018, the actress Nicolle Rochelle protested topless in front of the courthouse, the names of Cosby's alleged victims written on her naked torso in red and black ink. So the bare breast has served as an organ of protest for many decades and in many countries.

All this is political. It is the politics of the breast – and an indicator of lines of conflict that remain relevant today. One is the fetishization of the female breast as an erotic object, which serves to justify the unequal treatment of male and female nipples. Another is the revulsion inspired by the unfettered breast. As recently as 2019, the Italian press responded with outrage when German activist Carola Rackete, charged with illegally rescuing migrants in distress in Italian waters, appeared before an Italian court wearing – allegedly – no bra. The headlines were politically significant because, instead of focusing on migration policy, they drew attention to the 'shamelessness' of a woman who had dared to go braless. And this pattern is repeated over and over again. When the magazine *Wired* analysed Google search terms relating to the UK elections in 2019, it found that Lib Dem leader Jo Swinson appeared most often in the combination 'jo swinson boobs'.[6] Searches for 'jo swinson nipples' were almost as frequent. This quantifiable sexist undertone in public perceptions of female politicians is found regardless of specific political positions or agendas. As the *Wired* article goes on to say, attitudes to male politicians are quite different. For example, search queries on Boris Johnson's private life focused on his family ('boris johnson children'), not on his body.

Angela Merkel, the German chancellor from 2005 to 2021, is another woman and politician whose breasts made headlines. The story followed the same paradigm as the above-mentioned cases in other countries. Time and again, the debates revolve around the relationship between the body and power – and the breast is the site of negotiation. In 2008 Merkel suffered a similar fate to Janet Jackson and Jo Swinson when she appeared at the opening night of the Oslo opera house in Norway in an evening dress with a plunging neckline – not unusual in such a garment. The German newspapers were falling over themselves to produce the smuggest comment and the wittiest pun. During Merkel's term of office, the rather disrespectful title 'Mutti' (Mum) had become common in Germany. By evoking the stereotype of a respectable housewife with no clue about politics, the term belittled Merkel as a politician. At the same time, it tapped into the popular notion of an evil, dominant mother; as the most powerful woman in Europe, she clearly had power over men. These associations found a readily accessible symbol in Merkel's breasts. But their exposure – even just in the form of a low neckline – made people uncomfortable. In this case, the partially bared bosom signalled powerlessness – because it was obviously female. Given that women tend to occupy less powerful positions in patriarchal societies, 'femaleness' is not something that raises the status of a person associated with it. And this is not despite, but because of, a long-standing tradition in political iconography: the use of allegories and personifications of the (naked) female body to depict abstract values and virtues. Eugène Delacroix's painting *Liberty Leading the People* (1830; Louvre) is one of the most famous examples of a bare-breasted female figure embodying an abstract value – but it doesn't prove that real women enjoyed any political liberties at the time. The huge oil painting, 260 cm by 325 cm, was inspired by the events of the July Revolution of 1830, which led to the abdication of Charles X. Yet the artist's depiction of Liberty as a half-naked, combative young woman, placed at the centre of his composition, was in stark contrast to the reality of a society where women's civil liberties were by no means a given. Marina Warner's 1985 study *Monuments and Maidens: The Allegory of the Female Form* showed us that it is women's exclusion from political agency that makes their bodies the ideal canvas for the projection of the values – truth, beauty and goodness – that legitimate this exclusion. So when the female breast becomes visible not as an allegory, but as a real body part of a powerful woman, this upsets the gender hierarchy. The sight of an influential female politician's breasts does not cause controversy because it is somehow 'unseemly'. The agitation is fuelled by the paradoxical visual ubiquity of the naked breast in the realm of political symbolism, combined with the ongoing underrepresentation of women in politics.[7]

When it comes to breasts, it is striking how often we find processes of negotiation and practices of visibility/concealment. We will see many more examples of this in the first chapter. It therefore makes sense to pay special attention to visual material. The thesis put forward in this book is that no political history of this body part can be written without considering images of the breast. From the late 1960s, feminist artists realized this and created spectacular works exploring the societal connections between the (in)visibility of the breasts and gender politics (chapter 2). But pictures had produced political effects long before that. A seventeenth-century French pamphlet denouncing the décolleté contained an illustration in which the sinfulness of the naked breast was not only described but also shown (chapter 1, figure 5). Oscillating between attraction and repulsion, the cover of the tract displayed a combination of exposed breasts and the 'ugly' bodies of devils. This showed the depravity of the female body, arising in part from its power over the desiring gaze. Such images probably helped to justify the underprivileged position of women in many areas of public and private life: were their bodies not proof of their capacity to lead men to ruin? Visual material continued to play a crucial role in interpretations of the breast in nineteenth- and early twentieth-century ethnology and anthropology. Here the racist denigration of 'foreign' breasts was supported with corresponding images (chapter 2).

This book works on the assumption that visual representations are a core element of social discourses about the breast. In methodological terms, it is based on political iconography, a research framework developed by the German art historian Martin Warnke,[8] which regards visual representations as part of 'political action'.[9] This refers not only to artworks in the traditional sense, such as pictures hanging in museums, but to everything that produces an effect by visual means. Viewed in this light, such things as prohibition signs, scientific illustrations or protest marches (in which women appear topless as an act of defiance) can become visual agents of the political. They organize spaces and bodies in their relationship to one another: who is permitted to be where and in what manner? And this, if nothing else, makes the question of how breasts are revealed or concealed a political issue.

Today's arguments about the breast are part of broader debates, on the internet and beyond, about bodies, gender and feminism. This includes feminist critiques of body shaming,[10] the denigration of people whose breasts are either too big or too small, too visible or too invisible. Body shaming also includes the idea – discussed and deconstructed during the #MeToo debate – that women who dress too 'revealingly' have only themselves to blame if they are sexually harassed. At the other end of the spectrum is #bodypositivity:[11] a fierce, long-running debate about how to develop a 'positive' body image, which can hold its own without photo filters and cosmetic surgery – and the question of whether and in what circumstances this is actually desirable.

The stories about breasts that will be told here have been selected from this contemporary political perspective, inspired by a sense of bemusement at the agitation, unreasonable expectations and inconsistencies associated with this part of the body. The book delves into the past, seeking to explain the origins of a conflict that has resurfaced repeatedly in different times and places and is still with us today. It is not a complete or global cultural history of the breast from the Stone Age to cyberspace, but a selective look at a body part that has been highly politicized in Western culture.

Often people act as if the object of the conflict were always the same body, and as if everyone knew what was meant by 'breasts'. And yet this cannot be the case, as the many different opinions on the above-mentioned hashtags demonstrate. In order to assess and understand the conflicting positions, we need a historical view, and, above all, an awareness that the breast has a history of its own. Virtually the only constant in this history is that these very different debates all give direct insight into the theory and practice of gender relations. Apart from that, everything is in flux, and the breast is different every time.

There have been moments, for example, when breasts were not breasts, but weapons that could be used to rout enemies, as in the story of the Viking heroine Freydís Eiríksdóttir (chapter 4, p. 148). Or when goat udders became breasts for children whose mothers preferred to 'go out on excursions, attend theatres and balls', as claimed by a doctor in 1816 (chapter 3, p. 111). There have been times when breast milk came not from mothers, but from fathers, according to a report by Alexander von Humboldt in 1818 (chapter 3, p. 119). And there have even been times when breasts became organs producing unadulterated poison (chapter 3, p. 108).

This book examines aspects of the breast in different periods and contexts, concentrating on its transgressive potential. This conspicuous body part transcends boundaries between the sexes, between the natural and the unnatural, between humans and animals, and between geographies. In short, it is considerably more than what a Google image search might suggest. This 'more' is important, because it can help us to define more clearly what it is about the breast that is – in a positive sense – disconcerting. Almost all the breasts Google presents us with are quite young, quite white and quite eroticized. But what about all the others, the ones that disrupt the smooth, agreeable surfaces? These are the ones that have their own history and that reveal something about why the publicly displayed bosom is still so ambivalent and ideologically charged to this day. Which breasts count (as breasts)? Ageing breasts are rarely shown; they are regarded as a sign of decay and the loss of femininity, which is largely measured by sexual attractiveness. Nearly all the debates about toplessness in public spaces tacitly assume that we are talking about young breasts. In his study on the sociology of toplessness, Jean-Claude Kaufmann vividly describes the loathing inspired by old, naked breasts, quoting statements such as the following: 'When you see people of a certain age who have breasts that fall down to their navel, I think it's better to hide them.'[12] Seen in this light, it makes sense that most breast augmentations are carried out on 'young' bodies, not 'old' ones. In Germany, for example, the main age group is women between twenty and thirty (source: German Society for Aesthetic–Plastic Surgery). In the US, the country with the highest number of cosmetic breast operations, the largest age group is thirty to thirty-nine.[13] In this narrow time window, the equation between naturalness, attractiveness, femininity and breasts is critical. Incidentally, the 'natural appearance' which is high on the list of criteria for a successful operation refers exclusively to pert, youthful breasts – although crooked, sagging breasts may be far more 'natural'. Without the 'artificial' there would be no 'natural'.

The question of authenticity permeates the discourse on the breast in various ways. For example, the breasts of a trans* woman, assigned male at birth, are discredited as inauthentic because they have been produced 'artificially'. Conversely, the breasts of a trans* man, identified as female at birth, might be considered as proof that he is 'actually' a woman. Breasts = woman. End of story. The current debates on transgender issues can therefore be better understood in the light of this historical role of the breast – be it in the UK, where J. K. Rowling has been criticizing the 'current explosion of trans activism'[14] for some years, or in Germany, where similar debates are taking place. Reference is often made to 'cancel culture', and it is argued that increasing concern for the interests of trans* people is impinging on the rights of women. High-profile German feminist Alice Schwarzer recently argued along the same lines as Rowling et al., using the example of the breast. Schwarzer and her co-author Chantal Louis cited an English case in which clinics had allegedly instructed their employees to talk about 'chestfeeding' instead of 'breastfeeding'. Schwarzer and Louis saw this as an example of 'cancel culture' (pp. 131–4). Yet the new term, 'chestfeeding', was never meant to apply to everyone; it was supposed to offer an alternative for transgender people whose breasts or chest resisted clear categorizations.

All this suggests that the breast is a body part with incredibly narrowly defined boundaries. But since these are not as immovable as one might think, they help to impose order on society and thus have a political impact. And this is not just about beauty. Breasts are also an excellent indicator of other social hierarchies and a body part associated with racist denigration. Nineteenth-century texts about 'African peoples', 'Egypt' or 'Portugal' spoke of 'unusually large breasts which can hang down below the belly, be thrown over the shoulder or pushed under the arms'.[15] In 1904 the Austrian-Jewish sexologist Friedrich Salomo Krauss devoted a whole chapter of his book *Die Anmut des Frauenleibes* (The grace of the female body) to the breast.[16] The author placed the term 'racial differences'[17] in scare quotes, just as we would today. He criticized 'hard, apple-shaped breasts' – the only breast type to be valued – as an ideal of beauty that had little to do with reality.[18] Krauss's perceptive scepticism may have been partly inspired by the role of breasts in antisemitic discourses at the time. The antisemitic discourse on the breast (illustrated with many examples in Sander Gilman's well-researched 1999 study on the history of cosmetic surgery) appeared repeatedly in various writings on this body part and would certainly have been known to Krauss.[19] Proponents of this discourse insisted that the 'Jewish bosom' had characteristics that could be ascertained by measurements and calculations.[20] Around 1900, then, breasts were confined not only in corsets but also within anthropological ideas of race. On the imaginary scale of ideal femininity, some breasts became the norm, while others came to symbolize racist notions of 'primitivity'. The femaleness signalled by breasts was not seen as a shared characteristic of all breast-bearers, but was either valorized or denigrated by way of the breast. These racist attributions continue to have toxic effects, ranging from higher mortality rates among African American infants (which have been linked to the coercive use of Black women as wet nurses during the era of slavery) to the problematic impact of related beauty norms, whose oppressive effect is still manifested in advertising today (chapter 2, pp. 88–9).[21]

Given this cultural significance of the breast across so many areas of society, the indifference of researchers towards this body part is baffling. Yet this fits a cultural pattern that has recently been encapsulated by the term 'invisible women'.[22] Because male perspectives are presented as universal or neutral, women are not taken into account. In a collection of essays on the 'cultural anatomy' of parts of the body (in which the breast does not feature), one writer claims that 'probably no [body] part has occupied the cultural imaginary as persistently as the phallus'.[23] While it would be difficult to produce a cast-iron quantification of the cultural imaginary, the brief examples cited above are enough to show that the cultural potency of the female breast has been dramatically underestimated. From Sigmund Freud's 'penis envy' to Jacques Lacan's 'imaginary' and 'symbolic' phallus, the male member has always claimed too much space. It steals the theoretical limelight and diverts attention from the breast.

The vulva has experienced a similar fate: it was largely overlooked in cultural studies until the publication of books such as Monika Gsell's *Die Bedeutung der Baubo* (The meaning of the Baubo, 2001) and Mithu Sanyal's *Vulva* (2009). The breast received some attention slightly earlier: in an essay in 1990, the philosopher Iris Marion Young saw it as both representing and calling into question the highly overdetermined separation between motherhood and sexuality.[24] Young argued that this was what constituted the breast's potential for 'scandal' within Western societies. Yet it was only some years later, in 1997, that the historian Marilyn Yalom undertook the first major cultural history of this body part. Her seminal book *A History of the Breast* was one of the first to put the female breast on the map of cultural studies and cultural history. The year 2014 saw a further milestone in the exploration of the breast in cultural studies, the publication of the *Cultural Encyclopedia of the Breast* (edited by Merril D. Smith) and the *Cultural Encyclopedia of the Penis* (edited by Michael Kimmel,

Christine Milrod and Amanda Kennedy) as twin volumes. Here the penis and breast are seen as complementary. Instead of being assigned a fixed cultural significance, they are described, represented and evaluated differently in each case. Both are 'man-made', to borrow the term used by Nora Jacobson, a sociologist of scientific knowledge, in her 1999 history of breast implants, *Cleavage: Technology, Controversy, and Ironies of the Man-Made Breast*. The historian and theologian Margaret R. Miles studied the secularization of the breast from 1350 to 1750 in *A Complex Delight* (2008), while older titles such as Ingrid Olbricht's *Verborgene Quellen der Weiblichkeit: die Brust, das enteignete Organ* (Hidden sources of femininity: the breast, the expropriated organ, 1985) were guided not so much by historical interest as by psychological or medical interest. Lastly, Florence Williams, in *Breasts: A Natural and Unnatural History* (2013), examined the female breast from a natural science perspective, paying particular attention to the problematic effects of the industrialized lifestyle on this body part.

Because the breast is relevant to so many areas of society, there is, happily, no shortage of information about it. It is mentioned, for example, in the history of breastfeeding, in theology, in the development of cosmetic surgery or in fashion theory.[25] In all these places and far beyond them, research on the breast yields new insights. While a number of impressive and important studies have appeared on the subject, these are not as numerous as one might expect given the cultural significance of this body part. There is still much work to be done. Above all, apart from a small number of exceptions, there seems to be a strange unanimity (also extending to the literature cited above) that breasts are only relevant for 'women'. At most, men appear in the reference lists, for example as cosmetic surgeons, judges or artists. But surely the first astonishing aspect of current political debates about the breast is that the rigorous distinction between male and female breasts is based on the way we look at bodies rather than the bodies themselves? In any case, this is what the cartoon used in the German campaign to free the nipple ('Gleiche Brust für alle') suggests (figure 1). Numerous examples demonstrate that the breast has been a crucial body part in the history of the gender binary – and has been associated not only with women, but also with men. The mere fact that – right into the twentieth century – male lactation was seen as remarkable but undoubtedly possible suggests that the close and unambiguous links between femininity and the breast are more volatile than has been thought. The history of the breast, as told in this book, makes it clear not only that the boundaries between 'male' and 'female' – with regard to breasts – have been renegotiated again and again, but also that the associated practices (e.g. breastfeeding) have changed so much from century to century as to be barely recognizable. Insisting that breasts are only about women and femininity does not work, simply because the understanding of breasts has changed repeatedly, and masculinity has often played a remarkably significant role in these changes.

Speaking of change, Rudi Gernreich's design for the 'monokini' in 1964 (figure 2) comes across as a foretaste – in fabric – of the

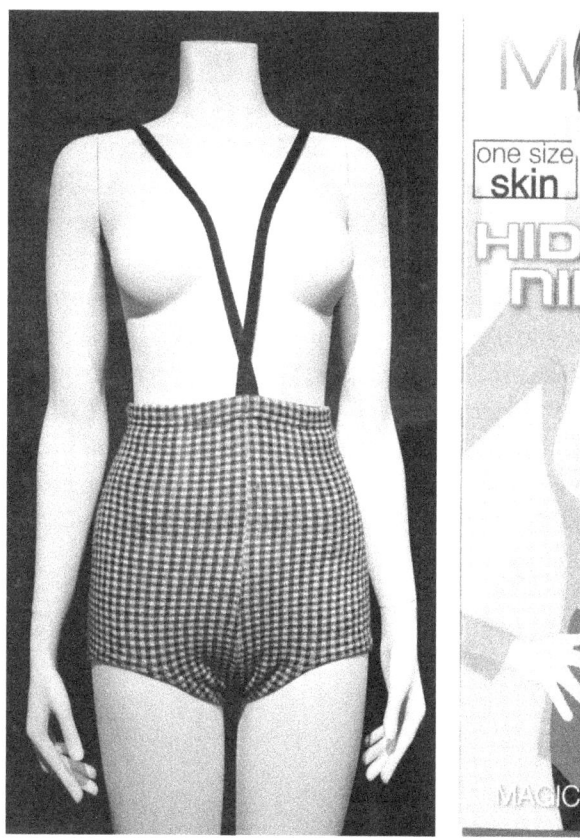

Figure 2 Show your nipples – Hide your nipples. Left: Rudi Gernreich's monokini, 1964. Right: 'Hide Your Nipples' (nipple covers, 2023).

recent court verdicts on the breast. The fashion designer, who had fled from Austria to the US to escape the Nazis, created a swimsuit with two long straps running between the wearer's naked breasts. The protests it triggered reverberated all the way to the Vatican: Pope Paul VI declared Gernreich an 'enemy of the church'.[26] And yet the monokini, designed at the time of the sexual revolution, offers an elegant statement against the hypersexualization of the female breast and a prototype for swimwear in an era of breast equality. The person wearing it does not have to take anything off and is therefore not 'topless' – in the same way that a man at the beach is not 'going topless' but simply wearing swimming trunks. The monokini has been back on the market since 2019 and continues to bravely resist the imperative to 'hide your nipples' – an imperative that Paul VI would no doubt have embraced (figure 2).

Long before public toplessness became an issue, the dressing and undressing of this body part was associated with a fundamental tension between visibility and invisibility. The question of toplessness – and of how female, male and other breasts are permitted to be visible in public – comes at the beginning of this history (or these histories). The first chapter considers these asynchronicities and documents the paradox of visibility and invisibility with reference to examples as disparate as religious art, fashion and anthropology. The second chapter turns to the emergence of powerful ideals of the breast (young, white, firm) and to the necessity and possibility of changing these ideals. The third chapter investigates whether breasts are fundamentally female. The final chapter discusses breasts, protest and power, and the realization that Amazons are not such good role models for 'free breasts' as one might suppose.

1

TOPS ON! TOPS OFF!
The ambiguity of the in/visible breast

The breast as a political organ: the role of in/visibility • Lust, vice, pain: visual narratives of sinful and virtuous visibility • 'Then' and 'now', as seen in clothing • The corset as a visibility machine • 'Artificial' and 'natural' visibilities: the enlightened breast • The 'liberated' breast makes itself useful: breastfeeding • New views: the breast as a medical problem • Modern breasts and new visibilities • The breasts of the 'other' woman: the new visibility of the breast as racism • 'White' breasts – 'Black' breasts

There is no such thing as *the* breast. The way breasts are seen, shown or concealed has been the subject of debate and scandal for centuries. We see this in the excited criticism of Angela Merkel's plunging neckline on her visit to the Oslo opera house, in the public fascination with Jo Swinson's nipples, in Janet Jackson's 'Nipplegate', and in the topless protests of political activists. In medicine as in art, the breast is always a political issue, because societies use the medium of the body to negotiate their own self-image. When it comes to breasts, however, there is no consensus: there are calls to reveal them, then calls to conceal them, and sometimes both simultaneously. An example from France illustrates this highly charged context. In 2016, shortly after the announcement of a ban on burkinis, photos were released which showed policemen forcing a Muslim woman to undress at the beach. In a justification of the ban, the French prime minister at the time, Manuel Valls, stated that 'Marianne [the symbol of the Republic] has a naked breast because she is feeding the people! She is not veiled, because she is free!' (figure 3).[1]

In this debate, the breast – not concealed by a burkini, but revealed by a bikini or swimsuit – is understood as a symbol of the 'progressive' West and its superiority over a supposedly 'backward' Islamic culture.[2] Yet the naked, visible breast, which Valls presented as a founding element of the French state, can rapidly change its meaning. In 2019, for example, when activist Carola Rackete, captain of the rescue ship *Sea Watch 3*, appeared before a court in Italy without a bra, the Italian

LA FRANCE RÉPUBLICAINE.

Ouvrant son Sein à tous les Français.

Figure 3 The 'free' breast stands for the free Republic. Engraving by Alexandre Clément, after a drawing by Louis Simon Boizot, *La France républicaine*, 1792.

newspaper *Libero* spoke of 'boundless effrontery' or 'shamelessness without limits'. Male journalists called for 'more decency'. In this case the visible breasts, or rather the nipples discernible underneath the T-shirt, were not a badge of freedom. Instead they were taken as grounds to challenge the freedom of the woman who had dressed in this way. Internationally, many women protested with the online campaign #freenipplesday, demanding the equal treatment of male and female breasts in public.

As recently as 2021, a teacher in Germany had to justify herself to her school's equality officer because she had dared to teach without a bra.[3] The worry was that pubescent schoolboys might have trouble concentrating in class if they were forced to see their teacher's unrestrained breasts. In response to an article about the case in the news magazine *Die Zeit*, a few women wrote letters to the editor recalling that second-wave feminists, particularly in the US, had 'often burned bras in public' (more on this in chapter 4) to protest against the sexualization of the female body. These letter-writers saw the bra as 'constricting the upper body' and reducing the wearer's 'freedom of movement and enjoyment of life'. Other readers, however, seemed to share the opinion of the school's equality officer. Some even demanded disciplinary measures for the teacher. Such readers felt she should not be permitted to display 'the erotically charged secondary [sex] characteristic of the breast'.[4]

The article and the related letters to the editor are examples of the current political and social discourses on the breast. Although bodily autonomy is central to the self-image of open, liberal, Western societies, it's obvious that women *cannot* actually do as they wish with their own breasts.

The breast as a political organ: the role of in/visibility

The aim of this chapter is not to give a comprehensive cultural history of the breast, but to explain these contradictions in current social attitudes to this body part. It is, by necessity, a fragmentary portrait, which takes as its starting point situations, images and conflicts in the contemporary 'Western' world. In general, people tend not to think about the body, in particular the breast, in terms of political categories. Yet personal experiences can also be political. The feminist movements of the 1970s coined the term 'body politics' to describe this. The private is political, to quote a well-known feminist slogan. This referred explicitly to the body and to what was done with it, from sexuality to clothing. Body politics is now a broad field of research, explored in many different academic disciplines, such as history, the social sciences, art history and literary studies.[5] Working on the assumption that the body is neither natural nor ahistorical, this book will focus on the political and social processes of negotiation that have sought to define it. This includes concrete political debates, as well as philosophers' arguments on the essence and purpose of Woman. It also includes the 'reform dresses' designed by women in the US and Europe around 1900 as an alternative to the constricting corset. The book is structured to focus attention on the present, and on those moments that highlight the political and potentially controversial role of the breast. Forays into the past will illuminate the diverse historical resonances of present-day 'breast practices' and their contradictions. This will allow us to reconstruct what the breast means in our societies, based on the historical evolution of this meaning.

A further aim of this chapter is to investigate what makes the breast so special. Why are there more disputes about this body part than about knees or shoulder blades? How are these disputes conducted? And what does this have to do with (body) politics? Supposedly obvious answers such as 'breasts are linked to sexuality' or 'breasts evoke motherhood' are too simplistic. They do not explain how the naked breasts of Marianne can justify forcing a woman to show her cleavage at the beach; nor do they explain why another woman should wear a certain item of underwear when working as a teacher. Yet these examples have one fundamental thing in common, which gives us a first clue to possible answers: the tension between visibility and invisibility that shapes Western attitudes to the female breast.

Of course, there are other body parts that are sexually and therefore politically and socially charged. But a cursory glance at them highlights the specific nature of the tension between visible and invisible breasts. The vulva has been described by cultural studies scholar Mithu Sanyal as the 'invisible sex / sex organ' (the German word *Geschlecht* refers to both).[6] The penis is the opposite. In the early 1990s Thomas Laqueur, a historian of science at the University of California, Berkeley, stunned his readers with an astonishing find:[7] in sixteenth-century anatomical drawings, the female genitals were represented as completely analogous to the male ones, with the vulva, vagina and uterus depicted as an inverted penis. So in terms of history (or the history of images) the penis, unlike the vulva, was not invisible, but functioned as a kind of visual paradigm, visible even in places where it was not actually present. A sort of imaginary hypervisibility. Humans as one race, but with two quality levels. The feminist theorist Luce Irigaray, writing in the 1970s, had already identified this as a fundamental problem of the Western philosophical canon. She spoke of 'this sex which is not one', observing that 'any theory of the subject has always been appropriated by the "masculine"'.[8] The feminine has, to put it somewhat hyperbolically, been made invisible. For all the criticism Laqueur later received for his 'one-sex model', this does not detract from his fascinating finding that the 'invisibility' of the female genitals is linked to the hegemonic visibility of the male genitals. According to this view, the distinguishing feature of the female sex organs is that there is *nothing* there, compared to the *something* that characterizes the male sex organs.

Regardless of this, one thing is true of both the vulva and the penis: as the so-called primary sex organs they are subject to more or less the same rules of non-visibility in everyday life. Men can wear tight trousers that display the size and shape of their genitals; women can wear miniskirts that excite fantasies of what might be found *underneath*, or leggings that reveal the outline of the vulva. But these body parts are not associated with all the intermediate stages of revealing and concealing that are linked with the breast. Nor are they subject to strategies of half-exposure, as seen in low necklines or see-through lace (or in nursing bras, developed to simultaneously cover and uncover the breast in public).

Even more crucially, the clothing and unclothing of the vulva and penis do not generate anything like the abundance of visual and discursive conflicts associated with the female breast. There are disputes over (excessively) visible breasts, but not about the public penis. In the above-mentioned cases, women from the German chancellor to a teacher have had to put up with public debates about how they clothe their breasts, yet there isn't a single comparable incident relating to the use of male underwear. A further indication that revealing and concealing, as two contradictory but paradoxically also mutually constitutive imperatives for dealing with the breast, are still relevant today. There is no comparable tendency to make any other body part a permanent object of scandal.

It will become clear that the dialectic of covering and displaying offers a crucial first key to understanding the political and social significance of the breast. The conflict-laden coexistence and clash between visibility and invisibility are played out discursively in very different fields. This applies to art, where feminist artists have deconstructed visual traditions for the representation of the breast. In 1976, for example, Ulrike Rosenbach used video projections to invite *Reflexionen über die Geburt der Venus* (Reflections on the birth of Venus) (chapter 2). It applies to techniques such as breast binding, which trans* men use to make their breasts, as a visible marker of femininity, invisible (chapter 3). And it also applies to the question of 'appropriate' clothing for powerful women, who are criticized for showing too much cleavage (chapter 4). It is this tension between visibility and invisibility that makes it possible to trigger a social debate by shifting these loosely interlinked boundaries. This is one of the reasons why the naked breast functions as an organ of protest, while the exposed penis does not. This is why there are topless protests where women display their naked breasts on cathedral altars to draw attention to the church's misogyny, but there are no comparable penis protests by groups of male activists – whatever their purpose might be (chapter 4).

Lust, vice, pain: visual narratives of sinful and virtuous visibility

The tension between visibility and invisibility, so fundamental to the cultural impact of the breast, can be retraced through images. These are always part of this tension, because they show but often problematize this showing. The worlds of ecclesiastical and religious imagery, which almost completely dominated the production of images before modernity, are a case in point. On the one hand, they suggest that looking at breasts is sinful; on the other hand, they actually invite viewers to do so, not least in the case of the bare-breasted nursing Madonna, *Maria lactans*. So the contemplation of the breast is simultaneously condemned and encouraged – just as Christian images of breasts simultaneously negotiate exposure and concealment.

In the post-classical period which is our focus here, the motive for depicting the breast was often deterrence. Early images of the breast are frequently depictions of pain. In medieval painting and sculpture, Luxuria, the personification of lust, one of the seven deadly sins, is repeatedly shown inflicting terrible mistreatment on her own breasts. She pierces them with a lance, as in a twelfth-century mural in the crypt of St Nicholas in Tavant in France, or pulls on them so violently that it hurts to even look at her. At the top of a pillar in the nave of Vézelay Abbey, also in France, the breast of a Luxuria figure is distorted into a wrinkled, pointed tube, hanging close to the head of a snake, which is winding around the figure's legs towards her breast.

The snake at the breast recalls the medieval motif of a woman suckling a serpent (the *femme-aux-serpents*). There the exposed breast is associated with the snake, the quintessential (female) symbol of temptation and evil. This may have been a Christian reinterpretation of the ancient tradition of the nurturing earth mother, Terra, transforming the breast from a positive symbol to a frightening emblem of religiously censured sensuality.[9] In any case, it seems that in the Christian context the desire to make the breast visible as a motif is paid for by ensuring that its contemplation is associated with pain and horror. So we can describe this type of representation as a kind of punishment for the gaze. Other images of Luxuria show her riding a goat, or beautifying herself with mirrors and combs to incite lust. The common feature of all these depictions is that they restrict the 'visualization of sexuality' to the female body.[10] There is no equivalent representational convention for the male body.

Besides the heavily sanctioned visibility of the breast, however, there was also a contrary strategy. This celebrated the visible breast, adding a new layer of ambiguous visuality. Contemplating the breast of the Madonna as she nursed the baby Jesus was not punished but, on the contrary, encouraged. Both the sinful breast of Luxuria and the holy breast of Mary were evoked in religious art, but each stood for a completely different type of visibility. While the grave sin of lust was visualized in Luxuria's bared breast and its mistreatment, Mary's youthful and pleasingly rounded breast signalled the overcoming of this and other sins with the help of God's grace. It also asserted the absence of the desiring gaze. There are certain representations of the breast – legitimated by Christianity – in which both strategies coexist. One is the often depicted story of Lucretia, a Roman woman who was raped and, in despair at the loss of her 'honour', took her own life by driving a knife into her chest. Here, contemplation of the wound inflicted on the naked breast is linked with a call to virtue.

Often the contemplation of the virginal breast became the actual subject of the image, for example when saints were shown kneeling before Mary in adoration, or donors were depicted alongside the mother of God. Here enthusiasm for the beauty of Mary's breasts was seen as a legitimate component of religious edification. In the thirteenth-century text *Les miracles de Nostre Dame*, the French abbot Gautier de Coincy praised the breasts of the Virgin Mary as 'so glorious and beautiful, so small and well-made'.[11] And in fact most images of the *Maria lactans* type do portray the breasts as Coincy describes them, with the baby Jesus attached. In general there is no breast milk visible, but there are some very interesting exceptions. One, from around 1480, is by an unknown Dutch master and shows Saint Bernard of Clairvaux kneeling before a *Maria lactans* (figure 4).

The stream of milk shooting out of Mary's right breast towards the saint's eye and forehead is clearly visible. In his writings, Bernard spoke of having an eye disease cured by divine intervention. In many other representations of this subject, from the Middle Ages to the modern era, the milk touches Bernard's lips, indicating that he is receiving spiritual nourishment from the mother of God. Other saints were even portrayed as drinking direct from Mary's breast.

Here Christian iconography was adopting ancient models, as it often did. In this case the models were from Egypt; we know of representations in which Egyptian kings are suckled at the breast of Isis and other goddesses. The story of the genesis of the Milky Way also finds its echo here. According to Greek myth, it came into being when the infant

Figure 4 The milk of the mother of God. Unknown artist, *Lactatio Bernardi*, 1480–5.

Heracles sucked too hard on Hera's breasts and she flung him away; the milk that sprayed out created the galaxy. Thanks to the divine breast milk, the Greek demigod Heracles (or his Roman equivalent Hercules) was blessed with superhuman strength. This is also the idea at the root of the Christianized version of the story: like Hercules, Bernard of Clairvaux received grace and enlightenment from the milk. Ordinary believers could share in this if they venerated the late-medieval relics of Mary's milk, preserved in liquid or powdered form. The milk of the Virgin (!) was only considered worthy of veneration because it was not associated with sexuality.[12] The problem with images of the virginal bosom was that they could potentially be read as sexually arousing. In the engraving of the unknown Dutch master, Mary's milk aims at Bernard's eye and forehead. This curbs any erotic associations that might have arisen if the milk had flowed into the saint's mouth, potentially leading the beholder onto sensuous and sinful terrain. The image counters this danger effectively on a visual level by ensuring that the stream of milk targets the eye and thus implicates the sense of sight. As a long-distance sense, sight is not associated with sensuous touch and seduction in the same way as a mouth opened to receive warm liquid. The danger is defused.

Without any connection to the Christian narrative of salvation, there was no reason to allow the breast to become visible. To this day, church authorities urge women to wear modest clothing and cover their breasts, with reference to relevant biblical passages: 'I also want the women to dress modestly, with decency and propriety, adorning themselves, not with elaborate hairstyles or gold or pearls or expensive clothes, but with good deeds, appropriate for women who profess to worship God' (1 Tim 2: 9–10).

Just a few years ago, the vicar and master of ceremonies at Cologne Cathedral, Tobias Hopmann, stated that when visiting a Catholic church a woman should cover up her shoulders and knees and avoid low necklines.[13] At least women in low-cut dresses are no longer threatened with excommunication, as they were under Innocent XI, pope from 1676 to 1689.

'Then' and 'now', as seen in clothing

The structure of this book is defined by frequent leaps back and forth between today's attitudes to the breast (and the related conflicts) on the one hand and historical examples on the other. These allow the past to illuminate the present and vice versa. Yet the links between such disparate phenomena as a medieval picture and the contemporary debates on breast visibility, fought with all the weapons of modern media, require a note of warning. Or, to put it differently: what is interesting is the differences within the commonalities. Because even if we can assume that the tension between visibility and invisibility is a constant in the cultural imagination of the breast in Western societies, the actual meaning of these two terms – including their meaning as bodily practices – has changed over time. In the Middle Ages, for example, a woman attending church might have looked upon a Luxuria while dressed – depending on her social status – in a simple, long robe with many folds of cloth, or in a luxurious tunic and a richly embroidered cloak. In either case, her chest would have been covered: the décolleté did not become common in women's fashion until the thirteenth or fourteenth century. For such a beholder, visibility would have had an entirely different meaning than it has for today's internet user, scrolling through her Instafeed of easily accessed and endlessly reproduced images of breasts on #freenipplesday.[14] Not only would the medieval viewer have had completely different, primarily sacred images of the breast in her mind's eye. She would probably also have had a different experience of the body, given that the loose, high-necked clothing of the Middle Ages did not require any special apparatus for the female chest. Conversely, the linking of the unclothed breast with sinful Luxuria would probably be difficult to comprehend for most of the women who protested when Captain Rackete was blamed and shamed for allowing her nipples to show through her T-shirt. Yet the linking of visible breasts and 'shamelessness', which rightly led to feminist indignation, has a history that reaches back to Luxuria. The fact that this link still functions has to do with its modernization – that is, with the fact that it means something different today. Rackete is not 'shameless' because her breasts signal proximity to one of the seven deadly sins, which most people would have trouble enumerating today. Rather, she can be discredited with a reference to her breasts because the linking of the female body with disgust is an inherent part of our cultural narrative on gender difference.

So while it's important to seek connections between old and new attitudes to the breast, it's equally important to identify shifts of the type described above, which are part of modernization. From the moment when the décolleté became an element of women's fashion, the visibility and invisibility of the breast came to play a new and central role. The corset was the crucial invention that allowed the eyes to be drawn to the breasts in a way that had not been possible before. Again and again, the dictates of fashion alternated between a low neckline and maximum visibility on the one hand and a flattened chest showing no cleavage on the other. In both cases, however, the bosom became something that was emphasized by means of clothing – in contrast to the Middle Ages, where no comparable distinction was made between outerwear and underwear. One way or another, the in/visibility of this newly discovered body part was always a subject of debate. *La Clef d'amours*, a late thirteenth-century adaptation of Ovid's *Ars amatoria* offering tips on the courtly art of love, recommended: 'If you have a beautiful bosom, you should not cover it up, but wear a low-cut dress so that everyone will desire it and dream of it.'[15] The inspiration for dreams came from the combination of visibility *and* concealment, because of course the low neckline did not reveal the whole chest, but only part of it. And the author of this early modern guide to romance even recommended that his female readers should blow out the candle before undressing for their lovers, since there are many aspects of the female body that are better concealed than revealed.[16]

Initially the corset was developed to flatten the chest, as if behind a shield. This created the impression of small breasts, and in fact made them nearly invisible. Very soon, however, rigid and tight-fitting constructions were used to press the breasts up as far as possible. The aim was to give an impression of youthfulness and, at the same time, push the top of the breasts above the neckline to make them partially visible.[17] Before the invention of the corset, no great need had been seen to design garments to support the breast, but this now changed. It is not altogether clear when exactly the corset became the standard undergarment. An English inventory from around 1300 mentions a corset belonging to the mistress of a royal household. But its fabrication and appearance are not described in any detail, so we don't know whether this garment resembled the corset of later centuries.

Histories of the corset usually refer to the Spanish court, which played the role of European trendsetter from the sixteenth century onwards, though only for aristocratic circles. For most of its history, the corset remained a garment for upper-class women: almost all models, from the early versions in the Spanish court to the nineteenth century, could only be put on with the help of servants. The servants themselves had to be able to dress and undress without assistance and were in any case unable to afford such garments. Quite apart from this, the rigid corset, laced up at the back, made movement difficult. This is why working women in the nineteenth century often dispensed with it, and only wore a corset – a simpler version – when dressing up to go out.[18] It was not until around 1840 that the construction of the corset was changed, allowing it to be opened and closed at the front and thus giving its wearers greater independence when putting it on.[19]

Before it became part of the clothing of bourgeois women in the nineteenth century, however, the corset was reserved for the aristocracy. The type of corset that was introduced at the Catholic Spanish court at the time of the Counter-Reformation, the first garment designed specifically for the breasts, hugely restricted the mobility of its wearer. The two rigid halves, connected at the sides, served as armour plating for the upper body. For both women and men, clothing was expected to be high-necked, with a preference for dark colours. The breasts were pressed flat and became more or less invisible.

The corset was occasionally part of male clothing too, but it was in women's fashion that it reigned supreme. And it was only among women that the rapid alternation between concealing and revealing occurred. The corset of the Spanish court, which subsequently found followers in the upper echelons of English and French society, rendered the breasts virtually invisible; the rigid components made the upper body appear as a more or less flat surface. There were, however, opposing developments: in the seventeenth century necklines slipped downwards again, and the breasts became more visible.

Like the corsets at the Spanish court, the low necklines of the Baroque and later Rococo period were aristocratic. The *grande toilette* of a noble lady included wide, hooped skirts, whose unwieldy shape meant that they revealed brief glimpses of otherwise hidden parts of the body, such as feet, ankles or knees, when she moved. It also included the erotically charged deep décolleté. Towering wigs and elaborate headgear, in the form of hats decorated with feathers, put the entire female body on display. This form of dress signalled the greatest possible distance from those strata of the population that did not share in the luxurious, extravagant and hedonistic lifestyle of the nobility. The body decked out in this manner could devote itself to erotic dalliance and the arts of seduction, but not to productive (paid) work – and nor was it expected to do so. The aesthetic appearance of the body expressed the ideals of the dominant class.[20]

The corset as a visibility machine

Throughout its history, the corset has attracted hefty criticism.[21] At first it was moral reasons that fired up the corset's (mainly male) opponents. Later, doctors expressed medical concerns, having discerned harmful effects on the female body. The most recent wave of criticism, in the nineteenth and twentieth centuries, was largely driven by the women's movement. This ultimately led to the virtual disappearance of the corset from women's everyday dress. In all these phases, gender politics and visibility went hand in hand.

The beginnings of the critical discourse on the corset concentrated on a thematic link we have already encountered in the representations of Luxuria: the breast and sin. Essentially, the hostility towards the naked breast that had dominated early medieval representations was still in place. The breast was the reminder that women, ever since Eve, had mainly acted as seductresses of men, and needed to be regulated as such. Much can be learnt about past fashions from the literature of the time, in which contemporary clothing practices were criticized. As we will see shortly, the breast is a central topic here, with arguments almost always revolving around how much breast it is permissible to show. The focus is not so much on women as on men, who need to be protected from the danger of seduction that emanates from the exposed bosom. At first, although breasts were seen as being as closely linked to desire and sexuality as the vulva, they triggered neither horror nor disgust. The aim was solely to curb certain 'excesses' of fashion, as manifested in the downward migration of women's necklines. Fifteenth-century French preacher Michel Menot censured ladies with 'chests uncovered down to the belly, with a white veil through which one can see everything distinctly'[22] – evidence that necklines were getting lower and that the naked skin was covered with more or less transparent pieces of fabric. It was only later that increasing numbers of writers began to refer to the breasts (like the vulva) as 'dirty', because of their ability to spark desire. In the mid-seventeenth century, the French Jesuit Paul de Barry described the fate that awaited the wearers of revealing décolletés after their death: 'If they could smell the intolerable stench that emanates from their breasts, encircled by serpents, swarming with worms and scorpions, and overflowing with suppurating abscesses.'[23]

In an anonymous pamphlet from 1686, an author inspired by this idea composed the following rhyme: 'Des Frauenzimmers blosse Brüste / Ein Zünder aller bösen Lüste' (Woman's bare breasts / Igniting all evil lusts).[24] Before that, another misogynist, the Paris priest Pierre Juvernay, born in 1603, had described breast cancer as the natural punishment for women's sinfulness, which resided in the breasts and could be detected by looking at them. Here too, the connection between pain and the breast remained a constant. In a polemic published in 1637, *Discours particulier contre les femmes desbraillées de ce temps* (Special discourse against the slovenly women of this time), Juvernay cited countless passages from the Bible to prove that women who displayed their breasts too freely on earth would face immeasurable torments in the afterlife.[25] Once again, the problem was not the breasts themselves, but the fact that women were using the corset to offer them up to the male gaze. In his tract *De l'abus des nudités de gorge* (On the abuse of the naked bosom, 1675), the Catholic theologian Jacques Boileau sums up this line of thought: 'The sight of a beautiful breast is no less dangerous for us than the sight of a basilisk.'[26] Basilisks are mythical animals whose gaze was thought to be lethal.

Luxuria's mistreatment of her breasts, as described earlier in this chapter, can be understood as an imaginary reference for these furious pamphlets denouncing the décolleté. Here, however, the punishment is no longer imagined as a self-inflicted injury but as an act committed by an external agent. The cover of Juvernay's tract illustrates this in drastic fashion (figure 5).

Figure 5 The sinful décolleté. Title page of Pierre Juvernay, *Discours particulier contre les femmes desbraillées de ce temps*, 1637.

The image juxtaposes two scenes which the author believes to be inescapably linked. On the left, an elegantly dressed lady is displaying far too much bosom; on the right we see the consequence: eternal damnation in the jaws of hell. The details are revealing. The winged devil grabbing the woman by her extremely low décolleté has breasts himself (or herself?), though these are pendulous and 'ugly'. The phallic object that the devil is holding under the woman's breasts refers to the 'evil lusts' ignited by the sight of the unclothed bosom. These lead directly to the mouth of hell, which is depicted in some detail: here a devil is driving a pitchfork into the belly of a naked female figure surrounded by flames. The long bodies of two snakes, winding upwards, give extra visual impact to the mouth of hell. Serpents are always part of any depiction of sinful femininity. Here they simultaneously form a sort of face, consisting mainly of a gaping mouth, with two large eyes looking out of the picture above it. The motif of eyes is very apt for the bared breasts and the 'lust of the eyes' which they incite, and it is no coincidence that the devil standing next to the female figure on the left, half-human, half-beast, is looking directly at us.

The moral demonization of the breast, with its focus on the low-cut dress, accompanied all the twists and turns of fashion. But despite the religiously motivated efforts to demonize and eradicate the corset, as the display case for the breasts, it maintained its place in the female wardrobe for another 200 years – along with the play between concealing and revealing. On the one hand there was the *fichu*, a type of scarf used mainly by women from the lower and middle classes to cover their throat and chest, while simultaneously emphasizing these features with gauzy, semi-transparent fabrics. And on the other hand there were generous displays of bare cleavage, which continued despite all opposition. These were, incidentally, a privilege of the nobility. In 1667 low necklines actually became compulsory at the court of Louis XIV, as proven by a decree dictating the wearing of the *grand habit*, a very low-cut dress.[27] Both these fashions were criticized. A very late critique of the corset, based on moral arguments, was produced by a German doctor, Christian Tobias Ephraim Reinhard, in 1757. Like its predecessors, this was a poorly disguised misogynist reckoning with the seductive power of women. He too emphasized the way clothing was used to make the breasts visible, and compared the revealing corset with a 'meat stall':

> Certainly females do not bare their bosom out of boredom, certainly they do not open their meat stall for nothing, and certainly they do not exhibit their wares without cause, just as the bird trapper never puts out his bait without reason, but always intends to trick the birds and lure them into the snare. [...], so I consider such females, who put the gifts they have received from nature up for sale, as nothing other than real whores.[28]

'Artificial' and 'natural' visibilities: the enlightened breast

Reinhard, the doctor who referred to the corset as a 'meat stall' and vilified women as whores, marked the end of a discourse based on the Christian-inspired understanding of the breast as a sign of sinful depravity. While the effects of this discourse can be felt even today, certain parameters changed in the eighteenth century, in the course of the Enlightenment. The naked breast became a symbol of freedom (figure 6).

Figure 6 The breast as a symbol of enlightened freedom. Louis-Simon Boizot, *Philosophy Unveiling Truth*, 1789–99.

An engraving from the years of the French Revolution shows Philosophy bearing a torch to bring light into the proverbial darkness of superstition and religion. She lifts a veil to uncover the breasts of a young woman seated on a chair. The latter figure, whose right foot is trampling a head with animal ears and a blindfold, represents Truth. The neoclassical décor contains numerous allusions to Enlightenment philosophy, most prominently a bust of Voltaire and a stone tablet with the inscription 'Contrat Sociale [sic]', a reference to Jean-Jacques Rousseau's 1762 blueprint for post-absolutist societies. Rousseau's key pedagogical work *Émile*, published in the same year, is also included: the book is one of several lying at the feet of Philosophy. And another bosomed figure appears: the 'many-breasted' goddess Artemis of Ephesus, serving as a reference to classical antiquity.

Although this engraving seems to depict self-confident women, liberated from the corset, raising the torch of Enlightenment, it would be a misunderstanding to interpret it as evidence of political partici-pation by real women. On the contrary, the female allegories that stand for statehood, truth or reason are essentially projections of a public order conceived as purely masculine.[29] The naked female body stands for the 'naturalness' and thus legitimacy of the ideals it embodies. Louis-Simon Boizot, who presents truth as a bare-bosomed woman in this engraving, also produced another series illustrating key concepts of the revolution. Here even 'la Fraternité' appears as a bare-breasted young woman. Contemporary women such as the revolutionary and feminist Olympe de Gouges noticed the contradiction between the many images of women, embodying all the things 'that were not only worth living for, but also if need be worth dying for',[30] and the exclusion of real women from political power and participation. De Gouges wrote her famous 'Declaration of the rights of woman and the female citizen' in 1791 and was guillotined in 1793.

The asynchronicity of the 'liberated' breast and the systematic oppression of women also applies to the fashion of the times: breasts were granted more freedom, but this did not mean any new political freedom for women. In the second half of the eighteenth century, women increasingly dispensed with tight corsets and wore high-waisted neoclassical dresses, with only a light veil over the breasts. At first glance one might be tempted to see this as evidence of liberation in a political sense. In paintings such as *Portrait of a Young Woman in White* (circle of Jacques-Louis David, 1798), the subject is enveloped in a light chemise of this type. The fine gauze barely covering her chest is so transparent that the breasts are not just hinted at but almost completely visible. This fashion, however, was soon displaced by the return of rigid corsets. A correspondent for the *Journal des Luxus und der Moden* (Journal of luxury and fashions), reporting from Hesse, observed with relief in 1805 that: 'The vile French nudity which was threatening to take hold a few years ago [...] and which gave much material for ambiguities and mockery, is disappearing more and more among Frankfurt's beauties.'[31]

Not only was the 'natural' fashion of the 'free' bosom very short-lived: even when it was first introduced and propagated, it was – like the female allegories – explicitly *not* about female participation in the freedoms promoted by the revolutionary ideas of the time. Quite the contrary. The 'natural' breast was seen by Enlightenment thinkers as an antidote to the now-despised lifestyle of the aristocracy, and found its echo in the clothing practices of female contemporaries. Yet it illustrates how the idea of liberation (of the mind, reason, mankind, etc.) that was associated with the breast's new visibility could simultaneously mean the restriction and curtailment of freedoms. Such 'ambivalences of visibility'[32] are made more than obvious in a series of engravings published in Göttingen in 1779–80. At the instigation of Georg Christoph Lichtenberg, the editor of the *Göttinger Taschenkalender* (Göttingen pocket calendar), the engraver and illustrator Daniel Chodowiecki contrasted bourgeois 'nature' with courtly 'affectation' in a series of paired images.[33] The proponents of the Enlightenment regarded the behaviour, clothing and habitus of the aristocracy as 'unnatural', and sought to illustrate this by juxtaposing them with new, explicitly bourgeois forms of interaction. The pairs of images, dedicated to topics such as 'The Greeting', 'The Conversation' and 'The Promenade', depict aristocratic body language as exalted and exaggerated. In the brief interactions, usually between two people, the aristocrats are conspicuous for their grand gestures, while the bodies of their bourgeois counterparts seem almost immobilized. The bodies of the women in particular take up far less space, dispensing not only with the Baroque splendour of wide, hooped skirts and enormous hats, but also with the most modest gestures. They appear passive and withdrawn.

Chodowiecki begins by contrasting nature and affectation in the images of two couples, making programmatic use of the motif of the naked breast as a symbol of liberation from the old order (figure 7). At first glance, the desirable state of nature represented on the left is most obviously manifested in the male figure, wearing only a narrow strip of cloth looped carelessly around his arm and hips. But his female companion is also naked, at least as far as her chest is concerned. Both are bareheaded and barefoot. Walking through nature, 'hand in hand, like brother and sister, purified of all lusts and without any affect,'[34] they demonstrate the imagined ideal of the disciplined bourgeois body and its behaviour – projected onto a couple straight from the Garden of Eden. They are, in every conceivable respect, different from the 'affected' couple juxtaposed with them. On the left we see a barely clothed human couple, not unlike Adam and Eve, gazing at each other in mutual absorption. On the right we see the complete opposite: the

Figure 7 Daniel Chodowiecki, *Nature and Affectation*, 1779, copper engraving in the *Almanac de Goettingue pour l'année 1780*.

lady, dressed in the Rococo fashion, has a hoop skirt so voluminous that it hardly fits into the picture, a tightly laced corset, an extremely narrow waist and a low neckline, emphasized by a large bow. Her companion, an elegant gentleman gallantly holding her hand, also wears court dress, including the usual wig.

Besides the differences that are instantly noticeable, a small and easily overlooked change is particularly significant. While the male and female posture is essentially the same in the 'affected' couple, the man and woman who have returned to 'nature' show different postures. Interestingly, the woman has retained the courtly foot position of the aristocracy. Her right foot is delicately placed directly in front of her left foot, and tipped slightly sideways. Her male companion, on the other hand, has abandoned the effeminate and mincing gait of the gallant courtier for a 'manly' stride. This suggests that a special, 'graceful' posture is naturally feminine. The corset-supported décolleté of the Baroque and Rococo periods had allowed better-off women to present their breasts as 'bait' and practise the art of seduction.[35] This power of seduction was now denied to them, paradoxically through the 'free' exposure of their breasts. The rest of the body is subjected to discipline in its behaviour and gestures, mitigating the terror inspired by the unrestrained breast. These engravings, according to art historian Ilsebill Barta's incisive analysis, offer 'ideal models and normative conceptions of male and female bourgeois behaviour.'[36]

The 'liberated' breast makes itself useful: breastfeeding

As ever, the breast remained a political issue. The new model of bourgeois female behaviour included the reintroduction of a breast practice that seems self-evident to us today, indeed the epitome of the natural: breastfeeding one's own children. It was Rousseau who championed this cause in the eighteenth century, arguing vehemently that children should be nursed by their own biological mothers. This view was part of the Enlightenment programme. Rousseau, as we saw in Boizot's engraving, was regarded as having a key role in the 'unveiling of truth'. And Boizot was not alone:

Chodowiecki was also well acquainted with the philosopher's work and contributed illustrations to Rousseau's novel *Julie or The New Heloise*. In 1762 Rousseau explained the usefulness of breastfeeding for the restoration of 'natural' morals and a gender order that would benefit the state:

> But let mothers deign to nurse their children, morals will reform themselves, nature's sentiments will be awakened in every heart, the state will be repeopled. [...] When the family is lively and animated, the domestic cares constitute the dearest occupation of the wife and the sweetest enjoyment of the husband. Thus, from the correction of this single abuse [i.e. the employment of wet nurses] would soon result a general reform; nature would soon have reclaimed all its rights. Let women once again become mothers [...]. There are [...] still some young persons of a good nature who on this point, daring to brave the empire of fashion and the clamors of their sex, fulfill with a virtuous intrepidity this duty so sweet imposed on them by nature.[37]

Previously it was customary in non-proletarian society for wet nurses to breastfeed the children of wealthier women. Infant mortality as a result of neglect was correspondingly high. But the breasts of women from the higher classes were meant for other things; breastfeeding would have compromised their function as erotic objects. The 'use' of the breast was a question of class. During the Enlightenment, however, women were urged to nurse their own offspring as part of a movement 'back to nature', and breastfeeding became a bourgeois virtue. This helped to establish the ideal of motherly love, which has been unmasked as a historical construction by philosopher and historian Elisabeth Badinter.[38] She showed that motherly love was first described – and thus invented – in philosophical and medical discourses in the late eighteenth century. Images of babies suckling or slumbering at their mother's breast, peaceful and oblivious to all around them, became the visual emblem of this feeling. From now on, the bared breast of a mother, offered to her child, evoked a new ideal of femininity as private maternal devotion.[39]

Just a few years after Rousseau's remarks on the benefits of breast-feeding, the artist de Saint-Aubin produced an image entitled *The*

Happy Mother (*c*.1800). This is no supernatural Madonna offering her breast to the son of God and any saints who might be present, but 'simply' a woman breastfeeding her children – not one but two of them, presumably doubling her happiness. In this representation, a young bare-breasted woman gazes fondly at the baby boy on her lap, who throws his hands in the air in joy. The image conforms to the heteronormative arrangement imagined by Rousseau, even if the father does not appear in this domestic scene (he is probably pursuing work outside the home). The mother's gaze is focused on the active boy, not the passive girl resting next to him. The genitals of both children are clearly visible, alluding to their role in future couples, where male and female complement each other, the male active, the female assigned to the reproductive sphere (as conceived by both Rousseau and Chodowiecki). The breastfeeding mother helps to ensure that these normative gender relations are reproduced in the bourgeois family.

The new visibility of the breast around 1800 also led to such spectacular objects as a 'breast cup' (*bol-sein*) resting on a tripod decorated with goats' heads. It was made for Marie Antoinette in 1787 by Boizot, mentioned above as the creator of the engraving *Philosophy Unveiling Truth*. The elaborately made object offered adults, who had long since been weaned, the experience of drinking milk from the breast. Admittedly it is only a breast made of porcelain, and its users did not suck on the nipple; instead they could drink from the cup in normal adult fashion. The cup glorifies the breast as the perfect milk dispenser, but simultaneously instrumentalizes it, since it is not attached to a woman, normally a prerequisite for producing milk. The shape dates back to the ancient Greek *mastos*, a drinking vessel modelled on the female breast. And while we're on the subject of breast-shaped drinking vessels: in 2014 the artist Jane McAdam Freud designed a champagne glass supposedly modelled on Kate Moss's breast. The form was described as 'abstract', however, and – unlike the breast cup of 1787 – the artist chose not to include a representation of the nipple.

It is very much in keeping with the Enlightenment's fascination with the breast that Carl Linnaeus, in the tenth edition of his *Systema naturae* (1758), invented the class of mammals (Mammalia, from the Latin *mamma* = breast), which is still in use today. In fact only half of the creatures thus designated actually have breasts with which they can can suckle their young (for a more detailed account, see chapter 3, pp. 101–2).[40] But despite this, the breast and its capabilities – in this case breastfeeding – had become the focus of natural history, philosophy and pedagogy. The breast became the supposedly natural reference for a new notion of femininity as motherliness, which could once again be linked to the body, this time with scientific backing. This is evidence that, as Belgian cultural studies scholar Michel Feher writes, 'a certain organ or bodily substance can be used to justify or challenge the way human society functions'.[41] Feher, co-editor of a multi-volume *History of the Human Body*, uses this formula to encapsulate a central finding of research on the body.[42] Body and society do not exist independently. Yet it is often asserted that they do, for example when writers such as Rousseau point out that women have breasts and (must) therefore 'fulfill with a virtuous intrepidity this duty so sweet imposed on them by nature'. In actual fact, the opposite is true. It is sociopolitical intentions that are seemingly placed beyond all discussion by reference to 'nature'. Often the 'nature' that is invoked is only created at the moment of its invocation, for example by images such as *The Happy Mother*. Her naked, 'natural' bosom stands for something that previous generations were not yet able to think and therefore see when looking at representations of the breast.[43] They may have seen the breasts of the Virgin Mary as representing the promise of divine salvation, but certainly not as evidence of a female nature, closely linked to the nomenclature of the biological sciences. References to a body part – in this case, the breast – always serve to justify, explain and make plausible a particular worldview.

Even today, the different 'breastfeeding fashions' reveal ideologies. In Germany in the 1960s, breast milk was considered inferior to 'modern' industrial baby formula. Now breastfeeding is back in fashion, and industrial formula is seen as unnatural and demonstrably worse for the health of the child. Yet the enthusiasm for breastfeeding does not mean that the breast is now a universally accepted sight. Or at least not in the US, where 'lactation suites' are provided for breastfeeding in public spaces. These are small, windowless boxes, for example in waiting areas in airports, which women can use to avoid baring their breasts in public. Naked breasts with naked babies, as shown in the engraving from around 1800, may still be charming, but they are not welcomed by the American public.

New views: the breast as a medical problem

The return to 'nature' established a new narrative of the breast. Besides the discourse on breastfeeding and the naked breast as an allegory of freedom, the eighteenth century brought a further innovation. While some doctors, as quoted above, were still vilifying women for the 'meat stall' displayed by their corsets, others, from the second half of the eighteenth century onwards, were increasingly evoking a previously neglected topic: the harmful effect of corsets on women's health. Interest would not peak until after 1800, but important groundwork for the subsequent debate was laid in the 1700s. The topic, which had previously found no place in discussions of the breast, now cropped up more frequently.

In 1770, nine years before Chodowiecki contrasted an 'affected' lady in a corset with a 'natural', bare-breasted woman, a book by the Jesuit priest Jacques Bonnaud sought to enlighten readers about the health damage caused by the corset. Its excessively long title conveyed its core message: 'The degradation of the human race through the use of the whalebone corset: a work in which it is shown that it goes against the laws of nature, increases depopulation and bastardizes man, so to speak, to subject him to this torture from the first moments of his existence under the pretext of educating him.'[44]

In his text, which did not have a lasting impact on the popularity of the corset, Bonnaud was able to refer to a number of valiant anti-corset campaigners – men such as the English physician John Huxham, who had already pointed out the dangers of the corset in an essay on fevers in 1750. All these predecessors, he argued, had proven conclusively that the corset was the source of an 'infinity of diseases'.[45] In Germany, the physician and Enlightenment thinker Johann Peter Frank wanted to have the corset banned in 1779, because it harmed unborn offspring and could even be used illicitly to trigger an abortion:

> The mother's belly already expands in height and width around the third
> month of pregnancy [...]: this means that a pregnant woman must lose

her 'waistline'. A corset is intended to achieve the exact opposite, and does so with such success that no further expansion of the womb and its vessels is possible, and all the force of taking breath and of every other pressure has an effect on the embryo and ultimately aborts it. Unmarried pregnant women seem to have learnt of this benefit from married women, and all too often they accomplish their sinful intention with this lacing up of their belly.[46]

Frank also reported that there were 'examples of deformed children', on whom one could see, after their birth, clear marks of the bottom end of 'busks', strips of whalebone, wood or steel that were inserted into the front of the corset to create a straight line from breast to groin. This is questionable but cannot be excluded altogether. As in the campaign for breastfeeding, then, the focus on 'women's health' was partly about population policy. 'Liberation' from the corset was not aimed at emancipation, but at imposing greater discipline on the female body.

Besides this aspect, which would remain relevant throughout the nineteenth century, the politics of the image is also significant here. This played a major role in ensuring that health-based arguments (which were voiced in the eighteenth century but never gained much traction) became so successful from 1900 onwards that the corset as a standard item of female underclothing was eventually abandoned.

The eighteenth-century texts that attacked the corset for medical reasons had relied mainly on written arguments. In other discourses on the breast that achieved social relevance (the breast as a symbol of divinity, a sign of sin, an allegory of freedom, etc.), visual representations played a major part. But for many years the physicians attempting to enlighten their readers lacked such images. How important these images actually were (and are) is clear from an early exception, Samuel Thomas von Sömmerring. In 1793 this anatomist had added a full-page illustration to the new edition of his text on the harmfulness of corsets, originally written as a competition entry and published in 1788. This set a new standard. Throughout the nineteenth and early twentieth centuries, nearly all texts on the corset took their cue from this image (figures 8 and 9).

The visual trick deployed by Sömmerring and his illustrator Christian Koeck was to allow viewers to look *inside* the body. This

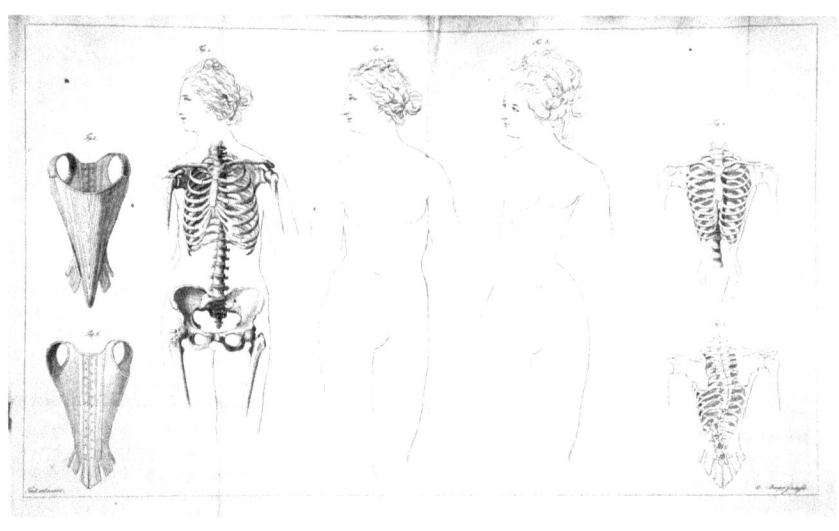

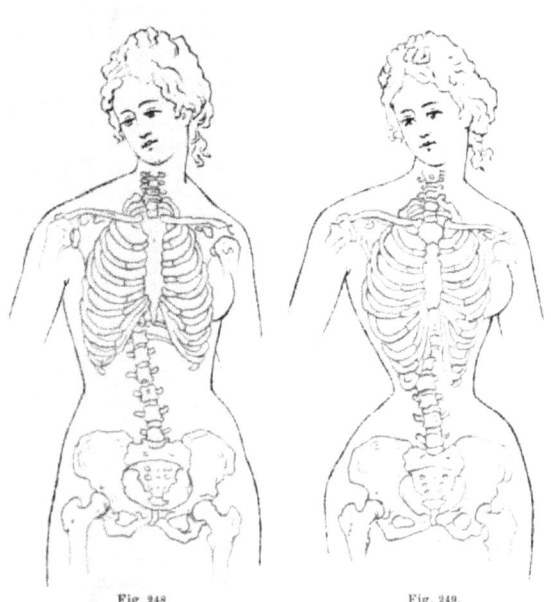

Fig. 248.   Fig. 249.

Fig. 248. Normaler weiblicher Brustkorb nach Sömmering.
Fig. 249. Durch Schnüren verdorbener weiblicher Brustkorb nach Sömmering.

Figures 8 and 9 Comparison becomes important – and the view into the body. Figure 8: Samuel Thomas von Sömmerring, *Über die Wirkungen der Schnürbrüste* (On the effects of corsets), 1793, p. 85; figure 9: Carl Heinrich Stratz, *Die Frauenkleidung und ihre natürliche Entwicklung* (Women's clothing and its natural development), 1904, p. 367.

instantly made the corset's deformation of the skeleton obvious. To achieve this, Koeck drew a skeleton inside the statue known as the Medici Venus, which Sömmering calls the 'true Greek Venus' (it was not known at the time that this was actually a Roman copy). The figure is at the centre of the illustration and serves as a starting point for the visual argument. As the author emphasizes, the beauty and perfection of this Venus as an ideal of the female body 'has been decided among connoisseurs, without a single exception known to me'.[47] The naked figure on the right vividly illustrates what a corset does to the beautiful female body. On the far right, a further illustration gives a view into a deformed ribcage, to 'represent very clearly how strikingly the skeleton must be modified (crippled) if it is to fit into a corset'.[48]

This 'clear representation' proved influential, playing a critical role in the ultimate demise of the corset. Thus the health arguments of the nineteenth and early twentieth centuries had become visual arguments. From then on, virtually every text on the negative effects of the corset on the female body included illustrations. The original image was gradually altered to intensify its impact. While Sömmerring's book had shown a rather confusing arrangement of several female bodies, later authors reduced this to just two bodies, to make the contrast between the natural and the deformed female ribcage more visually impressive.[49] In the decades that followed, this comparison became an integral component of modern attitudes to the breast.

Modern breasts and new visibilities

Despite changes in the details, Sömmerring continued to influence the specifically modern presentation of the breast in anti-corset campaigns for many years. As late as 1926, the Düsseldorf exhibition GeSoLei, an acronym for 'Gesundheitspflege, Soziale Fürsorge, Leibesübungen' (healthcare, social care, physical exercise), included a display showing the 'female body laced up by the corset' and the resulting damage.[50] The image created by Koeck and Sömmerring, of a deformed female body juxtaposed with a 'healthy' female ribcage, brought together all the different arguments against the corset into a successful visual argument that remained usable for more than a hundred years.[51] The increased visibility of the breast in the modern era enabled society to examine and criticize itself. The topic encouraged debates on the health and reproductive capacity of the population, as well as on emancipation and gender relations. The breast's new visibility targeted female viewers, who would immediately comprehend the *danger* highlighted in the images and act accordingly.

A striking example is provided by the debates about the abolition of the corset, which reached their peak around 1900. The development that really accelerated these debates was the advent of photography, which made it possible to show the harmful effects of this garment on the female body more clearly. Photographs meant a further increase in visibility; they appeared in their hundreds in the relevant publications (figure 10).

One title circulating at the time was the book *Die Kultur des weiblichen Körpers als Grundlage der Frauenkleidung* (The culture of

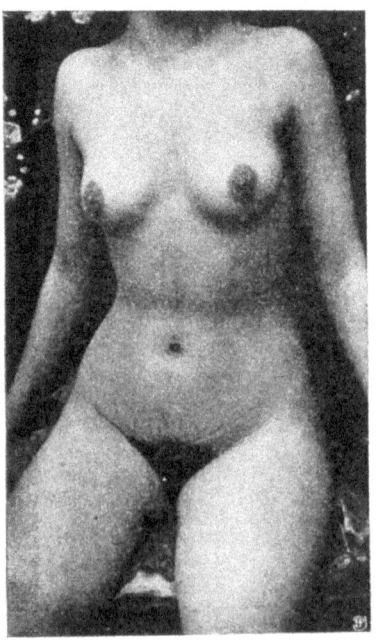

Abb. 27

Abb. 29

Figure 10 Educating viewers to 'look logically': Paul Schultze-Naumburg, *Die Kultur des weiblichen Körpers als Grundlage der Frauenkleidung* (The culture of the female body as the basis for women's clothing), 1901, p. 40.

the female body as the basis for women's clothing), published in 1901. The author was Paul Schultze-Naumburg, who would later became a Nazi art custodian and a member of the Reichstag for the Nazi Party. On nearly every page there are photographs, which – as Schultze-Naumburg himself admits in the introduction – essentially show the same thing again and again, but with a very specific intention:

> I gave the book the illustrations that were indispensable to produce those three-dimensional views that are necessary for the construction of completely new ideas of the body and therefore clothing. The linguistic evidence of such facts would not be convincing, firstly, and, secondly, would not have any practical effects. The great abundance of images, which apparently prove the same thing over and over, have been selected with well-considered intent, not to present the same evidence again and again but to educate eyes that have become accustomed to the deformation of the body through our traditional costume so that they recognize the true form of the body.[52]

The idea behind the headless torsos presented by Schultze-Naumburg was that nothing should distract the viewers from this educational mission. The above quotation shows the connection between the images and the persuasive aim of the text and proves that the sheer abundance of illustrations also played a part here. The new technologies of visualization envisaged a new type of female viewer, who would perceive her own breasts as a problem and – 'educated' by the pictures – abandon her corset.[53]

The anti-corset campaigns used pictures in other ways too: the illustrations were not just found in books, but also shown in exhibitions or used at lectures. The photos circulated. For example, a women's association for clothing reform in Frankfurt am Main, hosting an evening lecture, borrowed a pack of photographs that had previously been shown as illustrations in the relevant books.[54] The photos were subsequently reused by other women's associations. And then there were exhibitions: shows promoting corset-free 'reform dresses' displayed dressmaking patterns, finished dresses, and pictorial evidence of the dangers of the corset. Between 1900 and 1902 alone, five such events took place in Berlin, Dresden, Leipzig, Krefeld and elsewhere. Some were even organized by Schultze-Naumburg himself. The first such presentation, hosted in 1897 by the association for the improvement of women's clothing in Berlin, attracted over 8,000 visitors.

Although all this appears to be a concerted campaign to phase out the corset,[55] there was no consistent development, and those involved were not necessarily all committed to female emancipation. In fact there were so many associations, individuals, artists' groups, museum staff, physicians, writers, politicians and activists participating in these debates that it is easy to lose track. All these people had quite different interests. Opinions changed, too, and surprising alliances occurred. Some participants were very modern in some areas, but evoked reactionary ideas in others. For example, Schultze-Naumburg emphasized the similarity of male and female bodies at a time when other authors subscribed to the widespread belief that the female body was deficient. In 1901, an article by Baudelaire translator and author Margarete Bruns referred to this as the 'long known and recognized fact that the female body does not quite correspond to the laws of harmony'.[56] The sources for this supposed truth were Arthur Schopenhauer and his pupil Rudolf von Larisch, author of a book with the unambiguous title *Der 'Schönheitsfehler' des Weibes* (Woman's 'flaw', 1896). The female body was compared to the male body: 'Above all, the chest is very different.' It is 'the duty of clothing [...] to emphasize this characteristic disparity'.[57] This also seemed a plausible explanation of why most women were reluctant to dispense with the corset. Even among those who wanted to reform this garment, there were many who saw it as a necessary device to support women's upper bodies, which were perceived as *schlaff* – i.e. limp, saggy or droopy.[58] Schultze-Naumburg refuted this traditional denigration of the female body by stating that 'the plastic structure of the male and female body in its principal proportions'[59] was by no means as different as generally assumed. Elsewhere, however, he reactivated the old topos of the 'whorish obtrusiveness'[60] of the corset – a classic component of the largely misogynist discourse on the breast.

Thus the forced visibility of the breast around 1900 was linked with very different goals. In broad terms we can identify at least three groups involved in the corset debate at the time. First, there were voices from medicine, tirelessly producing richly illustrated works on the dangers of the corset. Non-physicians such as Schultze-Naumburg (an architect, among other things), who combined medical arguments with cultural politics and made them accessible to a wide audience, took inspiration from these medical works but were actually closer to the second group, the artists. These were people like Henry van de Velde or Anna Muthesius, on a quest to find an aesthetically pleasing reform dress which could be worn without a corset. And lastly, politicians and activists such as Minna Cauer and Anita Augspurg played a central role. They were part of the women's movements, which saw the corset primarily as a manifestation of women's oppression. In 1904 Cauer and her colleague Maria Lischnewska went to the minister of spiritual, educational and medical affairs in Prussia with a submission from the Federation of Progressive Women's Associations, demanding a ban on corsets in schools. They described the corset as a *Zwangsmaschine* (machine of coercion),[61] with reference to the social coercion imposed on women. Shortly before this, Anita Augspurg – opponent of the corset, women's rights activist, and editor of the magazine *Frauenstimmrecht* (Women's suffrage) – had launched a similar campaign. Augspurg provoked police to arrest her in order to draw attention to the fact that women in the German empire could be seized and subjected to a forced gynaecological examination if there was any suspicion of prostitution. History doesn't tell us what behaviour or clothing Augspurg (who, unusually for a woman at the time, wore her hair short) deployed to provoke her arrest. But, tellingly, the satirical magazine *Simplicissimus* alluded to the topic with a cartoon in which policemen are attempting to put corsets on recalcitrant women. The picture shows Augspurg in a reform dress, dragging a reluctant policeman behind her and demanding: 'Officer, come along now and kindly show me the law that says every female German subject must wear a corset.'[62]

Unsurprisingly, it was often women who pursued the anti-corset discourse from a feminist perspective. In 1903, for example, fashion designer Anna Muthesius published a programmatic text, *Das Eigenkleid der Frau* (Woman's own dress), demanding that women should take the nature and design of their clothing into their own hands and should no longer submit to the male-dominated dictates of fashion: 'Like trees that are cut into figures by a gardener, we are shaped into a sphere one year, and a spindle the next.'[63] She was referring to the ever-changing models for the female silhouette in the course of the nineteenth century, where high-waisted, corset-free neoclassical styles were succeeded by wasp waists.[64] In the middle of the century, the crinoline, a petticoat reinforced with steel bands, had turned women into 'spheres', as Muthesius put it. A handbook around 1908 stated that a 'beautiful bosom should be firm, hemispheric, pert, of great elasticity and suppleness', yet a glance at the changing fashions showed that this specification did not lead to a uniform presentation of the breasts. Some fashions pressed them together, some ignored them, others pushed them upward like a 'pigeon's crop'.[65] The only constant was that clothing for the breasts took the malleability of the female body as a given.

In light of this, Muthesius's approach really was revolutionary. Her contemporary Henry van de Velde had also campaigned for the reform dress, designed to make the corset superfluous. Yet he, very much in the tradition of the male artist, had spoken of women as 'material' waiting to be 'shaped'. In contrast, Muthesius self-confidently demanded: 'Every woman her own artist!' Male contemporaries had some trouble coping with this. A male reviewer of her book did concede that Muthesius's necessary criticism of the corset had caught women's attention, somewhat against their will. However, 'what Frau Muthesius was not able to say [was]: We, we men, want you this way; because we're the ones that matter in this question, no one else.'[66] This wasn't quite true, though: the sheer number of 'women's associations for the improvement of women's clothing' founded in many German cities towards the end of the nineteenth century shows that many women cared less and less about how men wanted them to look.

The breasts of the 'other' woman: the new visibility of the breast as racism

Many texts published in the early nineteenth century on the breast, the harmfulness of the corset and the 'beauty' of the female body remained on the market for a surprisingly long time. These were not marginal, specialist publications, but frequently sold and presumably much-read books, which played a defining role in discussions on the corset (and the breast) in their time. Schultze-Naumburg's text had been through five editions by 1922.[67] He was outstripped, however, by his contemporary, the gynaecologist Carl Heinrich Stratz, also a very prolific contributor to the corset debate. Some of Stratz's works – bearing titles such as *Die Schönheit des weiblichen Körpers* (The beauty of the female body, 1898), the Darwinistic *Die Frauenkleidung* (Women's clothing, 1900; from 1904 the title was changed to *Die Frauenkleidung und ihre natürliche Entwicklung*, Women's clothing and its natural development) or *Die Rassenschönheit des Weibes* (The racial beauty of woman; first published in 1901) – remained in print as late as the 1940s and went through up to twenty-five editions.[68]

Stratz is an example of the blatant racism that defined parts of this discourse. His writings racialized the breasts, inscribing them in a narrative of difference and inequality between the 'races'. This was, once again, a narrative of visibility and invisibility. Stratz stated, for example, that a European woman who is caught in the nude will typically cast her eyes down.[69] The assertion that hiding one's breasts and averting one's gaze are European characteristics is partially inspired by the fixation on the figure of Venus, which had illustrated the ideal bosom since Sömmerring and had reappeared in Stratz's work (figure 11).

Stratz also used the Medici Venus as a comparative illustration. He did so, however, not to criticize the corset-deformed bodies of the present day, like Sömmerring, but to distinguish the Venus from an Egyptian clay figure which covered neither its breasts nor its vulva. For Stratz, the latter was simply a 'fat woman', and he showed the figure only to lend plausibility to the 'sharp contrast' between the modest behaviour of European women and the shamelessness of the 'others'.[70]

The descriptions of the breast that are repeatedly presented in his book are therefore based on a racist ensemble of negative ideas derived partly from this 'fat' female statuette. The breast that is modestly veiled (but ultimately revealed) is beautiful; the breast that is 'fat' (or worse, simply *there*) is ugly. Stratz described the Papuans and Melanesians as 'mostly squat, somewhat stumpy figures, and among the women, not a single one with a European breast shape'.[71] All this was part of the author's racist convictions; he stated that 'not all human races are

Figure 11 Carl Heinrich Stratz was convinced of the connection between a lack of modesty and 'primitivity': Stratz, *Die Rassenschönheit des Weibes* (The racial beauty of woman) (1904) [1901], pp. 42–3.

equal; their level of development is lower or higher depending on the extent of their physical and mental attributes.'[72]

Stratz illustrated the 'Islamitic group' with two photographs, one of a veiled woman, the other of a half-naked woman lolling on a sofa. In the Orientalist visual fantasies of the nineteenth century, Western viewers had been presented with an 'imaginary Orient', which supposedly offered a glimpse into the harem and thus an opportunity to view the female nude.[73] The act of unveiling was part of Western fantasies about the harem as a place of female nudity inaccessible to outsiders. Stratz complained in the accompanying text that 'genteel Turkish ladies' were reluctant to be photographed in their 'domestic garb'. His solution was a 'model of Hungarian origin',[74] whom he presented in allegedly authentic harem dress. Thus a woman described as Turkish (but who might be Hungarian) became an item of visual evidence in an enlightened, 'Western' discourse, which understood cultural differences as part of a hierarchic history of development.

In the final third of Stratz's book on racial beauty, concerned with the 'Nordic race', we see a photo captioned 'Young Russian lady [Russisches Fräulein] from Podolia'. In the photo, this young 'lady of pure Russian descent from the upper circles of society' hides her face with a cloth draped over her eyes and nose. The fact that she 'decided to allow her beautiful body to be photographed' inspires the 'highest admiration' in the author.[75] As a member of the supposedly 'superior races', she was entitled to feel modesty. The cloth over her face signals this superiority, while the bared breast indicates her enlightened decision to overcome her modesty in the service of science.

It is worth mentioning – briefly at least – that the topic of the corset also influenced debates on cultural differences and hierarchies from a completely different direction. The European criticism of the (mis)shaping of the female body was noticed outside the West and sometimes used strategically against colonialist practices. Christian missionaries in China around 1900, fulminating against the practice of foot binding, were told that they should first ensure the abolition of the equally harmful corset in their countries of origin.[76]

'White' breasts – 'Black' breasts

Admittedly, women's bodies had already been used to make cultural differences visible and plausible before Stratz and his colleagues came along. Even before them, all breasts were not equal, and the showing and hiding of this body part were linked with the construction of cultural differences. In 1800 the neoclassical painter Marie-Guillemine Benoist had exhibited her painting *Portrait d'une négresse* in the Paris Salon (figure 12). The art historian Viktoria Schmidt-Linsenhoff, who has played a key role in integrating postcolonial perspectives into art history, offers a well-informed interpretation of the portrait,[77] a reading of the image that transcends a clear 'either–or'. The subject, depicted with a bared breast, does not simply represent an exoticist exploitation of the African model. This differs from Stratz's depictions of supposedly 'shameless' African women, whose nudity appealed to the voyeurism of his readers and was also intended to prove the 'primitivity' of the women exhibited. Benoist's painting, produced soon after the abolition of slavery in the French colonies in 1794 and shortly before its reintroduction under Napoleon in 1802, critically evoked the 'connection between the issue of slavery and the issue of women', as Schmidt-Linsenhoff shows.[78] The white dress wrapped around the young woman fully exposes her right breast. A red ribbon ties the fabric loosely below the breasts. These red and white elements, combined with the blue cloth covering the back and armrest of the chair she is sitting on, hint at the colours of the French flag. The motif of the loosely draped garment, covering the body with apparent negligence, had already been chosen by the artist around fifteen years earlier in her *Self-Portrait* (1786), which is interesting as a point of comparison (figure 13).

The half-bared breast and flowing hair evoke the motif of the Bacchantes, the wild followers of Dionysos. Benoist's contemporary Angelika Kauffmann had also painted herself as a Bacchante in 1785, suggesting a kinship with these mythological figures, who stood

Figure 12 Marie-Guillemine Benoist, *Portrait d'une négresse*, 1800. Louvre, Paris.

Figure 13 Marie-Guillemine Benoist, *Self-Portrait*, 1786. Staatliche Kunsthalle Karlsruhe.

(among other things) for the freedom and temperament of the arts. The motif was popular throughout the nineteenth century, with the Bacchantes generally shown entirely naked or at least topless. In Benoist's self-portrait, the nipples remain invisible, so this would generally *not* have been understood as a painting of a naked bosom. Yet the cloth draped around her and the soft fabric hugging the curve of the breasts emphasize these as a body part that is *almost* visible. The way the subject is sitting, with her legs slightly apart, also seems suggestive, but does not reveal anything to the viewer's gaze.

In contrast, Benoist's portrait of a young non-white woman, painted fifteen years later, shows the fully visible breast of her model. The hierarchic colonial relationship between the painter and her model was crucial for the interpretation and impact of Benoist's painting. Schmidt-Linsenhoff argues convincingly that the painter was ascribing 'a bourgeois, republican subjectivity to emancipated former slaves'. However, the mere fact that she presented the woman without a name, with the problematic title of 'négresse', makes it clear that she was doing so without 'granting [former slaves] the control over their own image which the genre of portrait painting envisages'.[79] Researchers now assume that the subject of the portrait was a young woman from Guadeloupe, whom the artist's brother-in-law had brought to Paris as a slave and/or mistress.[80] The woman herself, however, had no access to her portrait, which remained in the artist's possession until her death.

This shows an important difference between Benoist's self-portrait and the portrait of the woman she met in her brother-in-law's house: the manner in which the two women were able to control their own image. In Benoist's case, the representation of her body lay entirely in her own hands. In the case of the woman she painted, we have no idea what influence she had on her portrait. The fully bared breast, however, suggests that Benoist placed more emphasis on the physicality and sexualization of her model than she considered appropriate for herself.

Again and again, women whose bodies were read as 'Black' found themselves in the role of the 'other', for whom special rules about the naked body applied. Over time, they came to have greater scope to shape the related visual formulae themselves. Yet this remained a two-edged sword. When Josephine Baker danced topless in Paris and

Berlin in the 1920s, in the spectacular *Revue Nègre*, the newspapers were enthusiastic but betrayed their racism: 'But the theatre in which the Negroes perform is sold out evening after evening, for weeks in advance. Really, what the Negroes offer is distinctive, original, new. They are at their best in the areas where they are untouched by white culture, where they are wholly Negroes. They are an artistic, musical, naïve and childish people.'[81]

This praise is toxic: it signals that the bold, sexually explicit dance with which Baker captivated her audience was, above all, *not* white.

As in the racial ethnology behind books such as those of Stratz (which were still being published in this period), this review treats the uncovering of the breast as evidence of a supposed naivety, which can be equated with a lower stage of development. This is shown by the use of the term 'childish'. This primitivism allowed the 'white' public to perceive 'Black' womanhood as sexually exotic and fundamentally 'other'. Of course, Baker was not a naïve, childish woman, but a highly paid artist. Enthusiasm for her became a badge of modernity for those who were not content to look on in amazement as she danced, but sought a connection with her. Her contact with Le Corbusier is an example.[82] Baker was also a life-long political campaigner against racism, and research in recent years has focused on how she was able to subvert the primitivist expectations of the audience in her performances, for example by successfully opposing her designer, Paul Poiret, in matters of costume design.[83]

2

FROM VENUS TO PIN-UP AND BACK
The breast between art and pornography

Venus • Ideals of modesty • Modest or immodest? How female bodies become Venuses • Palaeo porn • The gender politics of the gaze • Another 'other' woman: the 'Hottentot Venus' • Nudes, power, pornography • Baring the breast: feminist provocations • Beauty • … and back to Venus again

Venus

Art produces idealized images of femininity. The figure of Venus, the Roman Aphrodite, has always been part of this process, a model against which real women are judged. For centuries, the beautiful, smooth, young body of a woman has been painted, chiselled in stone, and carved into wood. She often appears with her son Cupid, whose arrows can pierce any heart, even the most reluctant. Or she is depicted with Cupid's father, Mars, the god of war. Venus entered the world in classical art, portrayed in various positions: rising out of the sea foam (*Venus Anadyomene*), bending over to remove her sandal, or showing off her beautiful bottom (*Venus Kallipygos*). These and other motifs offered an opportunity to represent the female body in alluring poses. The vulva is never visible here, but the breasts are a key feature. Venus is an appropriate starting point for the following observations because she has served as an ideal of femininity from classical antiquity to the present. She has influenced the representation and function of the 'perfect' breast, which is inseparably linked with the whole female body.

Since depictions of the vulva have (generally) been taboo in Western art,[1] it is breasts that have served to inspire an eroticized and sexualized view of the female body. In depictions of Venus removing her sandal, she raises her leg and arm to draw attention to her breasts. In Botticelli's *Birth of Venus* (1484), which shows the goddess standing in a large seashell, her vulva is concealed by her long, flowing hair. Her chest, however, is only covered by one hand, leaving the left breast completely visible. The hand that hides is also the hand that shows. In iconographic terms, the seductive play between concealing and revealing begins here – or at least finds its first full expression here. Botticelli's painting, which actually depicts the arrival of the goddess in Cyprus, is one of the most famous images in art history and proves that Venus remained a fascinating topic even in post-classical art. Despite the displacement of classical figures by Christian subjects, as seen in the 'conversion from Venus to Mary', Venus became a core motif for Renaissance artists.[2] In the late fifteenth century, nobody believed in Greek and Roman gods and goddesses any more, but the subject offered a welcome excuse to depict female nudity. Venus with Cupid became a model that kept artists busy for many years. A few decades after Botticelli, Lucas Cranach the Elder painted the charming goddess eighty-seven times. In almost all these paintings, a transparent veil floats around the body, just a hint, painted so finely that the delicate white lines only emphasize the body visible beneath it. Venus' body is always painted in elegant, graceful poses, with slender, delicate limbs, the breasts set high and consistently hemispherical, as if this were the only possible shape.

The image of Venus rising from the foam seems to have regained its appeal in the nineteenth century. The youthful body and the hemispherical breasts remained unchanged, only the backdrop varied. Once again, the titillating combination of women and water proved a popular choice. The motif is based on the mythological narrative of Hesiod, in which Aphrodite emerged from the sea as the daughter of Uranus. The story is gruesome: Chronos had cut off the genitals of his father, Uranus, and thrown them into the sea. In doing so, however, he had created the prerequisites for unsurpassed beauty: semen and blood mingled with sea water to bring forth Aphrodite. The image of the female body, lying or standing in the water, can evoke 'the uncontainable ebbs and flows of female reproduction – and specifically [...] the taboo subject, menstruation'.[3] The topic was so popular that the author and art critic Théophile Gautier referred to the Paris Salon of 1863 as the 'Salon of Venus'.[4] One of the many works exhibited was a painting by Alexandre Cabanel entitled *Birth of Venus* (1863). It depicts a beautiful woman lolling in the water, with joyful cherubs flying above her. Her hairless vulva is a smooth, unbroken surface, visible and yet invisible. Her breasts, in contrast, are highly seductive. Art historians would soon dismiss this Venus of the nineteenth-century salon as kitsch, preferring modernized versions such as Manet's *Olympia*, also from 1863. Alluding to Titian's *Venus of Urbino*, Manet transformed the goddess into a modern Parisian woman. His contemporaries interpreted her as a prostitute, and scandal threatened – but then scandal soon became the *sine qua non* of modernist art. Even here, however, nudity was manifested in the presentation of the breast; it was still unthinkable to depict the vulva, which is covered by the subject's casually placed hand.

But the nineteenth century also saw the advent of a completely 'other' Venus: female bodies that did not look like the familiar Venus, but were given this name anyway. Big breasts. Bodies with vulvas. Bodies that were not slender and 'well-formed', but excessive and space-consuming. Bodies that were not positioned in the prescribed poses and did not follow any of the traditional patterns. One of these 'other' types of Venus, from 1810, was named the 'Hottentot Venus' and showed a Black female body in profile, a style of representation never used for the white ideal Venus. The images of the 'Hottentot Venus' established and propagated a racist view, giving the Black body the title of 'Venus' but simultaneously denying it all the qualities associated with this goddess: the ideals of beauty, purity and art.

Shortly after this, yet another Venus entered the stage: the *Vénus impudique* (immodest Venus), a Stone Age figurine discovered in France in 1864. Again, this is a female body that does not correspond to customary depictions of female bodies. There are no gestures of modesty, hence the name 'impudique', but it is still named after Venus.

The same goes for the more famous statuette found in Willendorf, Austria, in 1908 (figure 14).

This was not the end of the story of Venus and her images (and of course there *is* no story of Venus outside these images). In 1921 Paul Klee painted a *Barbarian Venus*, exhibiting both male and female genitalia. This can be seen as an echo of those 'deviant' Venus figures that served to make the 'other' bodies intelligible in the nineteenth century. Klee's drawing *Ageing Venus* dates from the same year. A clear sign of the subject's age is the 'sagging breasts', indicated by two semicircles with nipple-like markings at their lowest point. Otto Dix also showed the ageing female body in a 1923 painting, *Venus of the Capitalist Age*. Like Klee's Venus, Dix's has pendulous breasts and a grimacing face and is anything but the embodiment of an ideal. Venus is now permitted to grow old, but in doing so she becomes a vision of horror.

The surrealists, in contrast, turned Venus into a sexual provocation. One strategy was to confront the fictitious figure with real women. For the New York World's Fair of 1939, Salvador Dalí built a walk-in pavilion entitled *Dream of Venus*. A huge reproduction of Botticelli's foam-born Venus was mounted above the entrance. A photo documenting the creation of the pavilion shows this Venus, enlarged to immense proportions, surrounded by female models, many of them topless. *Time* magazine reported that there was more public nudity in Dalí's environment 'than any place outside of Bali'.[5] Many artistic experiments with Venus followed. For centuries, the theme was almost exclusively the preserve of men.

Ideals of modesty

While the figure of Venus is just one of many ideals of female bodies developed and explored in art, it is one of the most influential – simply because of its long history of fascination. Venus' sign, the stylized hand mirror (♀), marks all that is female in biology. In the 1970s it was combined with the raised fist and became the symbol of the women's movement. And the female nude, which has its origins in the Venus of classical antiquity, is unfailingly one of *the* main themes in the art of the modern era. In the 1980s the Guerrilla Girls, art activists concealed behind gorilla masks, protested against the fact that 85 per cent of all nudes in the Metropolitan Museum in New York showed a female body, while only 5 per cent of the works exhibited were created by female artists. Their campaign slogan was: 'Do women have to be naked to get into the Met. Museum?'

Things might have changed somewhat since the Guerrilla Girls' campaign. But even now, a woman visiting a major art museum will see large numbers of naked female bodies, displayed in a remarkably uniform manner. On the one hand, there is the almost total exclusion of the vulva, which has been analysed by scholars of culture and art.[6] On the other hand, there is the abundance of naked breasts. These signal eroticism, but are predominantly depicted in the same unrealistic way: as two perfect hemispheres. The standardization is striking, as is the similarity of the poses: there is the figure standing in *contrapposto*, the figure lying in a landscape or on a bed, and a rear view. All these are frequently reiterated poses of female nudes, and all of them, since the beginnings of art history in classical antiquity, have referred to representations of Venus. Venus is a visual formula without which large parts of Western art would be unimaginable. And though she has a counterpart, the male nude, he looks and behaves quite differently.

The Austrian art historian Daniela Hammer-Tugendhat uses a comparison between two works by the classical sculptor Praxiteles to explain the difference. In art, the presentation of the female body begins with modesty. While Praxiteles' Hermes of Olympia holds the infant Dionysus in his left arm, stretches his (truncated) right arm upwards, and presents his body openly, the same artist's Aphrodite of Knidos conceals her pudenda from our sight. It is our gaze that the goddess is avoiding, since the sculpture shows no one else she might need to hide from. Moreover, Aphrodite's body, unlike that of Hermes, is bent forward slightly and therefore appears unstable. The sculptures thus contribute to a 'polarization and hierarchization of the characters of the sexes': the standardized postures quickly become standardized ideas of femininity and masculinity – and vice versa.[7]

Over time, this modest pose of Venus/Aphrodite was intensified. While Praxiteles' goddess still had one arm free for something other than defending herself from 'shameless' looks, later versions had to use both hands for this. The breasts, initially uncovered, were now also half hidden. This female body was unable to take matters in hand, for the simple reason that it no longer had a hand free to do so. Instead, the protective gestures aimed at the parts of the female body with erotic connotations emphasized the defencelessness of this body and its role as an object, as well as its complete focus on this (defenceless, objectified) state. The Venus is self-referential and yet conditioned by the gaze of the (male) beholder.

This established a schema of the gaze which has remained influential to this day. In the 1970s, the feminist film studies scholar Laura Mulvey identified this regime of the gaze – 'men' watch, 'women' are watched – as the basic structure of Hollywood cinema.[8] Tracking shots over the female body re-enact this objectifying gaze over and over again. Here too, male bodies act, while female bodies are looked at. It is important to note that women can also acquire and apply this 'male gaze'. Furthermore, the example of Venus/Aphrodite demonstrates that this schema was created *art*ificially in the truest sense of the word – that is, in art. The female body is shown as a body that is looked at, or more precisely, a body that is there to be looked at. For all the historical differences between a Hollywood film and the Aphrodite of Knidos, we can nonetheless discern one constant, which forms the backdrop for various changes and modernizations: the 'female body in the nude portrait becomes the privileged object of the gaze.'[9] But at the same time this means creating a binary opposition conceived of as 'male' versus 'female'. This, as a glance at the history of philosophy shows, is influential not only in art, but beyond it:

> The gender difference is latently included in all the fundamental dualisms in which, as we know, the philosophical thought of the Occident has been rich since its beginnings, and seems only to have grown richer in the subsequent course of its history. Gender dualism is always implicitly present in the dualisms of culture and nature, soul and body, reason and emotion, public and private, having and being, the sublime and the beautiful. Conversely, this means that the fundamental dualisms of Western thought are inscribed in the concepts of femininity and masculinity. If asked, any person socialized in our culture would

'correctly' allocate the different categories to the two sexes, without doubt or hesitation. That women are closer to nature, while men carry out the work of culture; that women have more feeling and men more rationality; that women belong in the home (the private sphere), while the public sphere is reserved to men [...], etc. – all these are long-established gender clichés, which seem almost ineradicable.[10]

Modest or immodest?
How female bodies become Venuses

This rigid gender dualism could potentially have been turned upside down in 1864, when the aristocrat and keen archaeologist Marquis Paul de Vibraye found a Stone Age figurine in France. It showed a naked female body which looked completely different from the usual female bodies that had been painted, sculpted and exhibited so many times. The figure made no gesture of modesty, covering neither its vulva nor its breasts. But instead of taking this find as a stimulus to imagine a femininity beyond Venus, Vibraye did the exact opposite: he named the figure he had discovered the *Vénus impudique* or 'immodest Venus', by analogy with the modest *Venus pudica*. And this naming convention was retained: since Vibraye, all Stone Age female figurines have been referred to as 'Venus'. The Natural History Museum in Vienna, home to one of the most famous of these figurines, the Venus of Willendorf, presents it under the heading 'Venus Research'[11] (figure 14).

A particularly striking feature of the Venus of Willendorf is her colossal breasts. For modern viewers, whose gaze has been trained by art and mass media, the figure seems 'fat'; it contravenes today's beauty standards in various ways. In the 1960s, a small book on the history of the décolleté began by remarking on the Venus of Willendorf's 'monumental ugliness' and her 'two ungainly breasts'.[12] In 2014, the figure even appeared in a book about the history of plastic surgery. Here it was diagnosed with 'macromastia' (Greek *makros* = excessively large), a condition severe enough for the costs of breast reduction surgery to be covered by health insurance.[13] Yet these comments say more about modern attitudes to the breast and the associated norms than about the figure used as a foil for these norms.

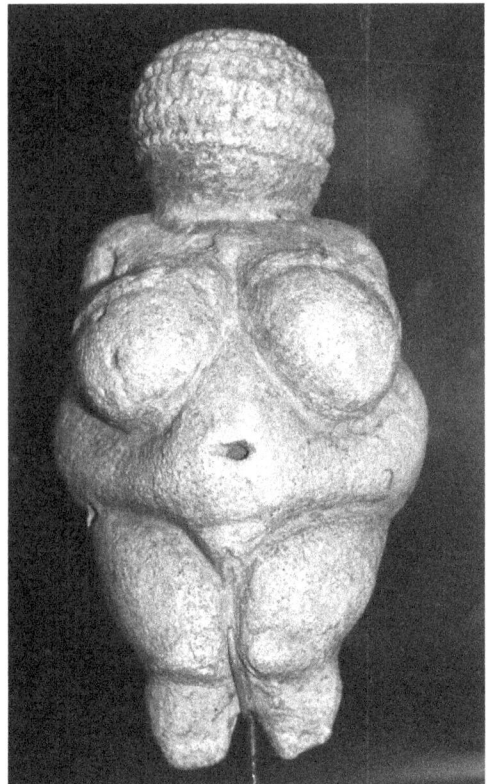

Figure 14 Venus of Willendorf, around 25,000 BC.

What were figures like this actually about? Prehistoric and proto-historic archaeology has yet to find a clear answer to this question. We will return to this later; first we will consider why these figures, which look completely different from the classical Venus figures, were given the name of the goddess in the first place. Obviously, the men who discovered them knew that these little statues could not actually be representations of Venus. There was no Venus in the Stone Age. In the second half of the nineteenth century, however, nearly every representation of a naked female body was most probably a Venus (see Gautier's reference to the 'Venus Salon' of 1863, incidentally the same year in which Vibraye found his *Vénus impudique*). And yet the name is strange, because immodesty signals the greatest possible divergence from the established model of Venus, whose basic condition is modesty.

Several factors come together here. First, the overpowering presence of a visual model of femininity that contains qualities such as modesty and youthfulness, distilled in the figure of Venus. In broad terms, every female figure was modelled on Venus, and if not, then she was not *something different from Venus* but, for the sake of simplicity, *a different Venus*. Another point is the nearly complete absence of other images of the body in art: the female nude at the time was essentially focused on the representation of the youthful ideal body. This is particularly clear when we look at the rare exceptions: images of female bodies that do not correspond to this ideal – for example, old bodies.[14] These are seldom represented in art, and if they are it is often as counter-images which reinforce the ideal, images designed to frighten or deter viewers. Lucas Cranach the Elder's *Fountain of Youth*, painted in 1546, is a paradigmatic example (figure 15).

Cranach's painting illustrates the notion that *all* female bodies should aspire to 'becoming Venus'. The idea of the fountain of youth, as the name suggests, is that one can regain one's youthfulness by bathing in its waters. An understandable wish, which men would presumably share. Here, however, it is only women who enter the water. On the left-hand side, where the landscape is bare and stony, dozens of women are being transported to the fountain in carts and wheelbarrows. On the right they emerge from the water, restored to their youthful form, and enter a lush, green landscape. There music, food and drink await them, along with the pleasures of love, as indicated by various couples – including the one hiding behind a bush in the bottom right-hand corner. Cranach's painting corresponds to an idea quoted by his contemporary, Rabelais: that men are rejuvenated by sleeping with youthful women. This would explain why they do not have to get into the water themselves. The topic of age is thus almost always associated with the female body. Hans Sachs, also a contemporary of Cranach, wrote a *Fastnachtsspiel* (a play to be performed on Shrove Tuesday) with the title *Wie man alte Weiber jung schmiedet* (How one forges old women into young ones), and the fountain of youth remained a popular motif in satirical stories into the seventeenth century.[15]

In Cranach's world, then, old age in men is not something that can be discerned from wrinkled skin, sagging body parts and toothless mouths. Male old age is wise and dignified, or simply a state a

Figure 15 Making young out of old. Lucas Cranach the Elder, *The Fountain of Youth*, 1546 (below: detail).

man enters if he doesn't die young. It is not subjected to aesthetic denigration, but is indicated by a shaggy beard or a slightly stooped posture. We do not get to see shrivelled testicles, pot bellies or wrinkled male bottoms. And the men disporting themselves with the rejuvenated women on the right are characterized either as beardless youths or as mature men who still have sufficient strength to dance. There is no naked male skin on display here.

This makes the stereotypical representation of female old age all the more striking. The crucial feature here, common to all the naked women on the left, is the 'sagging' breasts. And it is also the breasts that excite the attention of an older gentleman next to the fountain, whose red robe and spectacles, along with the large book under his arm, identify him as a scholar (figure 15). He bends down to inspect the breasts of a woman standing before him. The scholar represents us, the viewers contemplating the painting, and the small scene demonstrates what this is all about: the (male) gaze appraising the naked female body. The ideal aspired to by all the female bodies here stands in the midst of the bathing women as a sculpture: Venus with Cupid. This figure, central for an understanding of the painting, is small but placed in the middle of the artwork. In the fountain, the old, 'other' bodies become identical Venus bodies. So 'becoming Venus' is a topos that existed long before the naming of the Stone Age 'Venuses' (which Cranach would probably have positioned on the left-hand side of his painting).

The point of all these processes of transformation is eroticism and sexuality. If this wasn't clear before, it becomes obvious when we look at the couples that have come together after the women's successful dip in the fountain of youth. In the 1940s, the art historian Gustav Hartlaub observed 'certain lewd and somewhat bawdy details'.[16] The couples are locked in passionate embraces, or dance so wildly that the women's skirts fly up, or disappear behind bushes and trees, as indicated by fleeting glimpses of yellow-stockinged legs. Of course none of this is surprising, given the presence of the goddess of love and beauty. But it is interesting to consider that all this love and physical pleasure can only take place once the bodies match the Venus ideal. So the idea of Venus is a kind of framework imposed on art, which both defines an ideal of beauty based on the youthful female body and associates the idea of modesty with it. This implies that the female body must allow itself to be looked at, that it always somehow becomes a picture (and always has done), and is of course always subject to judgement. If a female body does not measure up to the fictitious figure of Venus, then the only possible conclusion is that it needs to become this figure – or that it is outside of everything that Venus embodies. This is, incidentally, consistent with the fact that the bodies in Cranach's painting do not gradually transform into the youthful ideal. We do not see any intermediate stages, where the breasts become a little firmer, the hair less grey, or the movements a little more sprightly – though this might have been artistically appealing. Instead all we have here is either/or: either a woman is an old hag and unlike Venus in every respect, or she *is* Venus, and the most interesting thing about her is her suitability as a sexual partner for men. No other roles are envisaged here, simply because there *are* no other bodies.

We can conclude from this that the *Vénus impudique* received her name because she threatened to disrupt this dualistic framework. The term *impudique* (immodest or shameless) points to the sexual connotations outlined above, which are alluded to in Cranach's painting. There the women's rejuvenation serves to make them sexually available for the older and ageing men, who can in turn be rejuvenated by physical relationships with the younger women. As Cranach depicts it, women's sexual desire is limited to this role.

When archaeologists discovered the figure of the 'immodest Venus' in the mid-nineteenth century, the prevailing ideas on femininity prescribed an equally strict division between male and female sexuality. In the context of a clear separation between the male public sphere and the female private sphere, bourgeois female sexuality was carefully contained, and female passionlessness was seen as the counterpart to active male sexuality.[17] The presence of non-reproductive female sexuality was denied or described as a deviation from the idealized norm. In post-classical representations of Venus, the fundamentally erotic figure of Venus had already been used to propagate virtuous modesty. Some years before the *Birth of Venus*, Botticelli had depicted Mars and Venus together, to represent the moderating influence of the female goddess on the fierce temper of the male god of war.

This reading of Venus was also influential in the nineteenth century. In a visual cosmos crowded with representations of Venus, where erotic titillation was always associated with this ideal of 'modesty' (closed body surfaces, hairlessness, modest gestures, lowered gaze, etc.), the representation of a female body with 'unshapely' breasts and a clearly visible vulva, a body that eschewed 'feminine' poses, could only be perceived as a counter-model, as something radically 'other'. In short, the concept of Venus served as the basis for two mutually exclusive but nonetheless interrelated constructions of femininity. The potency of this dualistic model can also be seen in its use in other contexts to racialize and denigrate female sexualities (for example in the case of the 'Hottentot Venus'). One of the men who discovered the Venus of Willendorf, the Viennese archaeologist Hugo Obermaier, noted that its 'fat', 'degenerate' female body resembled that of 'lazy Jewesses'. Around 1900, as the historian Sander Gilman has argued, the image of the 'fat' Jewish woman permeated fields as diverse as archaeology, cosmetic surgery (which specialized in the reduction of racialized, 'Jewish' breasts) and painting. Here the motif of Susanna and the Elders was used by artists such as Arnold Böcklin to evoke several antisemitic stereotypes at once (*Susanna in the Bath*, 1888, Oldenburg, Landesmuseum für Kunst und Kulturgeschichte).[18] The Venus of Willendorf thus acquired an additional function: it became the counter-image of an ideal, white (and in this case non-Jewish) female body.

Palaeo porn

People contemplating Stone Age female figurines in the nineteenth and early twentieth centuries took their large breasts as a sign of 'non-art'. This is one of the reasons why they are generally exhibited in natural history museums and not in art museums. The 'immodest Venus' was a woman/Venus who was positioned outside the Venus ideal and therefore outside art. She had – metaphorically speaking – not yet bathed in the fountain of youth. Even today, the large breasts of the Palaeolithic 'Venus' figurines seem to be the reason why they are still condemned as 'immodest' – albeit in a modernized way. From 'immodest' it is but a small step to 'porn'.

In 2009, archaeologists from Tübingen University in Germany discovered a Stone Age figure in a cave called Hohle Fels. In accordance with the usual routine, it was named the Venus of Hohle Fels. The features that were conspicuous in the Venus of Willendorf are instantly noticeable here too: the enormous breasts and the clearly visible vulva. In science communication, the figure was labelled 'Palaeolithic porno' with astonishing speed.[19] Based on the assumption that only men could be interested in it, the figurine was flippantly referred to as 'gentlemen's glossy portable statuary' and the 'world's first page 3 girl'. This may be understandable, given the need to attract clicks, but it is still sexist. For a start, there is no reason to assume that these figurines were created by prehistoric 'gentlemen', and solely for the use of other such 'gentlemen'. It is equally possible that they were created and used by women. Certainly, the idea that only men produced and consumed art in the Palaeolithic seems implausible; in any case, it has yet to be proven by corresponding finds or other sources. It is more likely that this conviction can be explained mainly by the reproduction of stereotypical concepts of gender, as the archaeologists April Nowell and Melanie L. Chang argue:

> It is [...] invalid to assume that female figurines [during the Palaeolithic] were made only by men. While the gender(s) of the artists who created Upper Palaeolithic figurines [such as the Venus of Hohle Fels] remain unknown [...], we believe that the assumption of male authorship is based primarily on the accepted wisdom that 'great art' has, throughout history, been made by men only and on the notion that the perceived sexual nature of the figurines would uniquely appeal to men.[20]

The assumption that the Palaeolithic Venus figurines were created for a purely male audience was widespread in art history and archaeology for decades, although the lack of rationale should have been instantly obvious. In 1978 the art historian John Onians and the palaeontologist Desmond Collins had declared, in the journal *Art History*, that the three-dimensionality of these figures predestined them to being picked up and fondled, 'in much the same way as [...] the buttocks or breasts of a real woman'.[21] They drew the conclusion that only 'adolescent, or adult, males' were worth considering as possible producers and users of the figures. No reasons for this were ever given. In 1984 the archaeologist Dale Guthrie stated apodictically that 'The bulging Venus figurines with enormous buttocks and pendulous teats, along with vulva drawn on the cave walls were undoubtedly male art creations for themselves or for other men [...] the drawings or carvings were made, touched, carved, and fondled by men.'[22]

It should be noted that the idea of a libidinous relationship between male cave dwellers and the artworks they created dates back to roughly the same period as the labelling of the Palaeolithic artefacts as Venus figurines. Not only were they given the name of a goddess from classical antiquity, who was not worshipped until tens of thousands of years after their creation; they were also associated with some of the stories about the goddess of love circulating at the time. One such tale, which used to be falsely attributed to Lucian, is taken as evidence of the charm and erotic attraction of Praxiteles' Aphrodite of Knidos. It recounts an incident of statuophilia, discovered when 'the trace of passionate embraces' (a suspicious stain on the statue's thigh) was found after a young male admirer had had himself locked in with the artwork overnight.[23] Thus the idea that the 'immodest' Stone Age figurines were made to be fondled by male users is a projection on the part of male archaeologists of the twentieth and twenty-first centuries and is not supported by any archaeological finds.

The gender politics of the gaze

Over the course of its history, then, the interpretation of the Palaeolithic Venus figurines has been shaped by sexist assumptions and visual conventions. The figures' large breasts have misguided interpreters into seeing them as potential candidates for plastic surgery, or as precursors of pornographized representations of femininity for heterosexual men ('palaeo pin-ups'). Yet these large breasts can also be interpreted quite differently. In 2012, the anatomist Gillian Morriss-Kay proposed a radical change of perspective. What if, she mused, the headless Venus of Hohle Fels were not the object of 'smut-hungry prehistoric proto-Germans,'[24] as has been assumed time after time, but evidence of female self-reflection? It could, for example, be the self-portrait of a woman shortly after giving birth:

> From the viewpoint of this interpretation, the portrait of the carver's body is not based primarily on what she sees; instead, the perceptions interpreted by her somatosensory cortex have contributed more than those of her visual cortex [...]. Her breasts are engorged with milk: their gradual enlargement during pregnancy has not prepared her for the sudden shock and discomfort of lactiferous engorgement. They feel unfamiliarly tight and enormous, hence their exaggerated size and raised position.[25]

These ideas have also attracted growing interest in archaeology and art history. As early as 1996, the art scholar LeRoy McDermott argued that the Palaeolithic Venus figurines

> represent ordinary women's views of their own bodies [...]. As self-portraits of women at different stages of life, these early figurines embodied obstetrical and gynecological information and probably signified an advance in women's self-conscious control over the material conditions of their reproductive lives [...]. I conclude that the first tradition of human image making probably emerged as an adaptive response to the unique physical concerns of women [...].[26]

These interpretations make it clear how strongly *all* interpretations are based on existing but unexamined patterns of thought. The stories that researchers tell depend on this predefined perspective. Or, as Samira El Ouassil and Friedemann Karig observe, 'Stories teach us how to live and how to love.'[27] This is exactly what the two 'breast stories' of the Palaeolithic Venus show. In one version, the Stone Age figurine 'tells' us that the origins of art lay firmly in the hands of heterosexual men, that men have always looked at women's bodies, big breasts and naked vulvas with a pornographic interest, and, above all, that there is/was evidently no room for any other desire or for a female view of women's own bodies. This allows a direct line to be drawn from the Palaeolithic to the pin-up girl. Regardless of whether the big breasts and the visible vulva of the Stone Age figures are labelled as Venus (nineteenth century) or pin-up (twentieth and twenty-first centuries), this narrative is always that of a heterosexual male gaze.

Hence the proximity to the subject of porn, which is so obvious in the descriptions of contemporary archaeologists. Porn is, after all, the place where 'immodesty' and 'shamelessness' belong. According to this logic, representations of women that cannot be assigned to the classical model of the *Venus pudica* remain 'Venuses' – that is, women's bodies that incite male lust. But they fall outside the framework of legitimate, artistic representations of nakedness.

The other narrative of the Venus of Hohle Fels as the self-portrait of a woman is a fundamental reversal of the gaze. It leads to an interpretation that attributes the origin of human art production to the bodily experience of women and their aesthetic response to it. In this version, the figurines no longer prove that, 40,000 years ago, sex-obsessed playboys and testosterone-driven 'hunters and gatherers' had power over highly eroticized and pornographized images of women, and used these artworks as sex dolls after a successful day's hunting. Instead, this version places the origin of human cultural production in female hands. The change of narrative is huge.

Incidentally, feminist artists in the 1970s experimented with just such a perspective. In an image by the US artist Joan Semmel entitled *Me Without Mirrors* (1974), the perspective on the body is similar to that of the Venus of Hohle Fels. The viewers take the perspective of the artist, who is looking down on her naked body. Her head is not visible because the self-portrait was created without mirrors, and the image 'begins' with her breasts, at the bottom edge of the picture. So here too we see a naked female body without a head, and here too, the breasts are in the foreground. Only the artist herself sees her body in this way. This could certainly be the perspective underlying the Venus of Hohle Fels. Mirrors were unknown in the Palaeolithic. The first mirror-like finds, small, polished metal plates, date from the Etruscan period, around 3000 BC. Apart from reflections in water, looking down was virtually the only possible way to look at one's own body. Semmel's visual strategy shows that it is by no means absurd to interpret the Venus of Hohle Fels as the self-portrait of a woman.

It is, however, essential to bear in mind that the motivations, experiences and body perceptions of the creators of the 1974 painting and the

Palaeolithic figurine were undoubtedly completely different. In no way can the comparison of these two representations of the female body suggest that they reveal a constant of supposedly female physicality. For a start, Semmel's work is a reaction to a long tradition of the image and the gaze, which she critically scrutinizes and subverts. Semmel is familiar with the many Venus figures from Praxiteles to Dalí. The creator (male or female) of the Venus of Hohle Fels, however, was working *before* the beginnings of this tradition. And what prehistoric viewers and users saw in the figure was undoubtedly different from what we see today.

The interpretation as a self-portrait did not go uncontested in archaeology. For example, it was pointed out that whoever carved the figurine would probably have been sitting or crouching on the ground while working on it, so it was implausible that the body would be represented standing.[28] Art historians also commented that the concept of the self-portrait, McDermott's leitmotif for the interpretation of the big-breasted figurines, is at the centre of Western culture and its focus on the individual. Since the contemporary gaze has been socialized by Western art and inevitably assumes the presence of a modern self, they argued, it is no wonder that this 'self' is detected even in places and times where it may not yet have existed.[29] Yet what the comparison between the Stone Age figurine and the mid-twentieth-century oil painting offers is a clue to the connection between gender and the gaze, even in the interpretation of archaeological artefacts. Researchers look at their finds with a 'Venus gaze', shaped by more than 2,000 years of conditioning.

Another 'other' woman: the 'Hottentot Venus'

A few years before the *Vénus impudique*, another 'other' Venus had entered the stage, a woman who became known in Europe under the name Sarah Baartman. She was probably born in the late 1770s as a member of the Khoekhoe population, in territory that had been colonized for over a hundred years and is now South Africa.[30] She was referred to as the 'Hottentot Venus', a derogatory term that reveals the dehumanization associated with it. A notice in the *Morning Post* in 1810 announced her arrival to the London public:

The Hottentot Venus. – Just arrived (and may be seen between the hours of One and Five o'clock in the evening, at No. 225, Piccadilly), from the Banks of the River Gamtoos, on the Borders of Kaffraria, in the interior of South Africa, a most correct and perfect Specimen of that race of people. From this extraordinary phenomena [*sic*] of nature, the Public will have an opportunity of judging how far she exceeds any description given by the historians of that tribe of the human species. [...] She has been brought to this country at a considerable expence [*sic*], by Kendrick Cerar [*sic*], and their stay will be of short duration. – To commence on Monday next, the 24th inst. – Admittance, 2s. each.[31]

What was being advertised here was the exhibition of a human being. In London and other European cities, humans were publicly put on show, and other humans paid money to see them, because they were bigger or smaller than the average, had tattoos, or were simply considered 'monstrous'.

So newspaper readers probably realized intuitively what this was about, even if the phenomenon and the term 'Hottentot Venus' were new. People knew what a Venus looked like, and tales about Hottentots had been told in Europe since the seventeenth century. The combination of the two promised to be a curiosity well worth seeing. Ideas about 'Hottentot women' had been introduced in travel accounts such as that of the German mathematician, schoolmaster and explorer of South Africa, Peter Kolb. His book *Caput Bonae Spei hodiernum. Das ist: Vollständige Beschreibung des africanischen Vorgebürges der Guten Hofnung* (Caput Bonae Spei hodiernum: That is, complete description of the African Cape of Good Hope), published in 1719, promised to give a detailed description of their 'customs and habits'. A defining characteristic of Kolb's account and those of other travellers was a 'contemptuous misogyny, especially towards "Hottentot" women'.[32] Their bodies were considered repulsive, as they typically featured two attributes that inspired particular horror: huge buttocks (steatopygia) and elongated labia (the 'Hottentot apron'). The third element taken as a sign of these women's 'ugliness' and otherness was their pendulous breasts. In the English edition of Kolb's travelogue, published in London in 1731, there is an entry on this subject with an accompanying illustration. There Kolb writes that these women's breasts are so long they can be thrown over their shoulder to breastfeed a baby tied to their back. This description is part of a discourse in which African breasts are compared with European ones.[33] Here the ideal of youthful and virginal breasts, round and firm, was the yardstick against which all other breasts were measured. In contrast, African breasts were seen as a 'perversion of the European prototype',[34] just as the *Vénus impudique* and the 'Hottentot Venus' were construed as perversions (Latin *perversus*: askew, awry) of the 'right', i.e. 'white', Venus. The ideal of a young, flawless, white body served to define otherness or foreignness.

The first pictures of female apes from the seventeenth century showed them with very visible, pendulous breasts, even though apes do not normally have breast tissue. This served to signal that pendulous breasts were to be associated with a 'primitive' nature.[35] Sagging breasts could reveal various kinds of inferiority and flaws; this did not apply solely to African women. In European women, drooping breasts were not only an indicator of advanced age, which was fundamentally devalued in women (see Cranach's *Fountain of Youth*). They were also – particularly from the nineteenth century onwards – seen as a mark of the lower classes, who wore out their breasts with hard work and prolonged and frequent breastfeeding. The motif of breasts that did not conform to the ideal shape – always a sign of something bad – was also evoked to vilify the Irish. For example, the Scottish traveller William Lithgow commented on the (in his view) unattractive breasts of Irish women, which were reminiscent of large bags. Similar remarks were made about the breasts of 'Hottentot' women; these were allegedly so big that they were to used make tobacco pouches, which were sold in great numbers at the Cape of Good Hope.[36]

The term 'Hottentot Venus', used in the London advertisement, also hinted at the motif of the 'Black Venus', which had featured in poems such as Isaac Teale's *The Sable Venus: An Ode* (1794).[37] It tells the tale of a Black Venus, whom the speaker of the poem meets on the Greek mountain of Helicon, the seat of the Muses. She asks him for a song in her honour, and he delivers it in the form of the poem. Yet despite the positive message of the text, which praises the superior beauty of the Black Venus, even here she is compared with the European ideal. This connection between Venus, the pinnacle of idealized white femininity, and the 'Hottentot woman' as her depraved 'other' was rendered plausible with the aid of visual inventions. This took place gradually. The print used to advertise the exhibition of Sarah Baartman in London showed 'Saartjee, the Hottentot Venus' in profile. There is no discernible reference to Venus in the picture itself, however, partly because this type of profile view is virtually unknown in the iconography of the goddess. Instead, the use of this type of representation situates the 'Hottentot Venus' in the ethnographic visual tradition. In other words, her posture alone indicates that she is not a goddess admired for her beauty, but the object of a racist gaze. The profile was used by ethnographers and went hand in hand with the measurement of bodies and the precise appraisal of their physical 'racial characteristics'. On a visual level, then, this print shouted 'Hottentot' very loudly and uttered barely a whisper about Venus. This changed a few years later, when a satirical etching by the British artist Charles Williams was published (figure 16).

It is based on the earlier version of the image, but diverges from it in important points. Besides the extended caption, 'Love and Beauty – Saartjee the Hottentot Venus', the figure is no longer in full profile. She now turns slightly towards the viewers, seeming to look directly at them. This makes both her breasts visible, while drawing slightly less attention to her posterior. The latter becomes a massive seat for the additional character added to the cast, a small Cupid shooting an arrow out of the picture. In a speech bubble above his little head, we read the warning 'Take care of your Hearts!!'. These few small changes are a decisive step towards Venus. In the literature on Baartman, surprisingly little attention has been paid to these visual modifications, although they could help to explain why Baartman's body was presented as a Venus in the first place. Cupid, son of Venus from her union with Mars, the god of war, is often depicted with a bow and arrow, as for example in Botticelli's famous painting *Primavera* (around 1482). Somewhat later (in 1509), Lucas Cranach the Elder was one of the first artists north of the Alps to paint the goddess naked. In his painting, the goddess tries half-heartedly to restrain her son, who stands at her feet and is clearly eager to use his bow and arrow (figure 17). In view of the desirable body displayed here, the warning given in Cranach's inscription seems unlikely to be heeded: 'Cast out the lusts

 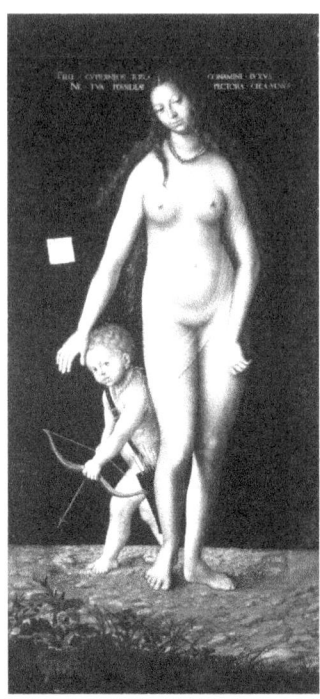

Figures 16 and 17 Love and Beauty. Figure 16 (left) Charles Williams,
Saartje the Hottentot Venus, 1822. Figure 17 (right) Lucas Cranach the Elder,
Venus and Amor, 1509.

of the flesh with all your strength, so that Venus does not rule over you
and make you blind.'

As we have seen, the satirical producer of 'Love and Beauty' added
a similar small Cupid to the depiction of the 'Hottentot Venus' and
also followed the tradition of issuing a (half-hearted) warning in an
inscription. The little Cupid is usually a playful and cheerful figure,
described in classical sources as a 'cheeky madcap'.[38] Here, however,
the winged god serves to discredit Venus. This is partly because his
use of Baartman's bottom as a seat emphasizes its size. But his position
also evokes the older topos of 'Hottentot' women whose breasts hang
down so far that they are supposedly able to suckle their children while
carrying them on their backs. Cupid's presence gives visual support
and confirmation to the verbal reference to Venus. But at the same
time, the mere idea of losing one's heart to the woman depicted here

is presented as a joke. It evokes a notion already found in Lessing's *Laocoon* (1766):

> The filthiness of the Hottentots is well known, as also the fact of their regarding as beautiful and holy what excites our disgust and aversion. The pressed gristle of a nose, flaccid breasts descending to the navel, the whole body anointed with a varnish of goat's fat and soot, melted in by the sun [...]: imagine all this the object of an ardent, respectful, tender love; listen to expressions of this love in the noble language of sincerity and admiration, and keep from laughing if you can.[39]

The argument here is that the very idea that someone could love the 'Hottentot', with her 'breasts descending to the navel', is laughable. And thus the discourse on Venus, even before it entered the archaeology of the Palaeolithic, was already part of a colonial racism. Although the name 'Venus' implied that female bodies which diverged from the classical ideal could theoretically be perceived as 'beautiful', this did not lead Western thinkers to recognize the relativity of their own norms. On the contrary, the philosopher Karl Rosenkranz, who published an *Ästhetik des Häßlichen* (Aesthetics of ugliness) in 1853, and who had read Lessing very thoroughly, argued: 'If there were no beauty, then there certainly would be no ugliness, for the latter exists only as the negation of the former.'[40]

Just how political a reference to beauty can be became evident around a hundred years later in the slogan of the US Black Power movement in the 1960s: 'Black is beautiful.' It reclaimed the concept of beauty for all those who were excluded from it or included only ambivalently for racist reasons, linked to the deeply problematic coupling of attraction and denigration. In 1992, the Black theorist bell hooks referred to the commodification of the 'other' in white mainstream culture as 'eating the other', as simultaneous consumption and annihilation. The fascination with the 'beauty' of Black bodies goes hand in hand with the masking of power disparities[41] – a pattern that is still discussed critically in contemporary debates on cultural appropriation, and is relevant for both sexes.[42] Historically, however, different references have been activated for the male body. There was never a 'Hottentot Adonis', and never could be, because in the Western discourse on art it was the *female* body that was given the task of (literally) embodying key concepts such as beauty and form. At the same time, however, this was always implicitly based on the assumption of a heterosexual male viewer, whose desiring or disgusted gaze was enacted in the image. The image is 'female', the gaze 'male'.

Nudes, power, pornography

This division between 'female' image and 'male' gaze has seldom been expressed more clearly than in a diary entry by Wassily Kandinsky from 1913:

> Thus I learned to fight the canvas, to get to know it as a being stubbornly resistant to my will (= dream), and to bend it forcibly to this will. At first it stands there like a pure, chaste virgin with a clear gaze and heavenly joy [...]. And then comes the desiring paintbrush, which gradually conquers the canvas, first here, then there, with all the energy it possesses, like a European colonist, who, with his axe, spade, hammer and saw, penetrates the wild maiden Nature, whom no man has yet touched, in order to bend her to his will.[43]

Here art is imagined as the (male) act of taking possession,[44] as a conquest and an act of violence. The sexual connotations are obvious. The 'desiring paintbrush' can be interpreted as a synonym for the penis, in accordance with a tradition that reaches back to the art literature of the early modern period.[45] And the triumph over the 'wild maiden Nature', which casts the artist as a colonial master, reflects the system of sexual exploitation that was a well-established component of colonialism.[46]

The idea that the (male) artist forces (female) material into a form, turning it into art, is not a modern concept. It can be be traced back to Aristotle, who codified the dichotomy of passive female and active male in his theory of reproduction. He saw the 'male' as 'possessing the principle of movement' and 'the female as possessing that of matter'.[47] This gender-specific allocation has continued to play a central part in the aesthetic opposition between form and material; Kandinsky is just one of many examples. In *The Nude*, first published in 1956 and still in print today, English art historian Kenneth Clark described the female nude as 'the most complete example of the transmutation of matter into form'.[48]

In the 1960s Yves Klein, an important proponent of *nouveau réalisme*, created a series of works entitled *Anthropométries*, using female models whom he referred to as 'living paintbrushes'. Having emphasized that he did not want to sully himself with paint (= matter), the male artist donned a suit and bow tie and gave instructions to the women, whose naked bodies then became images. The aggressive element inscribed into the process of art production in Kandinsky's description was also present here; in a subsequent performance Klein used a blow torch to burn the images produced by these 'living paintbrushes'. The transformation of the female body from matter to form also leads to the distinction between *naked* and *nude*. Only the nude constitutes art. Female bodies that undermine the rigorous process of transformation into the ideal form threaten art and risk crossing the line into obscenity. Art historian Lynda Nead argues that this line is largely drawn via images of the female body, with the 'good nudity' of art contrasted with the 'depraved nudity' of pornography. In both cases, though, it is the *female* body that is naked:

> At either end of the cultural register we have the images of high art and pornography. On the one hand, there is the fine-art female nude as a symbol of the pure, disinterested, functionless gaze and of the female body transubstantiated; and, on the other hand, we have the images of pornography, the realm of the profane [...]. Between these two extremes there lies a range of cultural distinctions and a sacred frontier which is drawn and redrawn along the lines of competing definitions [...].[49]

The naked female body is therefore threatened with the verdict of obscenity in a different way to the male body. In simplified terms, the separation between 'high art' (the ideal Venus, for example) and pornography (the 'other', 'shameless' Venus) is based on the appraisal of women's bodies. And this too is a reason why a woman who appears topless in public is condemned as disinhibited and possibly immoral, while a man appearing bare-chested is, at worst, ridiculed as a beer-bellied chav.

This double standard also became apparent in reactions to a performance by the US artist and former porn star Annie Sprinkle. Her *Public Cervix Announcement*, a performance combining medical, artistic and pornographic discourses, included an invitation to the audience to take a look at her cervix through a speculum. In 1990, police in Cleveland prevented her from performing by declaring her show obscene. The film scholar Linda Williams rightly described it as a 'fascinating comment on American culture' that Sprinkle 'was never visited by the vice squad' when performing live sex shows in the same city.[50] In 2017 Sprinkle ascended the Olympus of contemporary art when she was invited to Documenta 14 in Kassel. She has described the border between art and pornography, the site of her creative work, from the perspective of someone personally involved in both:

> [In art] there was no specific 'commercial style' or 'formula' one had to adhere to, as one does in the sex biz. There was total creative freedom, and far less censorship. For example, in a burlesque show you pretty much had to dress and act a certain way. Performances were always twenty minutes long, and there were strict laws about the sex and nudity. In art you could dress how you wanted, act how you wanted, and perform for as long or short a time as you wanted, and there didn't seem to be any very specific laws about the sex and nudity.[51]

From the perspective of a woman who exhibits her naked body to an audience, these differences matter. For Sprinkle, they mean liberation from a rigidly structured space of commercial sexuality and physicality into the 'openness' of art. Sprinkle is no longer perceived as a prostitute, but as an artist. If the transition from pornography is successful, the naked body ceases to be obscene and becomes art. If this does not succeed, as happened in Cleveland, sanctions follow. Apart from the self-determined and therefore more pleasant working conditions in art, the crucial difference is an increase in cultural capital, the term coined by sociologist Pierre Bourdieu for the broad field of social participation and influence.[52] It is fitting that Sprinkle claims to be the first porn star to have earned a PhD (awarded by the

Institute for Advanced Study of Human Sexuality in San Francisco in 2002).

Sprinkle's humorous approach to the unwritten rules of the porn industry has repeatedly led to political demands to withdraw funding from her 'obscene' art – particularly in the US. The key to this approach is that the showing of the female body is not the work of a male artist, nor does it conform to the conventions of the mass-produced images of pornography. Despite this, she always alludes to both fields and draws attention to the connections. For example, her *Bosom Ballet*, first performed in 1991, recalls on the one hand an absurd catalogue of artistic poses or attitudes which the female body has adopted in the history of the nude, and on the other hand the auto-erotic gestures of a striptease. With her upper body naked, the artist moves her breasts into a series of different positions, squeezing them together, covering them up or pushing them apart. Her elbow-length black gloves emphasize her movements.

Sprinkle is parodying this alternation of different poses in art – but also in striptease, a highly artificial performance. It is no coincidence that a number of special garments for the breasts have been developed for striptease, and that performers are required to learn special techniques for showing this body part.[53] But the fact that Sprinkle's performance and pictorial instructions cannot ultimately be used for instructional purposes makes her work recognizable as an artistic intervention. The individual movements seem not so much erotic as mechanical. She shows work with and on the breasts as a body technique, in both art and the sex biz.

Baring the breast: feminist provocations

The breasts are the focal point for the simultaneous revealing and concealing of the erotic body. There is, for example, the chastely raised hand, which covers one breast while drawing all the more attention to the other. Where this pattern is disrupted, conflicts occur. Or at least, conflicts and system malfunctions could occur, if the master narrative were not instantly reimposed. The Palaeolithic figurines, which do not correspond to the ideal of modest concealing and male-artist-led revealing, are labelled 'immodest' or 'shameless' and are nonetheless turned into Venuses. Other deviations from the rigorous ideal of this figure are projected onto the 'Hottentot woman' in racist images and practices. So it is not so much about *whether* body parts are shown as about *who* is permitted to show them, *when*, *where* and above all *how*. As the sociology of art has demonstrated, being an artist means occupying a certain position, from which one speaks *as* an artist. From this perspective, 'artist' does not designate an exceptional, creative personality, standing outside society, but a cultural figure that exists in and through certain discourses (e.g. the legend of the artist[54]) and institutions (such as art academies, biennial art festivals, museums and art history[55]). These discourses and institutions are not only subject to historical change, but also shaped in gender-specific ways. For example, the first European art academy was founded in 1563 in Florence,[56] but for centuries, all such academies admitted only men. In Germany, state academies were only opened to women when female suffrage was introduced in 1919. Clearly, 'artisthood' is not something that exists in a vacuum. Of course, there were always women who produced art. But for a very long time, in some cases even to this day, women as artists had only very limited access to the above-mentioned discourses and institutions. Often they appear only as astonishing 'exceptions' who confirm the rule. Even at the beginning of the twentieth century, the study of the naked body – especially the male body – was considered unseemly for women. As a result, female students were often not admitted to life drawing classes. Yet comprehensive knowledge of the human anatomy was the prerequisite for creating really 'great' art; without it, one might have to resort to less respected genres such as still life or flower painting. In any case, an artist whose training had allowed her no glimpse of a naked body would be unable to work in the prestigious genre of history painting.[57]

Presenting the human body, allowing it to be *seen* – on the one hand, this was long regarded as the artist's noblest task; on the other hand, this aspect of artistic training was reserved to men. As we have seen, early twentieth-century male artists such as Kandinsky imagined the process of painting as a highly eroticized battle of the sexes. In light of this, the argument of 'unseemliness' was a question of power in two senses. Admitting women to life drawing classes not only empowered them to enter new spaces in the real world, it also gave them greater power in the realms of the imaginary: now the female body of the woman artist could capture the male body on paper or canvas and take visual control. We must bear in mind, however, that erotic represen-tations of the male body by female artists are the absolute exception, both historically and in the present.[58] This makes the representations that do exist all the more interesting. In 1972, for example, there was a small uproar – but also amusement – at the annual meeting of the College Art Association of America. Speaking on 'Eroticism and the Image of Woman in Nineteenth-Century Art', the US art historian Linda Nochlin presented two photos. One is from the nineteenth century and shows a woman, naked but for shoes, stockings and a pearl necklace, holding a tray of apples in front of her chest. The caption of the soft-focus image reads 'Buy My Apples'. The breasts, and indeed the whole woman, appear as commodities on sale.[59] The second photo, taken by Nochlin herself, is based on the first, but instead of a woman, a man wearing only shoes and socks presents a tray of bananas in front of his naked genitals. This simple reversal does not work, however. While the presentation of the breast for erotic consumption is based on a long image history, no such traditions for the objectification of the male body exist. This may, incidentally, be a further reason why very few female artists have turned a sexualizing gaze on the male body.[60]

Feminist artists have worked to devise strategies that might thwart these attributions. The Cuban-American artist Ana Mendieta evoked the violence inherent in transferring a three-dimensional body to the flat surface of a picture by pressing a pane of glass against her upper body. Its sharp edges seem to cut painfully into the skin and deform her breasts (*Untitled: Glass on Body Imprints*, 1972).[61] The process by which the breasts become image appears here as a distressing attack on the integrity of the body.

In 1968 Austrian artist Valie Export had also deployed the breasts in a confrontational evocation of the way the female body becomes an image. Her *Tapp- und Tastkino* (usually translated as 'Tap and Touch Cinema') reversed the sensory experience of perceiving the breast in an image. Instead of using their eyes to see three-dimensional breasts as two-dimensional images on the flat surface of the cinema screen, passers-by could use their hands to touch Export's 'real' breasts, but could not see them. This was made possible with a portable box strapped to the artist's upper body. A curtain blocked any view of the breasts, but left openings for the hands of those who dared to accept the invitation to 'tap and touch'.

Working with Peter Weibel, an artist, theorist and later museum director, Export drew crowds on busy public squares such as the Stachus in Munich. A photo taken during one of her performances gives an impression of the atmosphere at the time. An excited crowd had gathered around Export and Weibel, full of voyeuristic interest but uncertain what to do. Some just looked briefly in passing, while others were braver and reached into the box with their hands. This and other photos of the event show only men. The division between the (female) object of the desire to see and touch and the (male) subject who mediates, explains and interprets also remained traditional. Peter Weibel used a megaphone to announce what the *Tapp- und Tastkino* was all about, encouraging passers-by to touch Export's breasts. And when the ORF, the Austrian national broadcaster, reported on the performance in *Apropos Film* on 12 September 1968, it declared smugly that the artwork permitted 'interested cineastes to take Valie's measurements, so to speak'. The report also pointed out that the artist was 'actually' called Waltraud Höllinger and was a mother. Whether Weibel was a father was of no interest to anyone. With its condescending tone (the artist is referred to by her first name, like a child), the commentary involuntarily demonstrates the sexism that Export's work unmasks.

By bringing the breasts into the public, urban space in this combative way, Export could be seen as carrying out an act of self-empowerment. Though she was charged with pornography after this performance, naked breasts were actually, surprisingly, much more present in public in the 1960s than they are today. But here too, the crucial question was *who* was showing them, and *how*. It was not showing breasts in public that was offensive, but the fact that a female artist was making her breasts 'public' according to her own rules, imitating and manipulating the everyday 'breast discourse' of the mass media.

The 'prudish' 1950s were not long over when Export strapped on her tactile cinema, but breasts were ubiquitous in magazines and cinemas. In 1969, the German television listings magazine *Hörzu* cited

Technik der körperlichen Liebe (The technique of physical love) as the number one hit film, followed by the Danish film *Without a Stitch*; another German film, *Kama Sutra*; the German-Italian coproduction *Marquis de Sade: Justine*; and the American group sex film *Come Ride the Wild Pink Horse*. The magazine's comment was 'Toplessness is always a drawcard.'[62] A glance at the covers of the German current affairs magazine *Stern* shows that the marketing of the (young) ideal bosom increased rapidly from the early 1960s. The front page for 14 July 1968 shows the rear view of a naked woman, turning sideways so one breast is visible. Opposite her stands a fully clothed policeman, who appears to be delivering a stern reprimand. The topic: 'Don't get caught – things that are fun are not allowed everywhere.' And a few weeks later the magazine sought to raise interest in the topic 'Are women really worse drivers?' with the barely covered torso of a naked woman. From 1970 onwards, bare breasts were a regular sight on the cover of *Stern*, supposedly illustrating completely random topics.[63] In 1978 this inspired Alice Schwarzer and her feminist magazine *Emma* to sue *Stern* for sexism. The case was dismissed, but it did trigger a debate about the issue.

As this short digression shows, the striking ubiquity of the breast in the mass media around 1970 was anything but a sign of emancipatory progress; instead, it was embedded in a culture of sexism. The permanent media visibility of the breast served purely to sell films and magazines. Valie Export's performance turned this around: suddenly the many images of breasts that could be viewed from a distance were replaced by the tactile confrontation with the artist's real breasts, which simultaneously remained invisible to the eyes. This must have been disconcerting for her audience. Export brought her breasts onto the street, but did not allow them to be thoughtlessly consumed; instead of being exposed, they exposed the voyeurism of the excited crowd.

Export's work remained an important point of reference for subsequent generations of female artists. In 1997, the Turkish-born artist Şükran Moral performed a multi-part work, *Bordello*, in which she appeared topless in front of a curious and nearly entirely male public in Istanbul. Holding a 'For sale' sign to her chest, she stood in front of a brothel, on which she had hung a sign saying 'Museum of Modern Art'. Commenting on her work, the artist mentioned the 'power of those who gape [*Gaffer*] and the passivity of those who are gaped at [*Angegaffte*]', which is the basis for 'the whole history of art'.[64]

Beauty

The carefully staged views of Venus impose strict norms. The 'beautiful bosom' of these ideal figures of art does not serve to innocently celebrate charm and grace, but to exclude non-white bodies, old bodies, trans* bodies, etc. Exploring and criticizing these normative ideals was a central theme of feminist art around 1970. The starting point for these works was the insight that there are certain visual patterns which strongly influence how we perceive ourselves and others, and especially how we imagine a 'beautiful' body and the 'appropriate' way to present it. On the other hand, however, these standardized images of the body also offer a target for criticism: they can be altered, subjected to irony, disrupted, or retold and re-visualized. This is exactly what feminist artists have been doing since the 1960s. As always happens in art history, however, the official historiography tends to under-state or totally ignore women's contribution. The case of the feminist avant-garde is no exception. This term has only become established in the last ten years or so, belated confirmation that the quantity and quality of feminist works around 1970 justifies their membership of the avant-garde of twentieth-century art.[65] Other art movements such as pop art or abstract expressionism are an established part of post-war history. For many years feminist positions were not included in this, but the pioneering nature of their works, in which the body is understood as political terrain, is now becoming clearer. French artist Annette Messager's *Les Tortures volontaires* (1972) shows all the torments that women submit to voluntarily in order to be 'beautiful'. Attached to dubious electric machines, which fix the legs, arms or head in grotesque devices, the women in Messager's multi-part photo series undergo the most unbelievable procedures. Bands, belts and suction caps are applied to the breasts to bring about some unspecified 'improvement'.

In the same year, in the cooperative artwork *I Tried Everything*, US artist Nancy Youdelman tried out certain gadgets of this type (promoted with slogans like 'Ashamed of your bosom?' or 'Increase your bosom! Yes you can have a big bosom!'), performed various exercises, and used a hormone cream that was supposed to increase her bust size. Her efforts were documented in fourteen photographs, and the advertisements, ointments and other remedies were included in the exhibition. In the words of the art historian Gabriele Schor, the documentary character of the work shows the breast 'soberly and without pathos, as the antithesis of the eroticized representation in advertising, historical paintings and sculptures'.[66] Other works that followed this matter-of-fact mode of conceptual art include Martha Wilson's *Breast Forms Permutated* and Friederike Pezold's *Brustwerk* (Breast work), both also from the 1970s.

US artist Wilson showed the breasts of various women in close-up, laid out in a grid. The presentation is reminiscent of scientific illustrations, suggesting that this supposedly objective discourse on the breast is interwoven with the eroticized visual language of art. In contrast, Austrian artist Pezold focused on her own breasts, manipulating them into sometimes painful-looking poses (as Annie Sprinkle would do later), as if she were working her way through an unknown set of instructions for breast handling. This leads to new readings. For example, when she makes a diamond shape with her index fingers and thumbs and uses this to push her breasts together, the result resembles a vulva. Pezold's project also uses videos and photos to analyse other parts of the body, such as eyes, nostrils, navel or thigh. It bears the title *Neue leibhaftige Zeichensprache eines Geschlechtes nach den Gesetzmäßigkeiten von Anatomie, Geometrie und Kinetik* (New bodily sign language of a sex according to the laws of anatomy, geometry and kinetics, 1973–6). The familiar term 'body language', which acknowledges that the body can be used to communicate, just like speech, becomes 'sign language' here. The way the body, in this case the breast, is presented in the image can be described as a sign, a code. Thus the youthful ideal breasts of Venus, in some cases modestly covered, signal a certain idea of femininity, just as the very differently presented breasts of the Venus of Willendorf do. Yet the breast does not necessarily appear in art as a sign that must be 'read'; instead, it is presented as something natural, as a part of the body that is depicted as it 'is'. Pezold's counter-strategy is to cut up and reassemble 'the old forms, images, drawings.'[67] Zooming in on the breasts, which are pushed, squashed and pressed into various positions, makes them part of a kind of taxonomy. It is not clear *what* the signs mean, and this cannot simply be 'read' by looking at them. But ultimately this applies to all representations of the breasts, and indeed the whole body. The attempt to take the body apart and then reassemble it on the level of the image, as Pezold writes, acts as a liberating assault on the many 'whole bodies'[68] produced by the history of art, and as an acknowledgement of the many conflicting meanings ascribed to the breast.

The aesthetic format of the grid, which feminist artists had chosen so often in their explorations of the breast in the 1970s, recently reappeared in advertising. In early 2022, the sportswear company Adidas launched an advertising campaign for its new sports bra range, claiming that it had a style to suit every possible breast shape. The ads, which appeared in social media but also on huge billboards in public spaces, show a series of frontal photos of female breasts of different ages, skin colours and shapes. As part of the current trend towards 'imperfection' in advertising, the photos include armpit hair, rolls of fat, and breasts that do not conform to the ideal. At first glance, the headless and therefore anonymous women's torsos seem a refreshing change from the usual seductive poses of perfect underwear models – especially as no underwear is visible here. It is probably no coincidence that this emancipatory impetus uses an aesthetic form which feminist artists had tried and tested nearly fifty years earlier. But what sets the bra ad apart from Martha Wilson's *Breast Forms Permutated*, Friederike Pezold's *Brustwerk*, or Youdelman's *I Tried Everything* is that the ad is intended to sell something. And, as is so often the case, it uses naked female bodies to do so. Critics of the campaign also noted that Adidas does *not* use close-ups of different penis shapes to advertise men's running shorts, for example. It is even quite hard to imagine a huge billboard with headless male torsos, from scrawny-chested runt to beefcake, as advertising for football shirts. And this shows that very different rules still apply to the presentation of male and female bodies.

The political significance of the Adidas campaign is by no means clear. Can it be seen as proof that feminist critique has become mainstream? Or are feminist positions being subordinated to marketing, which is ultimately quite indifferent to political goals? The Austrian journalist

Beate Hausbichler speaks of the selling out of feminism.[69] One of her reasons is that advertising campaigns such as this gloss over the differentiations and differences within feminism, which actually consists of many feminisms, pursuing divergent interests. While female artists such as Pezold, Wilson, Youdelman and others had drawn attention to the political dimension of the supposedly private body, the Adidas campaign implies that the aims of feminist body politics can be achieved if every woman attends to the very private matter of her own individual breasts. And it suggests that the multitude of non-ideal breasts in the world are now being taken care of by a sportswear company – and by each individual woman who buys a well-fitting bra. The campaign even generated a sales-boosting scandal: the billboard with the naked breasts was banned in the UK.[70]

... and back to Venus again

'The work on the image of Venus seems never-ending', wrote the German feminist artist Ulrike Rosenbach in the 1970s. 'I keep finding new pictures. [...] In advertising it's usually associated with tasteless, mass-produced items for the preservation of youth and beauty.'[71] Rosenbach recognized that the centuries-old images of the Roman goddess, which are reproduced again and again, play a significant role in ideas about what 'a woman' is, what 'a woman' looks like, and what 'normal' and 'real' femininity is. Simone de Beauvoir's often-quoted observation that one is not born a woman but becomes one referred to cultural norms and parameters which make people into women and men. In 1976, with the video *Reflexionen über die Geburt der Venus* (Reflections on the birth of Venus), Rosenbach produced a series of images in which she faded photos of her own body into projections of Botticelli's Venus in her shell, until the two were no longer clearly discernible and the 'real' woman and her image were indistinguishable.

It becomes clear here that there is no easy escape from the power of centuries-old idealizations of naked femininity. Other female artists in the 1970s also showed the disappearance of their own bodies behind popular visual formulae. In *Strip-tease occasionnel à l'aide des draps du trousseau* (Incidental strip-tease using sheets from my trousseau,

1974–5), French artist ORLAN used extravagant drapery to stage herself as various figures, starting with the Madonna, moving through Saint Teresa of Ávila and a bare-breasted maenad, and finishing with Botticelli's Venus. In the last of the photos, all that is left is the crumpled pile of sheets on the floor. The body has disappeared. Once all the poses have been taken, all the body parts shown, and all the drapery arranged, this is what remains of the woman: nothing at all. Without the drapery, without the visual formulae of the feminine, femaleness itself disappears.

In her video, Ulrike Rosenbach wears a tight-fitting body suit, black on one side and white on the other, which becomes a projection screen. When she turns to the black side, the image of her body disappears. In the place where Botticelli's painting shows the slim, white body of the goddess, Rosenbach's final shot contains a black silhouette, which diverges markedly from Botticelli's image. The hair is no longer visible as hair, but looks like part of the woman's bottom. It is not particularly likely that Rosenbach was consciously referring to the iconography of the 'Hottentot Venus' here; certainly, she herself never mentioned it. But there is nothing to stop us from incorporating it into our inter-pretation of the work. What is clear is that the last shot of the video sequence can be read as a representation of a Black body; it is equally plain that the white body from the first picture has thus become Black.

The remarkable thing, however, is that this was never explicitly mentioned. In the late 1990s, in a book called *White*, the cultural studies scholar Richard Dyer discussed in detail the invisibility of 'whiteness' as fundamental for the visual culture of the West.[72] 'Race' or ethnic difference is only evoked when 'Black' bodies appear in images, texts or films. For many years, 'whiteness' did not constitute a distinct analytical category, and yet it is, just like 'Blackness', subject to an elaborate process of construction. Except that this process culminates in the conviction that 'whiteness' is something that does not need to be mentioned. In simple terms, for example, the film *12 Years a Slave* 'is about Black people', while *The Lives of Others* is not about 'white people' but about East Germany. Whiteness and its representation is seen as 'normal' and as requiring no special attention. Dyer explains how film and photo (as 'light arts') participate in this tacit construction of 'whiteness'. But the black-and-white schema of photography and film can also be a metaphor for skin colours and ethnic difference.[73] In this sense, Rosenbach's video links visibility with the white side of her skin-tight suit, invisibility with the black side. The white Venus is accompanied by 'black' counter-images, which are a precondition for her whiteness but generally remain just as invisible. It is no coincidence that there is Venus (who is of course white) and then there is *Black* Venus (who is qualified as 'other' by the adjective). This blind spot can also be observed in the reception of Venus-themed works: in the literature, Rosenbach's video is regarded as a work concerned with the construction of an ideal female figure, but not specifically a 'white' ideal figure.

More about these blind spots can be learnt from works such as Renée Green's installation *Seen* (1990), which also highlights the relevance of historical discourses on the 'Hottentot Venus' for today's debates on racism. The work consists of a wooden platform which visitors can stand on. Their own bodies appear as silhouettes on a screen erected behind the podium, thus becoming images for everyone else in the gallery. Contemporary texts about Saartje Baartman and Josephine Baker (who was also referred to as 'Black Venus') are displayed on the ground, and the gaze of two blue eyes seems to follow visitors through a hole in the floor. One of the central experiences here is that of being observed while observing. The 'other' bodies of the Black women who were exhibited in the past remain invisible;[74] no pictures of their breasts or bottoms are shown. Given that the construction of Venus has always been about visibility, about the way Venus appears before an imaginary viewer (male or female), this refusal to show an image can be understood as a challenge to the Venus principle.

And one final example of how feminists have disrupted this consecration of Venus as the ideal, white body: in 2000, the US artist Jacqueline Hayden superimposed a nude photo onto a picture of an exhibition room in the Musée d'Orsay in Paris (figure 18). Cabanel's painting *Birth of Venus*, already mentioned above, hangs in the background. But in front of it is Hayden's montage. It looks as though the naked body of a middle-aged woman were reclining on a plinth. She acts as a counter-commentary, an objection to Cabanel's idealized female figure, lying passively on the waves. As if the Venus of Willendorf had come to life. And yet she does not claim to be a

Figure 18 Counter-model. Jacqueline Hayden, *Carol Venus* (detail), 2000.
Ancient Statuary Series, 1996–2000, XIII Carol Venus, 11.5 × 17 in.
platinum/palladium print.

'real' body, ready to tear down all the restrictive ideas about the
body produced in and through art for so many centuries. The figure
rests on two pedestals: on top of the high plinth with its geometrical
decoration lies the base of the sculpture, made of roughly hewn stone.
This, we are reminded, is the material from which the artist is able to
form a seemingly living body.

The conclusion we can draw from Hayden's montage is that all
female bodies, without exception, have always been put on a kind of
metaphorical pedestal. The process in which they appear and become
visible can never be simply 'natural', but – as in this case – has always
been judged against existing ideal surfaces and historical arrangements. Even if Cabanel's white, female body were not hanging on the
wall, it would inevitably still be in the back of our minds as an ideal
from which the figure in the foreground deviates. This is why we can
and should welcome the appearance of an older female body, whose
breasts do not conform in the least to the ideal prescribed by the
painting hanging on the wall behind her. And we can and should be

delighted that the space of artistic representation is being conquered by female bodies that are not merely about youthfulness and passive seduction. But the enthusiasm for more diverse images of the body is largely fuelled by knowledge and rejection of the ideal. It is only this that produces 'divergence'.

And so even in 2024 the ladies' razor 'Venus' is still on sale, successfully propagating – as a body practice for women and girls from puberty onwards – an ideal that was carved in stone over 2,000 years ago: the hairless smoothness of young, female skin. In 2021, incidentally, the company manufacturing these razors released several commercials alluding to trans* identities, colourism[75] and racism. One of the women who appears is trans*; another identifies herself in the film as 'African'. The ad was filmed – no surprises here – at a beach, a location regarded as particularly appropriate for the presentation of the female body ever since Botticelli. A few people are shown swimming in the water as the logo of the manufacturer and the name of the razor, 'Venus', are superimposed on the image. This constellation recalls the motif of the fountain of youth – and not by chance. It remains a matter of doubt how much empowerment (if any) is to be found in this apparently never-ending stream of female bodies, discovering their own beauty in, on or through water.

3

BREASTS AND OTHER ILLUSIONS OF THE NATURAL

Fantasies and fictions of lactation • Politics makes nature makes science: breastfeeding propaganda and the class of mammals • The asexual breast • Poison from the breast • Animal breasts – human breasts • Half breasts • Breasts and foreignness • Male nipples and male dignity • The ethics of the 'artificial' breast • Breastfeeding/chestfeeding and a law • Breasts, balls and other equipment • Scars

The breast is an overdetermined body part. Other 'secondary sex characteristics', such as facial hair, a deep voice or wide hips, also gender the body, but breasts are regarded as a sort of super-signal in comparison. They make it possible to read a person's 'femininity' even when the body is clothed, while their absence confirms a person's 'masculinity'. According to a 2022 handbook for women wanting breast augmentation surgery, breasts are the 'embodiment of womanhood'.[1] As early as 1904, the sexologist Friedrich Salomo Krauss, a colleague of Sigmund Freud, wrote that the breasts were the most important of the secondary sex characteristics and should actually be called primary rather than secondary. This introduces our topic here: the fate of the breast as the ultimate sign of femininity and as an indication of what Krauss called 'sex character' (*Geschlechtscharakter*). The connection between femaleness and the breast seems immutable:[2] the one appears to follow inevitably from the other.

The previous chapters have shown that this association is not set in stone, not least because the significance of the breast and people's perceptions of it have changed radically over time. Nonetheless, the assumption is that women have breasts, men do not, and it is only what people see in them that changes with the prevailing culture, politics, morality, religion or fashion. Breasts, according to popular belief, have always been female attributes.

The following chapter challenges this idea and calls into question the supposed naturalness of the breast and its unambiguous gender attribution. The belief that the presence of breasts enables one to 'tell a man from a woman at first glance' – as an advertisement for a cosmetic surgery clinic promises – is supposedly quite clear and simple. Yet it leads us into far more complicated but also more interesting realms. If the breast really is the body part that shows, most unmistakably, the difference between the sexes, then it can also show how this differentiation works (or doesn't), what purpose it serves (or perhaps doesn't), and why the breast is so well suited to this function. The aim here is to cast doubt on an unspoken principle underlying all studies on the female breast: the automatic linking of breasts and women. This doubt will be fed by looking at areas that are often cited as references for the obvious femaleness of the breast, such as biology, zoology and medicine. These prove to be a treasure trove of forgotten ideas, beliefs and questions, offering evidence that neither the breast nor femaleness are natural constants. The way each has been defined and the relationship assumed to exist between them not only have changed over the centuries but are directly linked to cultural and political attitudes. More than thirty years ago, the sociologist Claudia Honegger observed the 'positive legend' that the order of the sexes arose from a straightforward interpretation of nature. She argued that this legend 'has been instrumental in developing that thicket of theories, fictions and projections which still imprisons and inhibits us'.[3] Nothing has changed since then.

This chapter will show that even the seemingly self-evident connection between breasts, breastfeeding and femaleness is not a product of 'nature'. In reports by the naturalists and travellers of the eighteenth and early nineteenth centuries, men breastfeeding babies was a popular topic.[4] In the late eighteenth century, the British doctor

John Hunter reported on a father of eight who had hastened to help his wife when she had twins – by putting them to his own breast. In 1825 the *Dictionnaire classique d'histoire naturelle* reported that all Brazilian men were able to breastfeed. This suggests that milk production was seen as an exception worth reporting, but nonetheless a basic ability of the male breast. The theory of humours, which remained influential into the nineteenth century, was also open to the possibility of male lactation.[5] According to its proponents Hippocrates and Galen, milk and blood were bodily fluids which could change into one another. Around AD 600, Isidore of Seville gave an overview of the contemporary state of knowledge in his encyclopaedia. He was convinced that after birth 'whatever blood has not yet been spent in the nourishing of the womb flows by natural passage to the breasts, and whitening [hence *lac*, from the Greek *leukos* (white)] by their virtue, receives the quality of milk'.[6] The idea that the body's fluids could transform into one another quite easily, and that blood could turn into milk, made male lactation plausible. If the necessary organs were already there, i.e. the male body had breasts, then it was also conceivable that these breasts could produce milk. As late as 1908, a scientific study on 'human hermaphroditism' mentioned a 'man with milk in his breasts, who exhibited himself for money'.[7]

Fantasies and fictions of lactation

It is generally regarded as a 'biological fact' that breasts denoted as female are able to produce milk. The male breast is usually totally ignored in this context, partly because it disrupts the narrative of binary sex. If, however, we investigate the history of the technologies and institutions of lactation, a history that is central to this discourse of naturalness, the concept of the 'biological fact' soon becomes blurred. In the early 1990s, when the topic of body history was gaining ground in cultural studies research, the historian Barbara Duden described this moment of distance and estrangement from the 'naturalness' of the body:

> When I, as a woman, try to feel my way along the body into the past, I
> soon come to a place in which there is no longer any fibre of the body

that corresponds to my own feeling. The further back I go, the stranger the 'body' presented in the sources feels. Words, things, norms and meanings are no longer directly accessible to me. The vocabulary used to speak about the body in the eighteenth century points me towards matters relating to humans and animals, children, men and women, which are unfamiliar and leave me wordless.[8]

This applies not only to the man mentioned above, who exhibited his milk-bearing breasts to interested viewers for a small donation, but also to many of the following examples. Women feature here, but men – and animals – are equally important. Some reports on the breast may seem very strange. For example, the twelfth-century theologian who urged his readers to suck on Christ's breast to strengthen their faith. Or a puzzling will from mid-seventeenth-century England, in which a lawyer left one of his daughters £100 more than her sisters because 'her mother nursed her'.[9] What did a Frankfurt doctor mean when he noted, in 1806, that there was 'almost no part' of the body from which milk did not flow 'now and then': 'from the mouth, the eyes, the navel, the back, the curve of the leg, the feet etc.'?[10] And why, in 1815, did another doctor recommend buying a nanny goat and letting human babies drink from its udder?

All this is proof that the self-evident nature of 'biological facts' is illusory. Past actions, judgements and feelings relating to the breast were extremely changeable. They were based on fundamentally different conclusions from those that are drawn from the 'natural' abilities and properties of the body today. This further destabilizes the notion that birth, motherhood and breastfeeding are the essence of womanhood. The breast is a site of confusion, blurring distinctions between natural and unnatural, masculine and feminine.

In the late 1970s, the historian of religion Caroline Walker Bynum examined the fascinating texts of Cistercian authors, including the letters of Bernard of Clairvaux and his sermons on the Song of Songs.[11] There he urges readers 'suge non tam vulnera quam ubera Crucifixi' ('suck not so much the wounds as the breasts of the Crucified'), and describes religious instruction as the giving of milk.[12] This recalls the *lactatio Bernardi* mentioned in chapter 1, the miracle in which the saint was fed from Mary's breast, a popular subject in art. Bernard and other abbots and theologians used the breast as a reference for central theological and monastic concerns. Yet the breasts of the crucified Christ did not just bestow spiritual consolation in a metaphorical sense; they also found their way into art. Early Christian representations of Jesus between the fourth and sixth century represented the son of God as a very feminine man, strikingly androgynous, with long hair, a beardless face and occasionally even a hint of breasts.[13] This explains why a statuette of this type from the fourth century, showing Jesus teaching, was long believed to be a 'seated poetess' (Rome, Museo Nazionale, Palazzo Massimo alle Terme). In contrast, the texts of female mystics and other religious women authors tend to conceptualize the relationship to the divine in images not of milk-giving breasts but of flowing blood. Nuns, for example, imagined drinking from the bleeding wound on Christ's side.[14] While monks used and adapted the image of the milk-giving breast in various ways, religious women did not necessarily resort to the same female body images.

At the same time, medieval and early modern translators sanitized biblical passages with a clearly disturbing corporeality, in which God gives birth and has a uterus and a vulva: 'Listen to me, the House of Jacob and the whole remaining House of Israel, you who are carried by my uterus, you who are brought forth by my vulva' (Isaiah 46: 3–4). This corresponds to Jerome's fourth-century Latin translation of the Hebrew passage ('portamini a meo utero, qui gestamini a mea vulva'). In the King James Bible, this became 'Hearken unto me, O house of Jacob [...] which are borne by me from the belly, which are carried from the womb', while the New International Version is even more sanitized: 'you whom I have upheld since your birth and have carried since you were born'. In early medieval piety, however, comparable female images were still used intensively. In the first half of the twelfth century, in his exegesis on the Song of Songs, the Benedictine theologian Rupert of Deutz imagined a God with two breasts. One was responsible for the forgiveness of sins, the other for the distribution of mercies. Mary supposedly drank from these breasts after her ascension to heaven.[15]

Even outside the imaginary worlds of religion, there is other, later evidence that breasts did not necessarily have to be 'female'. For example, certain procedures were believed to diminish the difference between the milkless (= male) breast and the milk-giving (= female) breast. A late-seventeenth-century text on the art of midwifery criticized women who superstitiously believed they could dry up the flow of milk if they put on their husband's vest shortly after he had taken it off, while it was still warm.[16] The warmth of the male, milkless breast, stored in the yarn lying on the skin, was thought to transfer a property of the male breast to the female breast. This idea envisaged a clear female–male separation in the social role of the breast (breastfeeding vs not breastfeeding), but, at the same time, imagined a greater proximity between male and female breasts as body parts and perceived their properties as transferable. In contrast, the modern view is that men should definitely be involved in the care of babies, but that there is no longer any interchange between their breasts and those of their female partners when it comes to the ability to breastfeed. This reflects the exact opposite weighting: the bodies are totally different, but their roles much less so (at least in theory).

The history of breastfeeding – the object of considerable research in recent years – also casts doubt on the seemingly straightforward assumption that motherhood arises from giving birth to a child and then nursing it.[17] The mother has been a highly politicized figure for centuries, and still is today. The capacity of the female body to give birth and feed was seen as powerful and mysterious, but also controversial. The linkage between the milk-giving breast, femaleness and motherhood was by no means conclusively defined by the actual practice of infant care. The existence of the lactating breast led to the deduction that motherhood was 'typically female', yet there were contradictory views on the nature of this motherhood. If we consider one of the central topics of these debates, the question of whether babies should be fed by their biological mothers or by wet nurses, we find that attitudes to this issue underwent several fundamental shifts. While it was always considered better for a mother to breastfeed her own children, the image and role of the mother were extremely changeable.[18]

From the sixteenth to the mid-eighteenth century, the health of the breastfeeding mother was hardly mentioned, and interest was focused on the child's survival and welfare. After this, however, the discourse shifted to the positive effects on the mother. In the new ideology, breastfeeding was seen as healthy for the woman and necessary for

the prosperity of the state. These new campaigns were directly aimed
at mothers. While the authors had previously targeted midwives, wet
nurses or an unspecified audience,[19] they now sought to convince the
women themselves that it was good to breastfeed. This incorporated
the use of new media channels. Motherly love was propagated in
books, magazines and novels, but also in displays such as the 'Festival
of the Unity and Indivisibility of the Republic', celebrated in Paris in
1793. Here male delegates drank water that gushed from the breasts of
an oversized statue of Isis, known as the Fountain of Regeneration. We
saw in chapter 1 that the new visibility of the breasts in the eighteenth
century went hand in hand with advocacy for breastfeeding. But what
part did this visibility play when it came to establishing the breast as
a biological reference, a physical feature used both to justify women's
political role and to identify their 'sex character'?

Politics makes nature makes science: breastfeeding propaganda and the class of mammals

Politics turned breasts into (female) nature. Science contributed the
scholarly arguments. This is a very brief summary of the phase in which
revolutionary Paris gathered around the Fountain of Regeneration
and hailed the stone breasts of Isis. Spectacular festivals such as
this, devised to replace the calendar of Christian festivals after the
revolution, served to affirm the young republic and its goals. A high
point of the festivities of 1793 was a performance of the cantata 'Hymn
to Nature', by a choir of girls in virginal white, beside the Fountain of
Regeneration.[20] The male delegates then approached the fountain,
held up goblets to collect the water flowing from the figure's breasts,
and drank it. The women present were encouraged to breastfeed their
children, so that the national virtues being celebrated could go straight
into the hearts of France's infants with their mothers' milk.[21] Thus
nature and nation intermingled and became one.

However, this celebration of the breast went hand in hand with the
increasing exclusion of women from public political life.[22] Around
1800, references to nature were used to support a 'new theory of
the sexes', which made the 'extension of human rights to women'

seem unthinkable.[23] It also reinforced the conviction that the 'social usefulness of women lay in their capacity to give birth and breastfeed, in other words, in their biological bodily functions'.[24] Incidentally, it seems that before the eighteenth century it was fathers who determined the actual practice of breastfeeding: 'Husbands for the most part are the cause that their wives nurse not their owne children', as the Puritan William Gouge observed in 1622.[25] Yvonne Schütze has pointed out that in the *Conversationslexikon für das deutsche Volk* (Conversational dictionary for the German people), published in 1838, the article on 'love' mentions sexual love, parental love, filial love and brotherly or sisterly love, but not motherly love. Surprisingly, there is no entry at all for 'mother', although two pages are dedicated to the word 'father'.[26] Thus the political act of venerating the milk-giving breast was very much consistent with the trend at the time: to applaud the motherly nature of the breast while simultaneously reinforcing the ideal of the heterosexual family under patriarchal authority.[27]

The amalgam of breast, femaleness, nature and nation/society received decisive support from scientists. Then, as now, they did not conduct their research in splendid isolation, but communicated the truths they were discovering to society and were involved in these debates from the start. The Swedish botanist Carl Linnaeus, who introduced the term *Mammalia* (from the Latin for 'breast') in the tenth edition of his *Systema naturae* in 1758, had previously made his own contribution to the intense campaign for breastfeeding.[28] In his dissertation, published in 1749, he criticized the use of wet nurses with the comment that it was 'contrary to nature'.

The history of the term 'mammals' reveals that the purported connection to what is visible on the body actually only arose as part of a cultural habit of seeing. Using human, female, adult, premeno-pausal breasts as the reference for zoological nomenclature meant foregrounding an organ of the body which was, in parts of Europe in the late eighteenth century, highly politicized – as shown by the theatrical Fountain of Regeneration. In 1993, taking this observation as a starting point, the historian of science Londa Schiebinger investigated what actually caused Linnaeus to introduce mammals to zoological taxonomy. This designation is by no means self-evident, given that the class of vertebrates which Linnaeus called mammals (and which includes humans) has many other common features. One such feature is hair (so they could have been named *Hirsuta*); another is the number of bones in their ears. Until Linnaeus, the designation in use since Aristotle, *Quadrupedia* (four-legged), was still valid. But Linnaeus decided to put the breast at the centre of the nomenclature. Other researchers proposed alternative terms, such as *Tetracoilia*, based on the four chambers of the heart, another feature common to all mammals. But the breasts triumphed.

At first glance, making the female body, more specifically the lactating breast, the common point of reference for the highest class of animals might seem like an emancipatory move. But on closer inspection, as Schiebinger explains, it turns out to be a double-edged sword. *Mammalia* places humans and animals in the same category and emphasizes the connection between them. But in the same text that introduced the term *Mammalia*, Linnaeus also coined another term to maintain the superiority of humans over animals: *Homo sapiens*. This reestablished the distinction between humans and other primates, such as apes. While the female breast emphasized humans' animal nature, reason – a quality regarded as male – distinguished human qualities from animal ones. This is consistent with the fact that everything to do with milk production was situated in a field of transition and contact between human and non-human species, as shown by the myths of animals suckling human infants. Apart from the famous legend of the she-wolf who gave milk to Romulus and Remus, the twins who founded Rome, there were many other similar stories. Zeus, for example, was said to have been suckled by a nanny goat on Crete. Conversely, it seemed plausible that women would be able and willing to suckle animals. As a child, Saint Veronica Giuliani is said to have refused her mother's milk on days of fasting. As a nun, she allegedly took a lamb to her bed and suckled it to show her gratitude to the Lamb of God.

In the eighteenth century, the topic took on a new dimension, directly linked to the debates about reason and sentiment. Rejecting the view advocated by René Descartes, that animals are merely soulless machines and therefore fundamentally different from sentient humans, texts such as Claude Yvon's 'Âme des bêtes' (Soul of animals), in the first volume of Diderot and d'Alembert's *Encyclopédie* (1751), argued that animals could also feel and show emotions.[29] At the same time, paintings began to appear showing animals, in this case dogs, in close proximity to the female body. A work by Jean-Honoré Fragonard, for example (*Young Girl with Puppies*, painted around 1770), shows a young woman with two puppies in her arms. They nestle against her naked breasts, in a position not unlike that of human babies in their mothers' arms. The scene not only implies that baby animals could be interested in the human breast as a food source, but is also erotically suggestive. The painter had already evoked this two years earlier in his better-known painting *Girl with a Dog*, which shows a half-dressed young woman lying on a bed, balancing a white dog on her knees, which are pulled up towards her chest. The dog's tail lies close to her vulva. Again and again, paintings from this period show little dogs and naked female bodies between sheets and soft cushions, obviously enjoying each other's company. Diderot's encyclopaedia includes an entry on *jouissance*, which has the double meaning of enjoyment and orgasm. *Jouissance* comes about, he writes, when reason is made the slave of instinct, and nature is satisfied.[30] The representation of sexualized physical proximity between dogs and women fits this schema. It not only uses the female body to exemplify the overriding of reason to obtain physical pleasure, but also illustrates this with the transgressive proximity between human and animal bodies. The image of two puppies at a young woman's bosom gives visual form to Linnaeus's decision, a few decades earlier, to place humans and animals in the same class and to link this class, *Mammalia*, to the female breast.

The asexual breast

The eighteenth-century reorganization of zoological nomenclature resulting from the invention of mammals suggests a link with sexuality, as does the association of breasts and corporeality. Yet sexuality hardly featured in (popular) science texts on the female breast. Instead the breast was increasingly seen as an organ that could provide special access to the 'mystery' or 'riddle' of femininity (*Rätsel der Weiblichkeit*) (Sigmund Freud, 1933). As another Viennese doctor, Franz Liharžik, wrote some hundred years earlier, 'the tender female breast makes up such an important part of the whole female organism that its characteristic functions must have the greatest influence on the rest of the body'.[31] Understanding the breast enabled one to understand the entire body, the 'whole woman'. But the enormous significance ascribed to the breast in the understanding of femininity/femaleness – anatomically, physiologically, psychologically and socially – entailed a narrowing of the gaze. Liharžik's scientifically inspired ode to the breast was found in a book that was not about breasts but about the *Natürliche Ernährung der Kinder* (The natural feeding of children). The fixation on the breast's function as a feeding organ overshadowed everything else. An understanding of the 'whole body' thus meant that the body was only considered through *one* function of the breast, namely its ability to produce milk for children (preferably the woman's own children), at certain times and under certain circumstances. There were very few books that approached the topic of the breast from any other angle than that of infant care. One of the rare exceptions, in which the breast was not immediately linked to illness or motherhood in the title, was *Über die weiblichen Brüste* (On the female breasts) by the Frankfurt doctor Johann Georg Klees. The third edition of Klees's treatise was published in 1806 (figure 19).[32]

But it quickly becomes clear that Klees does not see the breast as an organ of female sexual pleasure. The author touches only very briefly on the 'well-known phenomenon of the hardening of the nipples upon a lustful sensation' – and never mentions this again.[33] Instead, any kind of sexual enjoyment of the breast seems to have a negative impact: 'Despite all their arts, young women of easy virtue have limp breasts from an excess of sexual intercourse.'[34] Women who masturbate are even worse off: 'A former self-abuser seldom has the strength to nurse her child; and if she did, her milk would never be good enough.'[35] Even in a book entitled *Ueber die Eigenthümlichkeiten des weiblichen Körpers in Bezug auf seine sexuelle Sphäre* (On the peculiarities of the female body in relation to its sexual sphere, 1870), the breast is only mentioned with reference to its milk-giving function. The 'wealth of venous vessels and nerves makes it capable of erection, which makes it easier for the newborn baby to access its food in the manner designed for it by nature'.[36]

ÜBER DIE

WEIBLICHEN BRÜSTE

VON

D. IOHANN GEORG KLEES.

Dritte vermehrte Auflage.

Frankfurt a/m
in der Andreäischen Buchhandlung
1800.

Figure 19 Klees's book *Über die weiblichen Brüste* (On the female breasts) (first published in 1795) is one of the few books on the topic of the breast: 'One finds them spherical, pointed like a pear, flattened like a pancake, cylindrical like a glove, or hanging and sack-shaped like the nests of the penduline tit' (Klees 1806, p. 32).

Decades earlier, an anatomy textbook had mentioned the 'numerous tactile corpuscles', which can produce a 'pleasant tickling sensation' – but only while a woman is 'fulfilling her motherly duty', i.e. during breastfeeding.[37] Thus the breasts became a preeminent symbol of femininity, but were at the same time desexualized and increasingly standardized. The prescribed sequence of a woman's life could be traced in her breasts, which not only reflected the female biography, but led their own life as the doppelgängers of the woman they were attached to.

In newborn infants they are a little swollen and soft, and exude a little lymph when pressed. At the time of sexual maturity, on the onset of menses, they awaken from their sleep, as it were: *they begin to live*; blood flow increases, they become plumper, firmer, grow in their whole substance and form hemispheres. [...] At the time of pregnancy they swell even more and become painful. After birth, milk is discharged; the milk ducts, previously collapsed, rise up from the sucking on the nipple. They no longer look cartilage-white, blue-white and smooth, but become pitted and uneven. On weaning, they rest again until the next pregnancy. At the end of menses the breasts lose their sensitivity, they become thinner, wrinkled, withered. *The breasts thus go through a life of their own.*[38]

This seamless merging of a body part with a typical female life course tightened the connection between the idea of the 'natural' and the breast.

And of course, the breast could only be of sexual interest in a heterosexual setting, in which 'the lustful eye of the young man rests on it with pleasure.'[39] The focus lay solely on the male desire inspired by the breast. It was only in the 1920s that surgeons performing breast operations began to try to preserve not only the nipple but also the vascularization of the tissue, so as to maintain the erotic function of the breast as well as the ability to breastfeed.[40]

But before that came to pass, many quite different topics would be discussed: *natural* wet nurses and *unnatural* mothers, suckling nanny goats and poisonous breast milk.

Poison from the breast

Despite the numerous recommendations and exhortations to mothers to breastfeed their children themselves rather than using the services of a wet nurse, the breast lauded as a 'natural' source of food in the nineteenth century was not the same thing as it is today. When modern campaigns for breastfeeding assert that 'breast is best', they are referring to the scientifically proven benefits of human milk. The favourable impact of breast milk on infant health seems to prove that what is natural is always good. A doctor called Friedrich Christian Strahsen made the same claim in 1831: 'Nature has imposed a duty on mothers: not to deny their children the breast. [Nature] created the organs for this and in them, with habitual motherly care, prepared the most necessary and suitable food.'[41]

Strahsen's book, however, bears the title *Ueber die Eigenschaften, welche eine gute Amme besitzen muss, und über das Verhalten derselben beim Stillen* (On the qualities a good wet nurse must possess, and on her behaviour while breastfeeding) and contains a surprising warning. Within the first few pages, the writer states that one of the worst apparent causes of infant mortality is not wet nurses (who take second place), but the 'coddling effect [*Verzärtelung*] of well-meaning motherly love', which puts infants at risk.[42] The text is very critical of the use of wet nurses, and sees it as justified only in exceptional circumstances, when a mother is unable to breastfeed her children 'for natural reasons'.[43] However, it does not contrast the 'biological' mother with an 'artificial' wet nurse. Instead, it is natural but 'excessive' motherly love that endangers the child.

Thus the fact that women have been advised, for centuries, to breastfeed their own children does not prove that breast milk has always been seen as natural and therefore healthy. On the one hand, there were a surprising number of reasons to use a wet nurse, and on the other hand, it was believed that the breast milk of the biological mother could potentially have devastating effects. Even in the nineteenth century, it was seen as possible that the milk flowing from the breast could transmit characteristics, feelings and moral shortcomings from the breastfeeding woman to the child. There seemed to be ample evidence of this. The legendary cruelty of the Roman emperor Caligula was said to have been caused by suckling from a bloodthirsty wet nurse, who had daubed her nipples with blood. Furthermore, human milk was not something that came only from the breasts of women. It was reportedly found in 'people who were not supposed to have any: children, virgins, men and old women'.[44] Nor did it flow only from breasts. Under the influence of humoralism, it was assumed that the different fluids in the body could transform into one another; this meant that milk could in theory be discharged from anywhere on the body. And milk could look quite different from usual; occasionally it came out as 'thick, pitch-black moisture'.[45]

Even if these reports were being cited less frequently by the end of the nineteenth century, the breast remained a portal through which all possible evils could enter. Here the mother's breasts were not seen as any better than those of wet nurses, whose services were still frequently used in wealthy circles in the nineteenth century. The potential dangers for the baby were the same, whether it was fed by a wet nurse or its biological mother. For example, both wet nurses and mothers were urged to avoid breastfeeding immediately after experiencing intense emotions.[46] The danger was that violent emotion might be detrimental to the quality of the milk, or that negative feelings might be directly transferred to the child.

This was why the 'manifold deceits with which wet nurses conceal their state of health' were so problematic. According to Strahsen, 'given the moral corruption of that class of humans from which wet nurses are usually chosen',[47] it was unavoidable that 'these [women] usually bring the temperamental faults proper to this class [...] into the circle of their masters and thus become unfit for their business as wet nurses'.[48] In other words, it was feared that the child would absorb the 'moral corruption' of the wet nurse with her breast milk. Strahsen therefore advocated a public authority which would keep wet nurses 'under strict supervision'.[49] Women's milk was considered potentially dangerous and, at worse, poisonous: 'Sexual intercourse, lustfulness, and the monthly period spoil the milk [...]. Intense passions of the wet nurse, rage, vexation, indignation, can change their milk so much that it acts as a poison, causing vomiting, diarrhoea, convulsions, epilepsy and death.'[50]

Here, too, the wet nurse and the mother were not seen as different in essence; the only difference was the possibility of preventing these harmful effects before they came about. The mother knew that both 'vexation' and 'lustfulness' could turn her milk to poison, and was encouraged to make use of a wet nurse in such cases. So alongside the continued idealization of the mother's breast, there were numerous arrangements in which other breasts were regarded as just as good and often a better choice. In some cases, those 'other breasts' might even belong to a nanny goat.

Animal breasts – human breasts

Given the absolute necessity of feeding infants, people sometimes resorted to using animals. This was not a marginal practice or a source of embarrassment, but could, on the contrary, be an arrangement that was both pleasurable and useful for all those involved, as proven by a report from the early nineteenth century:

> In Brückenau, the wife of the shoemaker Kaspar Happ died in child-birth, leaving him a healthy child. The poor father was at a loss to know how he could raise a child. Friends advised him to let a nanny goat suckle his child, and he was forced to take this course. A start was made immediately and an animal was found that was willing. The nanny goat was let into the living room every time; she would always jump onto a bench by the window, and enjoyed looking out of the window, which also amused the passers-by.[51]

As late as the early twentieth century, there were conditions that made it seem advisable to allow children to drink straight from the udders of goats and other mammals.[52] This practice was occasionally justified with reference to mythological narratives in which abandoned children were suckled by she-wolves. As mentioned above for human milk, it was assumed that attributes of the animal could be transferred to the children they fed. This could have positive effects. A text from 1819 recounted that Achilles was suckled by a lioness, thus gaining 'the courage to attack all ferocious monsters'.[53] This meant that it was vital to have a precise knowledge of the character traits of the animals being used to feed children.

There were many reasons for the use of non-human breasts. One was to avoid infection in the case of diseases such as syphilis, which infected children could pass on to their wet nurses. Some orphanages and hospitals had stables specifically for this purpose, where animals were kept so that these children could drink straight from the udder. To treat the children, mercury was fed to the goats or applied to open wounds on the animals' skin. The idea was that the poison added to their milk would cure the infants. The survival rate of the children (but not of the goats) rose as a result.

But the goat as wet nurse was not confined to orphanages or other such settings in the outer suburbs of society. In 1816, the German doctor Konrad Anton Zwierlein recommended this practice to all 'delicate, weak and suffering women, as well as vain and fashionable ones'. This challenged the sharp moral divide between mothers who were not capable of breastfeeding because of physical infirmities and those who simply had no desire to nurse. The nanny goat, which Zwierlein praised as the 'best and cheapest wet nurse', thus became the third option – alongside the mother and the human wet nurse (figure 20).[54]

Figure 20 In 1816, the doctor Konrad Anton Zwierlein recommended *Die Ziege als beste und wohlfeilste Säugamme* (The nanny goat as the best and cheapest wet nurse). He regarded mothers who cared only for their own pleasure as 'unnatural' (p. 1).

Adding the animal to the mix, however, further blurred the clear distinction between the supposedly 'natural' process of feeding at the mother's breast and the 'unnatural' nutrition supplied by a wet nurse:[55] 'It is, however, a true misfortune for the young creature who is neglected by the vain, frivolous mother, caring only for her own pleasure, and who receives, from his *unnatural* mother, a milk that does not make him thrive but acts as a poison.'[56]

Once again, breast milk is potentially poisonous, and there is talk of an 'unnatural mother'. This refers to neither the wet nurse nor (still less) the nanny goat, but to what might be called the 'natural' mother today. The 'natural' mother becomes 'unnatural'. Clearly it did not take much for the human breast to be regarded as unsuitable for nursing (and thus unnatural), in both wet nurses and mothers. If we add up all the cases in which women were advised against breastfeeding, this leaves very few women who could put their child to the breast without hesitation. It was all too easy for the milk to be spoilt, and to have 'the most detrimental, sometimes even toxic effect on the infant'.[57] Motherly love made no difference. 'Older mothers, cantankerous or fretful mothers' were advised not to breastfeed, as were those 'who take part in all parties and excursions, attend theatres and balls; who are dedicated to fashion and addicted to gambling, and can therefore find no time for their child'.[58]

If the natural function of the human breast was compromised in this way, it could be replaced by the animal breast of the nanny goat. All the emotions and distractions which turned the milk of the human breast into pure poison were a matter of indifference to the goat. Nanny goats were seen as gentle animals, 'untroubled by any passions'.[59] This was one of the reasons why Zwierlein (who gave practical hints on keeping these animals in a city apartment) saw them as ideal. Another was the fact that they were not as stupid as sheep. Zwierlein went a step further, though: another advantage of goats, he argued, was that their character was strikingly similar to that of human females. He asked rhetorically: 'Does not the nanny goat, in its mood, flightiness and changeability, strongly resemble our young ladies?'[60] Instead of lapdogs, he suggested that young mothers should keep 'lap goats'. They should also consider having their hair done in the same style as a goat: 'Won't that be amusing, when the heads of the lady of the house and her daughter look just like that of their lap goat?'[61] The external resemblance thus corresponded to the inner similarity of woman and she-goat, and the potential danger inherent in a bodily fluid led to the conception of a species-transcending femaleness. As a result of Zwierlein's book, the use of nanny goats as wet nurses enjoyed a certain popularity in European countries for a few years.[62]

But the tone changed in the decades that followed. So did the meaning of 'natural'. It came to be associated more and more closely with the human female body, and in the second half of the nineteenth century the nursing mother became an indispensable part of the bourgeois family. Animals were no longer relevant. Descriptions of the relationship between the baby and its mother – as a unique bond and simultaneously an idealized image of the feminine – rose to ever loftier heights:

> What a sublime, sacred image of life is the sight of a mother nursing her child! Could any husband, even if he were one of the rough, good-hearted children of nature, ever have failed to feel an impression of moral beauty [...] when he saw his wife with the baby at her breast, the breast that gives living nourishment? Must not this image of a happy mother carrying out her sweetest duty of nature radiate through the whole life of the family, harmonious and sweet [...]![63]

The quotation is from the military doctor Hermann Klencke, in a book published in 1870, *Die Mutter als Erzieherin ihrer Töchter und Söhne* (The mother as the educator of her daughters and sons). Here Klencke romanticized the mother, presenting her as a mystery which the father can only observe in amazement.

Under the Nazis, this topos of the 'naturalness' of the breasts became part of a racist ideology. *Die deutsche Mutter und ihr erstes Kind* (The German woman and her first child), written by a woman doctor, Johanna Haarer, was purged of overly obvious Nazi references after 1945 and remained in print into the 1980s. In the 1941 edition, the relevant chapter begins with this command:

> German mother, you must nurse your child! From your breast flows the nourishing source, which the wise creator has endowed with all

properties [...]. This source of your body is fully attuned to your own child, flesh of your flesh, blood of your blood. [...] German mother, if you breastfeed, you are not only doing your duty to your child, but fulfilling a racial obligation. [...] So consider the responsibility that you bear towards your more distant descendants, indeed towards your nation and its future.[64]

This exhortation to breastfeed was combined with warnings about children growing up *führerlos* (without a leader, without guidance)[65] and about 'overly loud and vehement manifestations of maternal feelings'.[66] The iron rule for the 'maintenance' of the infant is as follows: 'The child is fed, bathed, and changed, but otherwise left alone completely'.[67] This mixture of rigid routine and lovelessness ('let it cry!'[68]) was combined with the reference to the breast as a 'nourishing source'. In other words, breastfeeding did not automatically lead to a particularly close, pleasurable, tender – or *natural* – relationship.

Half breasts

In the eighteenth and nineteenth – and even into the twentieth – centuries, the female breast was, in many respects, an 'other'. It was a potential source of poison; it could be replaced by the udder of a nanny goat; and it could take on the properties of another breast, a male breast, just by the application of a male garment still warm from the wearer's body. It was a body part whose capacity for sexual arousal was carefully concealed. Furthermore, breasts and the differentiation between the shape of male and female breasts were critical for more general questions of human existence, such as how someone could have more than one sex or gender, and why men could also have breasts.

Artists in the twelfth and thirteenth centuries had developed a format for the depiction of non-binary bodies, in which the breast signalled the simultaneous presence of 'male' and 'female' elements.[69] Such figures, referred to as hermaphrodites, were inspired by Pliny's first-century *Natural History*. Here the Roman scholar told of a mythical African nation of hermaphrodites, for whom he used the term 'Androgyni': 'Beyond the Nasamones and adjacent to them Calliphanes records the Machlyes, who are Androgyni and perform the function of either sex alternately. Aristotle adds that their left breast is that of a man and their right breast that of a woman.'[70]

The linguistic image of the chest that was simultaneously male and female fell on fertile soil: several images have been preserved in which hermaphrodites are characterized by a single female breast. These include an illustration in *Marvels of the East*, a manuscript from the twelfth century. The text repeats the assertion that hermaphroditic humans bear this name because both sexes appear in them: a male breast on the right and a female breast on the left. The manuscript also states that they can beget and bear children alternately. Strikingly, however, the visual representation shows *only* the upper body as two-sexed. The figure's left breast is female, the right breast male; the body appears to be divided vertically. But the question of the primary sex organs is neither asked nor answered visually, as there is no sign of genitalia.

The same goes for a bestiary produced slightly later, a thirteenth-century compendium on animals found in Westminster Abbey, London. Here, too, the representation of a two-sexed figure is divided vertically into a male part with a flat chest and a female part with a rounded breast. Again, however, the figure has no genitals. On the side with the female breast it wields a large pair of scissors, and on the other side, a large sword. Obviously, these objects can be read as proxies for female and male activities, but their shapes also evoke the vulva and the phallus respectively. These organs are not shown on the body, but they 'appear' in the form of objects that point to social gender roles and thus make the curious case of the double body visually comprehensible.

The historian Leah DeVun recently analysed in detail the history of non-binary genders from the Middle Ages to the Renaissance. In medieval discourses, she explains, gender was not primarily the product of physical properties, but of social perceptions and inter-actions. Fighting with a sword or cutting off a thread evokes gender not as a body but as action in accordance with social roles. In the 1990s, in the influential book *Gender Trouble*, Judith Butler talked of the 'performativity' of gender, referring to it as something that one not only has, but also does. DeVun links this insight with the medieval images of half-breasted hermaphrodites. They too tell more about gender-specific tasks than gender-specific bodies.[71]

Several hundred years after the medieval representations of these double-breasted beings, in 1631 to be exact, another artwork used a breast to evoke the question of gender. Although completely different from the medieval images, it draws on them and at the same time points forward into the nineteenth and twentieth centuries. This is Jusepe de Ribera's spectacular portrait *The Bearded Lady*, commissioned by the viceroy of Naples, Don Fernando Afán de Ribera y Enríquez (1631).[72] The topos of the bearded woman had already been alluded to in hagiographies such as that of Saint Wilgefortis, who prayed intensely to escape marriage with a heathen bridegroom and grew a beard as a result. Her father had her crucified to punish her, inspiring a number of depictions of a bearded woman nailed to a cross. But one of the most famous pictures of bearded women in art history is Ribera's work.

The painting shows a woman named Magdalena Ventura with her husband and a baby, which she is holding to her right breast. Since her body is enveloped in a splendid, floor-length garment, both the breast and the beard stand out as physical features. Unlike the medieval illustrations showing hermaphrodites, the aim of this image is to identify the subject as a woman. The inscription, presented on a stone stele, records her story. She is described as a woman from the town of Accumoli, near Naples, and a wonder of nature ('Magnum natura Miraculum'). After giving birth to three children, the inscription states, she grew a beard at the age of thirty-seven. Modern medical knowledge suggests that she probably had an androblastoma, a tumour that leads to increased testosterone production. Ribera's portrait depicts her at the age of fifty-two,[73] making the baby at her breast doubly confusing. At this point, none of the children she had had before her beard started to grow would have been so small. So who is the child? And why is Ventura, as a woman aged over fifty, presented as a breastfeeding woman/mother? Perhaps the painter was using the bared breast as evidence of his subject's femaleness? Simply portraying Ventura with naked breasts would have been considered unseemly.[74] But a breast offered to a baby was an established visual topos, allowing this body part to be exposed without dishonour. Moreover, it becomes evident on closer inspection that the baby is not feeding, but just has its mouth near the woman's nipple. So the aim is solely to indicate that this breast *has* served to feed babies, even though Ventura's appearance is otherwise completely masculine.

The second strange thing in this image full of strange things is Ventura's anatomy. Her breast, which she holds up to the baby's cheek, hardly looks like an organic part of her body. Rather, it appears as a kind of free-standing object, protruding from high up on her torso. There does not seem to be a second breast, as no bump is discernible under the smoothly hanging garment. This was clearly not because Ribera was unable to present bodies in a naturalistic way – many of his other paintings demonstrate this ability.

At around the same time (1630–3), Ribera's contemporary and fellow countryman Francisco de Zurbarán produced a painting of Saint Agatha, a third-century Sicilian saint, whose breasts were cut off after she refused to marry a heathen. In accordance with the centuries-old iconography of this saint, the breasts appear as extraneous, even detachable objects. Like Ribera, Zurbarán was not concerned with anatomy; his aim was to use the breast as a reference to something else, in this case the saint's martyrdom. In Zurbarán's painting, the severed body parts show no signs of violent mistreatment, and Agatha presents them calmly and serenely as two perfectly rounded hemispheres on a silver tray. To this day, cakes in the form of breasts (known as *Minne di Sant'Agata*, Saint Agatha's breasts), looking remarkably similar to those in Zurbarán's painting, are eaten in Sicily.

The presentation of the breasts as something that the saint has control over has encouraged associations with current debates on transgender identities. In 2023, for example, Katayoun Jalilipour, an artist from Iran, offered a queer reinterpretation of the image in *Study of Saint Agatha as a Boy*. Here the artist interprets the removal of the breasts as an exercise in bodily autonomy, and the voluntary renunciation of this body part as a form of self-empowerment.[75] The severed breast, which Zurbarán's painting presents as something that is no longer part of the body, does not cause Agatha grief or pain. Rather, the organs presented on the tray bear witness to the fact that the saint, in a difficult situation, chose to subject her body to the torture of amputation in order to reconcile her physical and spiritual identity – as a virgin and a Christian. This link to the topic of transgender identity, which will be discussed in more detail later, is no coincidence. The political and cultural debates on this topic are concerned with bodily self-determination: they challenge the idea that secondary and primary sex characteristics form the basis for a clear identity, which is fixed forever and cannot be influenced by the individual.

The nineteenth and twentieth centuries saw an increasing reliance on anatomically plausible representations of the body as a means of tracking down the uncertainties of gender in and on the body. This is not the point of Jalilipour's work, however, just as it was not a key concern in the medieval images of hermaphrodites or Ribera's *Bearded Lady*. The focus here is different. The breast literally becomes a foreign body; it serves as a symbol of femaleness which is detached from the body or must be authenticated by evidence located outside the body. The breast depicted in the portrait of Ventura, appearing as a single organ affixed to the body, is thus closer to the conventions for the representation of hermaphroditic ambisexuality – where the singular breast served as a prop to create ambiguity – than to the 'real' body.

Ribera's inscription notes that the woman's beard would better befit a 'bearded master' (*magistri barbati*) than a woman who has already given birth to three children. *Magister* is a title that implies dignity and economic success and is associated with masculinity.[76] So here, too, the artist is emphasizing social aspects of gender difference. Breastfeeding (quoted rather than actually shown) is presented as a task for humans with breasts, not as a function of the body part at the moment of its representation. A spindle at the right-hand edge of the picture, lying on top of the stele bearing the inscription, further emphasizes the subject's social role as a woman. Ribera's picture is linked to the considerably older images by the anatomically improbable breast and by the reference to social activities which help to interpret the bodily signs of gender. The glitch between masculinity and femininity, which is given visual form here as the contrast between breast and beard, anticipates later evocations of breasts and gender difference.

Breasts and foreignness

The non-binary figures of the medieval texts ran counter to dualistic ideas of gender and signalled an outside, a beyond. The 'monstrous races of the earth', as shown in bestiaries, books of monsters and *mappae mundi* (world maps), were positioned at the furthest edge of the inhabited world and showed their separation from 'us' through their association with the 'others'.[77] This linking of spatial and bodily difference remains a constant with regard to male–female breasts. From the beginning of the nineteenth century, there was increasing discussion of gynaecomastia, the growth of feminine breasts in men. Just as the combination of male and female breasts made some figures in the Middle Ages appear ambiguous, so too did men with this condition destabilize categorizations. The gender confusion was further intensified by the fact that they often succeeded in breastfeeding babies. But while no one had ever seen the mythical half-and-half hermaphrodites found in medieval book illustrations, men with breasts did actually exist. This makes it all the more striking that the literature focuses on cases based on hearsay. These hazy origins made it possible to elaborate wildly on their astonishing characteristics. This was because the stories about male breasts and their abilities were associated with geographical foreignness. They most often appeared in travelogues, suggesting an inevitable connection between foreign anatomy and foreign countries. Francesco Saverio Claverigo claimed in his *Storia Antica del Messico* (1780/1), a history of pre-Columbian Mexico, that all men in the New World had been able to breastfeed ('nel nuovo Mondo quasi tutti gli uomini abbondano di latte nelle mammelle').[78] He also asserted that the men, and not the women, had taken responsibility for bringing up children. In 1818 Alexander von Humboldt quoted this claim and dismissed it as an absurd misconception. This did not, however, stop him from contributing new stories on the same topic. Like Claverigo, Humboldt had not seen the breastfeeding men himself, but had to rely on eyewitnesses and written reports such as the following:

> In this village lives a labourer, Francisco Lozano, who presented a highly curious physiological phenomenon. This man has suckled a child with

his own milk. The mother having fallen sick, the father, to quiet the infant, took it into his bed, and pressed it to his bosom. Lozano, then thirty-two years of age, had never before remarked that he had milk: but the irritation of the nipple, sucked by the child, caused the accumulation of that liquid. The milk was thick and very sweet. The father, astonished at the increased size of his breast, suckled his child two or three times a day during five months. He drew on himself the attention of his neighbours, but he never thought, as he probably would have done in Europe, of deriving any advantage from the curiosity he excited. We saw the certificate, which had been drawn up on the spot, to attest this remarkable fact, eye-witnesses of which are still living. They assured us that, during this suckling, the child had no other nourishment than the milk of his father. Lozano, who was not at Arenas during our journey in the missions, came to us at Cumana. He was accompanied by his son, then thirteen or fourteen years of age. M. Bonpland examined with attention the father's breasts, and found them wrinkled like those of a woman who has given suck. He observed that the left breast in particular was much enlarged; which Lozano explained to us from the circumstance, that the two breasts did not furnish milk in the same abundance. Don Vicente Emparan, governor of the province, sent a circumstantial account of this phenomenon to Cadiz.[79]

All these descriptions contain latent hints of the cliché of ethnicized feminization and enfeeblement. Humboldt mentioned that the indigenous peoples of North America had been described as 'weak' because a striking number of the men were able to breastfeed their children. He argued that this was false, however, because 'a white person of European descent' had also nursed his children there. People of European descent were associated with strength and masculinity; if these were present, then even breastfeeding could not 'weaken' such men. Humboldt took a very similar approach to the numerous reports on the prevalence of male wet nurses in Russia. Some reports claimed that nearly all Russian men were able to breastfeed children. Humboldt referred to anatomists in St Petersburg, who had allegedly dissected large numbers of men with lactating breasts. But since 'the Russians have never been deemed weak and effeminate', he viewed this as further evidence that breastfeeding men were not necessarily a sign of weakness in a nation.[80]

In other travelogues, men with 'women's breasts' nonetheless remained the epitome of foreignness. One example is John Franklin's *Narrative of a Journey to the Shores of the Polar Sea*, published shortly after Humboldt's report. Franklin tells of a 'Chipewyan Indian' who put his child to his own breast after his wife's death and found that milk actually began to flow. The story contributed to the impression that the people in the areas where Franklin was travelling were astoundingly different or 'other'.[81] If such cases were not 'discovered' in distant countries on expeditions by European travellers, but were found in Western countries, they were usually described with reference to ethnic alterity: 'A stout man of forty-five was found to have hugely developed breasts, which hung down like those of Hottentots. He had never been able to marry because of this deformity'.[82]

Here the presence of male breasts immediately signified the man's potential de-Europeanization – just as, in many other texts, the breast was viewed as an indicator of 'primitivity'. We saw in the first chapter that breasts were excellent indicators of racist denigration: at the beginning of the twentieth century, the gynaecologist Carl Heinrich Stratz turned the breast into a body part that revealed 'primitivity' and foreignness. In the classifications that were eagerly undertaken on the basis of the breast, 'race' and 'sex' were intermingled as two decisive categories, produced simultaneously and kept in balance.

Male nipples and male dignity

The issue was complicated. The 'presence of nipples in men has long embarrassed the philosophers', as Alexander von Humboldt observed in 1818. Why did the male and female breast share this striking feature? Humboldt quoted a report by the Academy of Sciences in St Petersburg, published in 1735, which explained that 'nature denies one sex the ability to breastfeed, because this activity is incompatible with male dignity'.[83] Humboldt evidently did not find this explanation convincing. But a sceptical remark was not enough to banish the idea that female breasts were a kind of demeaning morphological phenomenon, which women's bodies had so that they could fulfil the childcare tasks assigned to them. Decades after Humboldt, men's lack of breasts was still seen as a visible sign of their relative perfection. The influential Austrian anatomist Joseph Hyrtl was convinced that a man's 'large, broad chest' was an 'expression of physical strength'. In contrast, 'a narrow, sunken, long, keeled' chest was 'a sign of weakness and infirmity'. He continued: 'There is a deep meaning in our use of language, which situated courage, boldness and warlike valour in a man's powerful chest, while women, who were not born to be strong, exhibit the expression of their dependency and weakness in the undeveloped form of their ribcage, and the prevalence of their soft additions.'[84]

The 'soft additions' (*weiche Zugaben*) were the breasts. And the term 'prevalence', which comes from medical statistics, highlighted – subtly but insistently – the status of female attributes as medically divergent. The male nipple was regarded as proof of men's superiority. In evolutionary terms it was interpreted as a 'remnant of foetal life' and was compared with the clitoris. Anatomists saw both as 'memorials of prehistory, when the individual had both sexes', as one writer stated in 1819.[85] This assumption that the clitoris was (like the male nipple) essentially functionless was very much in line with the exclusion of any sexual element in interpretations of the female breast.

The term 'secondary sex characteristic', now found in every textbook, was still brand new around 1800. It ensured that breasts and other non-genital sex differences could become objects of scientific study in their own right when it came to investigating the origins of sexual development – which were still shrouded in mystery at the time.[86] Once again, scholars engaged less in discovery and description and more in interpretation – and in a very specific direction. It was the above-mentioned John Hunter who first spoke of the breast as a 'secondary organ', in his 'Account of an Extraordinary Pheasant', published in 1780. His reports of breastfeeding men are no longer of interest to today's anatomists, but the term he coined, 'secondary sex characteristic', was highly successful, as shown by its continued use.

Surprisingly, Hunter's interest in the female secondary sex characteristics was focused not so much on their reproductive abilities as on a hierarchy: 'Every female, just at the age of maturity, is more like the young of the same species than the male is observed to be; and if the male is deprived of his testes when young, he retains more of the original form, and therefore is more similar to the female.'[87] Hunter's view, then, was that while male humans developed further and further from a child towards an adult, the secondary sex characteristics showed that women at some point stopped progressing along this path, or at least did not get as far as men. Thus female breasts signalled a proximity to childishness and became a 'natural' sign that allowed a hierarchic interpretation of difference.

Despite all attempts to associate weakness with the soft, female breast and strength with the 'big, broad' male chest, this categorization still required interpretation – just like the many other things that the breast was believed to demonstrate. One example was the claim that male nipples, though generally not suited to breastfeeding, could sometimes produce milk after all. Well into the nineteenth century, the public was supplied with reports of breastfeeding men. In 1876, readers of a Bavarian magazine were informed of a Pomeranian doctor who could 'stimulate lactation in any human being' and thus procure both female and male wet nurses.[88] In specialist medical literature, however, doctors and anatomists increasingly assumed that these stories were largely 'fables', and reports about male breastfeeding soon faded from view. Instead, the focus shifted to how the existence of the male breast could be adequately explained in scientific terms.

In his 1866 book *Über die männliche Brustdrüse und über die Gynaecomastie* (On the male mammary gland and gynaecomastia), the Austrian anatomist Wenzel Gruber compiled and illustrated such cases.[89] The doctor had set himself the task of cataloguing the cases described in the literature and known to him personally. This included a critical review of Humboldt, which rejected the reports of male lactation. It also included meticulous documentation of specially conducted 'mass examinations of the male breast and mammary gland on living bodies and cadavers'.[90] Gruber found his subjects in a military school and a military hospital. In the long lists resulting from this study, he described the 'size, colour and shape of the nipple', down to the millimetre, classifying the shape as 'sloping-elliptical' or 'nearly vertical'.[91] He distinguished between true and false 'gynaeco-masts' (men with female-looking breasts). The 'true' ones had enlarged breasts as a result of medical disorders, while the 'false' ones had bigger breasts because of natural fat deposits, due to old age or excess weight.

Figure 21 A 'true' gynaecomast, who died of a stroke in Mariinsky Hospital
in St Petersburg. Wenzel Gruber, *Über die männliche Brustdrüse und
die Gynaecomastie* (On the male mammary gland and gynaecomastia),
St Petersburg, 1866.

The only illustration in Gruber's study (figure 21) shows a patient
he had met at the Mariinsky Hospital in St Petersburg in March
1866, and who had died of a stroke soon after. The patient was a 'true'
gynaecomast with 'enormously developed breasts'.[92] Questioning
revealed that he had become a soldier at the age of fifteen, had since
become an alcoholic, and was also blind. There was nothing unusual
in the fact that the patient sat for a portrait. Although photography
had long since been invented, scientific literature did not necessarily
use photos as illustrations. In many cases, scholars appreciated the
artistic possibilities offered by drawings – the ability to highlight
things that were considered important and downplay others.[93] In

this case, the artist made use of this freedom by not even hinting at the part of the body below the nipples. In the place where the man's navel should have been, we read the inscription 'Gynaecomastus'. This allowed attention to be focused on the appearance and position of the breasts, in contrast to the head. The close-cropped hair and dark stubble attest to masculinity, while the breasts signal its disruption. Thus the illustrator selected a very similar combination to Ribera in his portrait of Magdalena Ventura: beard and breast. But unlike Ribera and his predecessors, he was able to omit any further references to the social gender of the subject. Neither sword nor scissors were required, neither babe-in-arms nor spindle, because the 'female' breast and the 'male' beard were now readable as bodily signs of gender, which automatically supplied their own social significance.

And so the problem of the male breast changed yet again. The strangeness of other places and mythical life forms and the amazement at male wet nurses 'in our midst' faded away. Instead, a scientific, supposedly objective perspective gained the upper hand. Yet the male breast still inhabited a precarious and shadowy zone, as psychiatry and criminal anthropology reveal.

For example, the psychiatrist Hans Kurella saw male breasts as a typical feature of the criminal character. He explained this in his *Naturgeschichte des Verbrechers* (Natural history of the criminal), published in 1893, based on the findings of Cesare Lombroso.[94] In psychology, the 'male breast' was mentioned as a cause for neuroses of all kinds. In his 1912 study *Über den nervösen Charakter* (On the nervous character), the Austrian psychologist Alfred Adler cited the case of a patient in whom 'strong development of his Mammae', among other things, had led him to believe that 'he could even be a girl', or at least, not a 'complete man'.[95] Breasts and suckling meant, for him, a feeling of 'inferiority as female'. In his study on the history of cosmetic surgery, Sander Gilman uses this example to highlight how much attitudes to the 'male breast' changed within just a few decades. In the early 1910s, Adler regarded talking therapy as the method of choice to assist the patient. By the mid-1930s, however, he saw plastic surgery as the best way to stabilize the psyche of a person suffering from their physical appearance.[96]

This was a change that would have radical consequences. For many years the male breast, unlike the female breast, had been explicitly spared any surgical interventions. Medical textbooks of the nineteenth century regularly described the pathological enlargement of male breasts. A typical observation was: 'This condition seldom reaches such a degree that surgical assistance becomes necessary, which, incidentally, would be provided in the same way as in the case of hypertrophy of the female breasts.'[97] Even in 1877, a report on a 'case of gynaecomastia' from Stuttgart in the *Medicinisches Correspondenz-Blatt* ended with the words: 'Naturally no therapeutic intervention had been undertaken.'[98]

The ethics of the 'artificial' breast

Nowadays surgical removal of breast tissue in men is a routine operation in modern cosmetic surgery and is among the top three treatments requested by male patients. But while the aim of breast modifications for women is to preserve, restore or optimize femininity, the aim for men is to eliminate female characteristics. The term itself – 'male breasts' or 'man boobs' – designates a body part that conflicts with a 'real' male physique. There are also huge differences in the way surgical work on the female and male breast is judged. When it comes to the male breast, there is no differentiation between an objectionable fixation on exaggerated ideals of beauty and a legitimate desire for breast surgery because of illness. The removal of 'man boobs' in cis men (i.e. men whose gender identity coincides with the sex assigned to them at birth) is viewed as an absolutely legitimate desire. Nor is it described as a 'gender-affirming' operation or 'gender reassignment surgery', as is the case for a trans* man's mastectomy. It is simply breast removal. Similarly, chest binding, a practice in which trans* men and non-binary people compress their breasts to give the impression of a flatter chest, is sometimes referred to as 'gender-affirming', while a minimizer bra, used by cis women to make their breasts look smaller, is not characterized in this way.

All these things exacerbate the double moral standards applied to trans* people. In 2011, Germany's Federal Constitutional Court decided that requiring trans* people to undergo surgical intervention was a breach of the constitution (*Grundgesetz*). But while German health insurers routinely pay for surgical breast reconstruction after cancer treatment for cis women, the Landessozialgericht Berlin (the court responsible for health and welfare issues) refused a trans* woman's application to have the costs of a breast augmentation covered by her health insurer. The rationale for this 2011 decision was that there was no general entitlement to 'as close an approximation as possible to a supposed ideal' (L 1 KR 243/09).

Overall, there are substantial national differences in the number and type of 'cosmetic' procedures carried out, as a few figures will show. The US accounts for the highest number of breast augmentations: in 2021, 22.5 per cent of the global total of these operations took place in the US. Germany was in fourth place with 4 per cent. Brazil, which took second place with 10.6 per cent,[99] is worth mentioning in this context for two reasons. Firstly, because access to *plástica* is much easier here; in many cases it is available for free. Even children affected by bullying are regarded as a target group for cosmetic surgery.[100] The second reason is that the nature and extent of the procedures performed are closely linked to ideas about ethnic difference. As in many other countries, breast augmentations are the most popular cosmetic surgery procedure, but historically there has also been a high demand for breast *reductions*. In the upper middle class, the reason was the association of big breasts with lower social status and Blackness.[101] Although the physical visibility of different origins has positive connotations, there are still more or less subtle value judgements, even today. The operations generally change the body 'in the direction of Europe, not Africa', as Brazilian surgeons admit.[102]

In Germany, breast augmentation is considerably more common than breast reduction, but there were signs of a turnaround in 2021: the proportion of breast reductions increased by 12.4 per cent, while that of breast augmentations fell by the same value. At the same time, the number of facelifts in women increased by 80.4 per cent.[103] The professional associations of surgeons cite Covid as the explanation: the increasing frequency of online meetings led patients to seek treatment 'because something bothered them about their own video conferencing image.'[104] Breasts, of course, are not usually visible in this context.

Even in the early days of modern breast surgery, there were 'improvements' that were considered objectionable and therefore not carried out. Although the Viennese surgeon Joseph Gersuny argued in 1903 that the prevailing ideas of beauty had more to do with the ideal bodies of classical antiquity than with normal human beings – an argument that could be seen as a defence of 'normal' bodies – he nonetheless made fine but significant distinctions. While he had no problem correcting a 'hooked nose' in a male actor who had trouble finding suitable parts, his views on the breast were quite different: 'Old coquettes hungering for beauty wanted me to remove the first wrinkles from the withering skin, to restore the youthful turgor of the drooping breasts – I could not bring myself to accommodate these desires and to extend the boundaries of our art – downwards.'[105]

Where did this division between 'good' and 'bad' surgical breast modifications come from? In many cases it was based on the opposition between 'natural' and 'artificial'. Everything that was natural was good. Everything that was artificial, fake or false was bad. And yet the boundaries of these concepts were very elastic. One of the most striking changes in the history of breast operations since the nineteenth century is the question of the 'right' size for breasts. Until well into the first decades of the twentieth century, large breasts were regarded as 'primitive', and not only in Europe. The first procedures in modern cosmetic surgery at the end of the nineteenth century (the first 'modern' procedure took place in 1897) were therefore breast *reductions*.[106] 'Excessively large breasts can in some circumstances even make amputation necessary', noted the anatomist Joseph Hyrtl in 1847.[107] At this stage there was no talk of breast augmentations. Breast reductions continued to predominate until the mid-twentieth century. It was only from the 1940s that larger breasts gradually came to be seen as more erotic, leading to a significant rise in breast *augmentations* in the US and Europe.[108] In all cases, the guiding principle was the self-declared goal of plastic surgery, as articulated by its spokesman Eduard Zeis in the *Handbuch der plastischen Chirurgie* (Handbook of plastic surgery) in 1838: to correct the 'repugnant sight' of a mutilated body part.[109] Of course neither large nor small breasts were actually mutilated, yet first the one and then the other were perceived as disfig-urements. Surgical reduction was understood as the reconstruction of a bosom that no longer bore any marks of ethnic difference, but corresponded to the 1920s ideal of the 'new woman', with her bobbed hair and small breasts.[110] The same then went for breast augmenta-tions, which were also seen as something that 'restored' femininity. The difference was that large breasts were now seen as necessary to achieve this.

From the end of the nineteenth century, the demand for a 'natural' effect meant that the post-operative breast was expected to show no scars and to have a nipple. For many years, however, the nipple's erotic function was treated as irrelevant. It was not until the mid-1920s that the 'natural' function of the nipple was expanded to include not just the ability to breastfeed but also the capacity for erotic stimulation.

This is consistent with the fact that ageing female breasts were denied surgical rejuvenation, and that procedures of this type were seen as debasing the art of medicine. One of the reasons why boosting the erotic charm of an 'old coquette' seemed so outrageous was that this would have meant acknowledging female sexuality beyond idealized youthfulness. In the rare cases around 1900 where patients were granted a breast augmentation, mention of their occupation served as a justification. The Heidelberg doctor Vincenz Czerny has been named as the first surgeon to carry out a breast reconstruction (in 1895). He did so by injecting fatty tissue from the patient's back into her breast after treatment for a benign tumour.[111] The comment that the patient was an actress legitimated the intervention as necessary for the continued exercise of her profession.

Joseph Gersuny (the doctor reluctant to treat 'old coquettes') exper-imented with paraffin, which he not only injected into the breasts but also used to correct the shape of the oral cavity or nose. This turned out to have a number of side-effects, however, so new materials were sought.[112] Silicone, originally a material used by the American military for electrical insulation, also seemed promising in the context of breast enlargement. In the history of cosmetic surgery, silicone is directly linked with sex. The material was evidently first used on Japanese prostitutes, who were injected with it to meet the US soldiers' demand for big-breasted women. The literature suggests rather cryptically that the silicone injections were later sold on the black market to US women in the 'entertainment industry'.[113] Articles from a strongly feminist perspective talk of 'sex slavery'.[114] Tragically, illegal silicone injections still happen today and can cause dramatic health problems, such as ulcers and necrosis – often years after the actual treatment. In 2004 the US National Coalition for Lesbian Gay Bisexual Transgender Health pointed out that trans* women are particularly affected by this. Since the silicone injections can be had for a fraction of what proper medical treatment would cost, they mainly attract poor people who cannot afford medical insurance.[115]

Despite all the health concerns, the injection of silicone remained legal in countries such as the US and Germany well into the 1970s. Advertisements in magazines claimed that 'bosoms can be increased two inches – without pain' in a 'ten-minute medical procedure'. Up to 50,000 women are believed to have undergone this procedure between 1940 and 1970 in the US alone. One of them was Carol Doda, a topless dancer in the Condor Club in San Francisco. Allegedly the first woman to perform completely topless (i.e. without nipple covers) in US strip clubs in the 1960s, Doda became extremely popular.[116] Her decision to have her breasts enlarged with silicone injections was reported in the media with corresponding photos, contributing to the growing popularity of the treatment.[117]

Despite the obvious association of silicone breast enlargements with the sex industry, 'marital happiness' was often cited as the purpose of a breast augmentation in the 1950s and 1960s. A psychiatric study from the 1950s included the husband's satisfaction with the new breasts as a separate category.[118] To this day, judgements about the same operation on the breast are based on a moral distinction between the fulfilment of marital duties and debauched sexuality. Since 1992 there have been medical warnings in the US against silicone implants, which had replaced direct injections. But while they were completely banned for 'cosmetic' use, they were still allowed to be used for plastic recon-structive surgery after cancer treatment.[119] The argument was that they should continue to be available for those 'who have an urgent need for breast implants', in the words of the Food and Drug Administration (FDA).[120] Apart from the question of why it would be more 'urgent' for a woman to have two breasts than to avoid the harmful health effects of implants, we could also ask why the need for two breasts should be less urgent for people without cancer or for trans* people.

Matters of health policy, for example the funding of such operations, are also influenced by these considerations. The distinction between 'reconstructive' and 'cosmetic' procedures is not just about money. In 'reconstructive' surgery, the operation is treated as the legitimate 'restoration' of a female body by recreating 'normal' breasts. In 'cosmetic' surgery, it is seen as a vain whim, with the morally dubious aim of increasing one's own erotic attraction. This distinction is blurred in the case of trans* women. For them, the prerequisite for a breast operation is pathologization. A study by Spanish sociologists pointed out that the exact same medical procedure is judged differently depending on whether the patient is a trans* woman, a woman who has had cancer treatment, or a woman who wants to increase the size of her healthy breasts for other reasons. The judgement depends on 'whether or not the person demanding the feminizing operation is considered properly feminine'.[121] And also, they add, on what is regarded as normal, beautiful or desirable.

Unlike other services offered by cosmetic surgery, breast augmentation is also tied to another boundary: the line between 'normal', 'natural' femininity on the one hand and hypersexualization and the grotesque on the other. The French porn star Lolo Ferrari, whose pseudonym combined the French slang for breasts (which is also the baby word for milk) with the name of an Italian brand of high-horsepower cars, clearly overstepped this line with her enormous bosom. After dozens of operations, Ferrari made it into the *Guinness Book of Records*. She then died in her thirties from an overdose of antidepressants. The circumstances of her death were mysterious, and for a time her husband was suspected of involvement. But there was also a tendency to associate her death with her breasts: there were rumours that she had suffocated under them in her sleep, or that they had exploded in a plane due to a drop in pressure. 'Death by Breast', as the Australian cultural studies scholar Meredith Jones calls these derogatory, sexist legends.[122] But Ferrari herself actively appropriated the artificiality of her creation: 'I'm like a transvestite [...], I've created a femininity that's completely artificial.'[123]

Breastfeeding/chestfeeding and a law

'Artificiality' remains an emotive term. In November 2024 a new law came into force in Germany. Under the name *Selbstbestimmungsgesetz* (Self-Determination Act), it replaced the Transsexuals Act, which had been in place for forty years. Until 2009 this law had stipulated that married couples had to divorce if one spouse changed gender, and until 2011 it had contained the iniquitous requirement that sterilization must take place before an official change of gender.[124] Importantly, the new law dispenses with legal proceedings and medical assessments. Anyone can now change both their first name and their gender in a simple procedure at the registry office.[125] This is a substantial and positive change for those affected, even if they are (justifiably) critical of some aspects.[126] Heated discussions preceded the passing of the Act. These are part of a wide-ranging debate, which the sociologists Ruth Pearce, Sonja Erikainen and Ben Vincent have dubbed the 'TERF wars'.[127] 'TERF' (trans-exclusionary radical feminist) applies to all those who saw dangers in the planned law change, for example that 'fake women' (i.e. men) would 'sneak' into women's toilets and changing rooms and molest women. This argument has also been aired repeatedly in other countries. The debate surrounding British author J. K. Rowling even made it into the glossy magazines.[128] It started in 2020 with a tweet in which she criticized a phrase used in a newspaper article: 'people who menstruate'. She wrote: 'I'm sure there used to be a word for those people. Someone help me out. Wumben? Wumpund? Woomud' (Rowling on X, 6 June 2020). The ensuing debates were extremely acrimonious. In 2024 Rowling lambasted a visually impaired trans* woman who was participating in the Paralympic Games in Paris, accusing her of 'cheating'. The 51-year-old athlete, Valentina Petrillo, openly took part in the competition as a trans* woman and did not win any medals. So her 'cheating', from Rowling's point of view, can only have consisted in 'pretending to be a woman' although she was 'actually' a man. This way of thinking has been vehemently rejected from a trans-activist perspective.[129] Not just because it denies – without any explanation or justification – that trans* women, whether in toilets or at the Olympic Games, are women (and not 'in reality' men). But also because it ignores the fact that trans* people are, in the vast majority of cases, the victims and not the perpetrators of (sexual) violence.

The wide-ranging historical dimensions and legal intricacies of this debate cannot be dealt with adequately here. There is, however, *one* highly topical aspect of this huge debate that we need to look at more closely. This is a focal point for the politicization of the breast, and shows that there is a still a powerful desire to unequivocally link femaleness, breasts and naturalness. While the debates around Rowling mainly played out in social media, and heated tweets on X allow little space for deeper exploration of the issues, in Germany Alice Schwarzer, the editor of the feminist magazine *Emma*, devoted an entire book to the debate. This is the polemic *Transsexualität* (Transsexuality), published in 2022, edited by Schwarzer and her colleague from *Emma*, Chantal Louis. Their contribution brings together many of the arguments touched on by Rowling and develops them in more detail. Like Rowling, Schwarzer and Louis are perturbed by an alleged 'trans trend', which denies the biological foundations of the difference between the sexes (a 'simple and obvious fact'[130]). The following example is taken as evidence of this: 'At the beginning of 2021, several English university hospitals instructed their midwives to use the "inclusive" term "chest-feeding" instead of the word "breastfeeding", and to replace the term "breast milk" with "human milk". The justification was that "elements of the current narratives and discourses around birth are biologistic and transphobic".'[131]

Chantal Louis argues that women are 'disappearing'.[132] As is so often the case in similar discussions, it is implied (with varying degrees of subtlety) that certain terms are no longer 'allowed' to be used, or that people are 'instructed' to speak in a certain way. In actual fact, however, the 'instruction' quoted above is explicitly directed at staff who work with trans* or non-binary people.[133] Of course, mothers are still allowed to put their child to their breast, but this should also apply if a trans* man (that is, a person who was identified as female at birth and now lives as a man) has a child and wishes to nurse it. It should be obvious that such a person would not recognize their own experience in the standard terminology. The cultural studies scholar Karen Fitts describes language in a sexist society as a 'loaded gun', capable of inflicting deep wounds.[134] Years ago, studies showed that the use of obviously gender-specific terms such as 'breasts' and 'breast milk' was felt to be hurtful by trans* and non-binary parents and could actually have negative effects on their health.[135]

The breasts that are supposed to identify 'real' women are perceived in very different ways – as shown in this book by the many technologies of the breast practised over the past centuries. It can be an organ that is wonderfully suited to feeding a baby, and yet not be perceived as evidence of femaleness by the person whose body presents this feature. One of the reasons Schwarzer and Louis's contribution has been criticized by associations such as the LSVD (Federation [for] Queer Diversity in Germany) is that it 'is ultimately a plea for making things as hard as possible for trans* people, for pushing them into invisibility and presenting them as a problem and as unequal'.[136] Not only does the book rigorously exclude certain experiences of having breasts, it also denies the (feminist) history of breastfeeding, which has revealed the connection with questionable 'moral ideas about the role of women in society'.[137] There is no danger that women will disappear if trans* men 'chestfeed' their babies. What could disappear is the idealized, normative ideas of femininity that have been proven to be associated with breastfeeding.

One of Schwarzer and Louis's central arguments, incidentally, is that the new legal status of transgender identity, which makes it easier to change gender, reproduces traditional gender roles. They argue that 'non-conforming young girls' in particular are 'recklessly' (*leichtfertig*) encouraged to believe the following: 'You just have to have the right body to fit your state of mind. Instead of saying to them: You can be a girl who is passionate about maths, likes playing football, or falls in love with her best (female) friend – and yet has a female body. There's no incompatibility there'.[138]

This is misleading for three reasons. Firstly, it is implausible because even the authors do not provide any concrete proof that girls who want to play football are being 'told' they are trans*, and that large numbers of children who like kicking balls around are being pushed into becoming transgender. But even if we understand this exaggeration as a rhetorical device, the argument has very little substance. Because – secondly – this suggests that it is trans* people's efforts to combat legal discrimination in our society that sustain outdated gender ideas and misogynist ideologies. The gist is that no sooner have girls started to play football and take an interest in maths than they have to go under the knife. Yet the opposite is actually true. Because – thirdly – it was the legislation existing prior to the Self-Determination Act (legislation which Schwarzer and Louis defend), including assessments by doctors, psychologists and judges, which encouraged such normative concepts of gender. As the trans* activist and sociologist Felicia Ewert writes, those subjected to such assessments had to 'embody cis-normative ideas as convincingly as possible'. If their appearance or demeanour was perceived as 'ambiguous' this could be regarded as unconvincing, resulting in a negative evaluation.[139] Subjecting people to constant scrutiny of their gender identity is much more likely to lead to the reproduction of stereotypical ideas of gender than dispensing with these procedures. The cultural and media studies scholar Josch Hoenes rightly pointed out that the legal regulations in place prior to the law change 'strictly adhere[d] to the criteria of unambiguousness, permanence and coherence'. Again and again, they confirmed the 'basic assumptions of the heteronormative gender binary' – even though the very possibility of changing gender reveals the absurdity of these assumptions.[140] In other words, the previous legal requirements for changing gender, which Schwarzer and Louis defend, actually promoted the normative, simplistic categories of gender binarism (e.g. 'football is for boys') that they seek to criticize. Under the new law, there is no longer any debate about whether a person who wants to change their gender at the registry office is 'feminine' or 'masculine' enough to do so. And that is something that feminists of every kind should welcome.

Breasts, balls and other equipment

It is worth dwelling on the example of the football-playing girls a little longer, since sport is a key area in which gender, body and social conceptions are closely interconnected. The idea of trans* women infiltrating sports contests to the detriment of 'real' women shows that the question of what a woman or man is has particular relevance in sport. The sports sociologists Gabriele Sobiech and Gian-Claudio Gentile argue that gender classifications and social hierarchies are accentuated and magnified in sport.[141]

This becomes particularly obvious in the combination of breasts and balls. In 1955, at the request of the Lower Rhine Football Association, the German Football Association (DFB) announced a ban on women's football. One reason for this was breasts. Looking back, Hubert Claessen, a member of the DFB board at the time, sums up the concerns that led to the ban: 'That was a mortal sin, having the girls running across the field with their breasts bobbing and then, on top of that, kicking the ball or fouling each other.'[142] The women who wanted to play football with bobbing breasts risked being condemned as immodest or shameless: 'In the fight for the ball, feminine grace disappears, body and soul inevitably suffer harm, and the displaying of the body violates decency and propriety.' This was the DFB's justification for its ban, which it maintained until 1970. Why did the sometimes fierce (cultural) battles around women's football concentrate so much on the breasts? One of the reasons, undoubtedly, was that this was the body part that made the players' femininity particularly obvious, in a sport that was (in Europe) viewed as typically masculine. The focus on breasts in the debates and practices relating to women's football persists to this day. Lewd jokes about shirt swapping have accompanied women's football from the start, and there is still a myth in circulation that female footballers – inspired by the legendary breast amputations of the Amazons – bind their breasts. The implication here is that this part of the body must be subjected to rigorous treatment before a woman can kick a ball.

One particularly puzzling fact is that, in contrast to the European belief that breasts and balls are incompatible, the exact opposite view prevails elsewhere, for example in the US. There soccer is regarded as a female sport, even a 'womanish' one; this explains why successful US men's teams are a rarity internationally. 'Real' men prove themselves in American football, where women play a peripheral role at best and are subjected to similar hostility to that experienced by women in German football.

Even after rescinding its ban, incidentally, the DFB ensured that women's alleged physical inability to play football in the same way as men remained tangible and visible for both spectators and players. At first the female players had to play with lighter youth balls and were only allowed out on the pitch in 'good weather conditions.'[143] And their game lasted only seventy minutes, instead of the usual ninety – another concession to their 'weaker' nature. These restrictions were not lifted until the early 1990s.

Today female players are expected to think of ways to make women's football more popular. Tragically, they seem to have accepted the idea that the best way to do this is to show their 'female charms', so as to avoid any associations with man-hating Amazons. In a study in 2018, sports scientist Karolin Heckemeyer quoted a female footballer as saying that a sexy appearance made it possible to attract spectators, 'especially male ones, because they then take an interest in the players.'[144] This does not work, however, as shown by a series of photos published online by a German television magazine in 2020. Seemingly oblivious to the #MeToo debates, the magazine ran a story on 'The most beautiful female footballers in the world'. One photo showed Kaylyn Kyle, a former member of Canada's national team, in a bikini. The comment was: 'We admit that we don't know much about this blonde's football skills. But with photos like these, Kaylyn can have a place on our team any time, even if she can't even manage a two-metre pass to a team mate.'[145] As we can see, presenting 'feminine charms' does not contribute to the acceptance of women's football. On the contrary, it encourages men to deny women's competence altogether. The rule, to this day, seems to be that displaying a 'beautiful body' gives rise to doubts about a woman's sporting ability.

Sportswomen thus find themselves caught in a virtually inescapable dilemma. When it comes to the breast, projections, ideals and distortions are still activated wherever needed. The 'bobbing breasts' that the DFB officials fantasized about to justify their ban on women's football recall related ideas about female bodies in sport: the breastless Amazon and the 'mannish' woman, also breastless. Yet women with breasts cannot be 'real' athletes either, because attractive breasts supposedly make real sporting activity impossible. A circular argument which, despite its obvious lack of logic, continues to influence the actual practices of sportspeople, journalists and spectators.

The perceived plausibility of such ideas may have to do with the flood of literature (pseudo-scientific, from today's perspective) produced in the first decades of the twentieth century on the topic of women and sport. Of central interest here was the 'effect of physical exercise on the female constitution, birth and menstruation' (the title of an article published in 1929).[146] This discourse was based on the unexamined premise that 'the physical activity of women is – and should be – fundamentally different from that of men', as the (male) author of a book on women's sport and women's bodies asserted in 1930.[147] This assumption formed the framework into which all reflections on this subject had to be fitted. Every movement permitted to female humans had to be subordinated to the 'fulfilment of woman's natural vocation', i.e. having children.[148] The authors (nearly all men) who wrote on this topic focused on the impact of sport on the reproductive organs. But the breasts, which were needed to nurse offspring, also seemed to be in danger. It was suggested, for example, that swimming while breastfeeding might have an unfavourable influence on the volume and composition of the milk[149] – a distant echo of the supposedly poisonous breast milk of women whose behaviour did not conform to norms. This still resonates today in tales of breast binding in women's football.

The 1930 text argues that breasts are 'quite cumbersome during sporting activity due to their configuration' and need to be 'tied up' (*hochgebunden* – the same word that would be used for tying back one's hair). 'Tying up' the breasts, however, leads to an 'unfavourable positioning of the glandular tissue'. This results in such sad cases as the 'dry, trained type of the long-term athlete', who, 'very frequently exhibits a sagging of the breasts'.[150] It comes as no surprise that the writer of these sentences 'must categorically reject football for women', with the rationale that it is 'too robust and too rough' for them.[151] Today there is a vast range of special bras for sport, first invented in the 1970s in an attempt to defuse the argument that the female breast was an obstacle to movement. But even before the invention of special sports bras, there were women who engaged in sport and who argued persistently against the idea that their bodies were fundamentally unsuited to these activities. In 1925 a small book on the subject of women and sport noted that 'the anatomical differences between men and women are not so substantial that a woman's sporting activity needs to be restricted because of them.[152] The book makes no mention of breasts. It does, however, contain numerous photos of women doing sport, such as 'Fräulein Lingner [...] the best female forest runner in Berlin', holding the 800-metre record of 2:36.4.[153]

In the eighteenth century, when Rousseau's theories on education inspired various writers to turn to the subject of physical exercise, women and girls were fundamentally excluded. This was taken as so self-evident that no explanations were felt to be necessary. In 1793 the philanthropist Johann Christoph Friedrich Gutsmuths wrote a treatise on gymnastics for youth, which he understood as a 'contribution to the necessary improvement of physical education'. The book talks about boys a great deal and frequently mentions that strengthening the body through exercise serves to increase the manliness of those who do it. This was linked with a deliberately political argument – boys had to engage in sport because physically demanding activities in politics awaited them: 'He needs to play his part in the state'. What is interesting is the fear repeatedly evoked in the text of a softening and feminizing of male bodies that do not engage in sport. This is because the 'excessive delicacy of the female nature is transferred all too easily to the young male sex'. Gymnastics ensure that 'the male character can once again become dominant'.[154]

What did the author mean? Art historians such as Abigail Solomon-Godeau and Mechthild Fend have spoken of a 'crisis of representation' and of the 'limits of masculinity', which were becoming ever more visible at the time.[155] Both things can be seen in a number of images from around 1800, showing androgynous male bodies, whose posture, delicacy and expression often suggest femininity. If Gutsmuths had seen Anne-Louis Girodet-Trioson's 1791 painting *The Sleep of Endymion*, depicting the lover of the moon goddess Selene, he would undoubtedly have recommended a few rounds of vigorous gymnastics. There is no female breast on display in the painting, but the subject is supine, with one arm raised behind his head. It is a posture with a long iconographic tradition from the nude to the pin-up, usually used to present the female breasts to the viewer's gaze. Girodet-Trioson's painting not only gives Endymion a feminine posture, but also pale skin, slender, unmuscled, hairless legs, and a passive pose on a forest floor padded with cushions and blankets.

'Feminine' male bodies such as these were a source of anxiety around 1800. The fear that male bodies could succumb to the 'excessive delicacy of the female nature', as Gutsmuths called it, was also a fear of gender confusion. Sport, which was only just becoming fashionable at the time, was seen as a way to avert this danger. This is particularly interesting given that, even today, bodies that transgress or blur their supposedly natural gender boundaries are still a source of fear in the world of sport.

In sport, the breasts as a sign of femininity are precarious, regardless of whether their largeness (bobbing) or smallness (mannish woman) is thought to prove the natural unsuitability of the female body for sport. What matters is that they are constructed as a problem in relation to a 'normal' gender order. This is perhaps most obvious in bodybuilding. While the male pectorals can turn into male breasts after intense training (or the use of anabolic steroids), female bodybuilders face the opposite danger, the 'masculinization' of their breasts.[156] Both are problematic, but the latter sometimes leads to restrictive countermeasures on the part of the judges, who strictly monitor the observance of gender norms. The Black female bodybuilder Renné Toney, who holds the world record for the largest biceps ever measured in a woman, was once told to let her hair (which she wore short) grow to a 'conventional length', because her muscular, small-breasted body would otherwise lack 'femininity'.[157]

This is part of the obsessive quest for clear categorizations, even though the way bodies look and the changes they undergo as a result of sport are actually extremely diverse. The judges' demand that Toney grow her hair long was meant to differentiate her from a man, and yet for her, the reference to the male body was fundamental:

> [...] when I visualize the kind of physique that I want for myself that I'd like to display to the world, actually it's the body of a male bodybuilder; and I'm not trying to be a man by no means by lifting weights ... I kind of like looking androgynous. That's going to cause controversy, I know that. That's going to raise some eyebrows.[158]

Such statements contrast with the kind of image-oriented body-building[159] that appears under hashtags such as #girlswholift, between pole dancing and heterosexual relationship advice, and celebrates hypersexualized images of femininity. There is no room here for any in-between, ambiguous or androgynous body images, as cultivated by Toney. Muscles are optional, but breasts are compulsory.

Scars

It's a fine line. Too much artificial bosom exposes 'womanliness as a masquerade', as the psychoanalyst Joan Riviere famously put it in 1929. It leads to devaluation. For a person who was classed as male at birth but now identifies as female, getting 'artificial' breasts involves a number of legal and social hurdles. It may also be seen as fraudulent and arbitrarily discredited.[160] But deciding not to get 'new' breasts, for example after cancer treatment, can cause problems too: absent breasts are also a subject of debate. Special clothing and accoutrements are designed for them, and perceptions of them vary hugely.

Until well into the twentieth century, the standard treatment for breast cancer was a full mastectomy. Today this operation is only carried out on around 20 per cent of patients (who are not all female; in Germany around 700 men per year are affected by breast cancer[161]). Before the use of anaesthetics became routine in the second half of the nineteenth century, the procedures were drastic: red-hot irons were pressed onto 'suspect' areas.[162] But after successful treatment, the – now absent – breast(s) remained the focus of attention. The first patent for a breast prosthesis was granted in the US in 1873; hundreds more followed.

Surgical procedures originally developed for breast augmentation were and still are used to 'restore' the lost breast. But this practice began to meet with resistance in the 1980s. The assumption that women who had lost a breast to cancer would inevitably wish to replace it was criticized by the women themselves. The Black writer and activist Audre Lorde denounced the normalizing effect of prostheses and reconstructive surgery in her *Cancer Journals* in 1980. She argued that they reinforced toxic stereotypes of femininity, which prioritized women's looks above all else – and thus prevented an exploration of trauma and vulnerability.[163] Today, over forty years later, there is a more nuanced view (also among feminists) of the rigorous refusal of prostheses and reconstructive surgery. But it is Lorde's enduring legacy to have raised the question of whether and why a 'restoration' of the breast is necessary.

Visual artists also contributed to this questioning, pursuing similar tactics of making the invisible visible. They used their works to highlight the way prostheses and operations conceal the trauma experienced, and to deliberately show the damaged state of the breast. In the late 1970s the New York performance artist Hannah Wilke created a double portrait: a photo of her mother, Selma Butter, who had cancer, next to a photo of herself, both bare-chested. The young and beautiful body of the artist contrasts disturbingly with that of her mother, marked by illness. Her scar is visible, as are the small red blotches on the skin that signal the return of the tumour. Wilke echoes these in the small, pistol-shaped objects that she places on her own breasts. The artist, who was to die of cancer herself in 1993, also processed her own illness in her art, in a series entitled *Intra-Venus*. In the double portrait with her mother, her young and healthy body still seems far removed from this.

At first glance, Wilke's juxtaposition of old and young female bodies resembles an established visual motif in art, as exemplified by Cranach's *Fountain of Youth* (see chapter 2). Sometimes these are even combined in a single body, for example in a wooden statuette carved around 1480 in Ulm, Germany, entitled *Garstige Alte* (Horrible old woman) (Liebig Haus, Frankfurt am Main). The figure is identified as a hag by her toothless mouth and wrinkled, sagging breasts, which – in the style of a *Venus pudica* – she tries in vain to cover with her right hand. From the rear, however, she appears to be a much younger woman. The statuette, an ingenious optical illusion and puzzle, uses the female body to convey a warning about the transience of earthly beauty. In contrast, Wilke's double portrait focuses on the cross-generational relationship between two women.[164] In its temporal dimension, this may imply ageing and potential suffering, but it also highlights the women's mutual care and concern.

The strategy of drawing attention to missing breasts, damaged breasts and scars is an attempt to regain agency and scope for action. The British photographer Jo Spence was diagnosed with breast cancer in 1982 and took photos documenting her stays in hospital – including mammograms, doctors' rounds and operations. Her work sought to give visibility to the body *after* traumatic treatment but also to show medical processes from the perspective of the person undergoing them. The pictures call for self-empowerment in the face of a medical practice that 'controls women's bodies', as Spence wrote. She saw her work as a 'research project on the politics of cancer'.[165] What medical procedures, devices, touches and directives does the body have to submit to? How does the woman who has to endure these things look at them? One photo shows the artist during a mammogram, the radiographer having been persuaded to take the photo ('She was rather unhappy about it, but felt it was preferable to my holding the camera out at arm's length and doing a self portrait').[166] In a snapshot taken by Spence from her bed, doctors and students in their white coats are visible from behind. We sense that the men are about to turn to the patient and look at her, but for the time being *she* is still in control of the gaze. In these and many other pictures in the series we can see and feel the frightening experience, the dependence, the waiting, the relinquishing of control over one's own body and time. These do not conform to the visual modes of education and/or advertising that are usually served up to us.

Spence's work never attracted as much mass-media attention as the photographs of the feminist artist Matuschka around ten years later. One reason for this is probably Matuschka's promise to reappropriate standard beauty poses and aestheticize physical harm. She shows a poignant overcoming of adversity rather than humdrum hospital routine. Her campaign began with a spectacular photo on the cover of the *New York Times Sunday Magazine* in 1993, presenting the artist in a specially designed evening dress. The asymmetrical cut of her white dress reveals the long scar left by her mastectomy. The gauzy white fabric that covers her left arm is also wrapped around her head, evoking a bandage. Many years later, the art director responsible for the issue, Janet Froelich, remembered: 'No one had seen this scar before, unless you had it, or a close family member had it. We were riveted by the images.'[167]

The photo was part of a health policy campaign about breast cancer, modelled on the AIDS activism of the 1980s.[168] The aim was to criticize the assumption that women's main concern after breast cancer treatment was to look the same as 'before' as quickly as possible. The activists drew attention to the high incidence rates, the underfunding of research, and the tortures of breast cancer treatment.[169] And they criticized the 'cultural truism that a woman without breasts is worse than no woman at all'.[170] But while Matuschka favoured an image that insisted on the beauty of the amputated body and evoked heroic echoes of the Amazonian motif, Spence was not interested in this. In one of the photographs taken after her surgery, she does not demand a 'positive' view of her damaged body, but asks how this body becomes visible at all, and what happens if it does not meet conventional expectations. The key element here is the attribution of 'ugliness' to a female body with 'deformed' breasts. Spence throws open her green surgical gown and stands there naked, inviting viewers to read the word written across her chest: 'MONSTER' (figure 22).

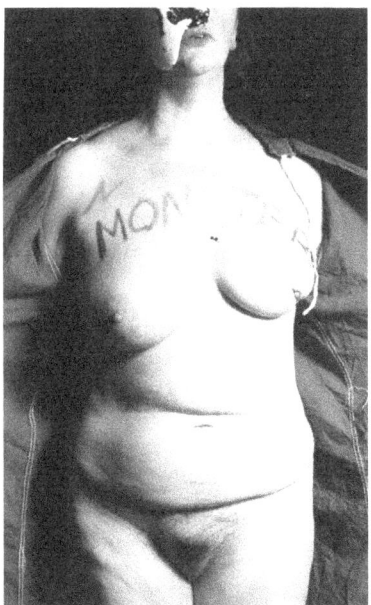

Figure 22 View of a post-operative body. Jo Spence, 'Exiled', from the series *Narratives of Dis-ease*, c. 1985. © Jo Spence Memorial Archive, The Image Centre.

The gesture of the opened gown is an explicit visualization, similar
to Matuschka's work. Spence, however, does not reveal the traumatized breast as an affirmative statement ('I am what I am – deal with
it!'). Instead, 'Monster' refers to the process of 'othering'. And this
process produces attributions, value judgements and classifications.
When this body becomes an image, it becomes a 'monster'.

But 'monsters' are also able to transcend boundaries, as the feminist
cultural studies scholar Marsha Meskimmon explains. On the one
hand, the clinical gaze, in combination with existing beauty norms,
makes 'monsters' of all those who do not meet these norms. On the
other hand, these bodies are situated outside such attributions.[171]
They defy the norm. It is no coincidence that it is mainly figures coded
as female who are judged to be monstrous or grotesque. In a study
entitled *The Female Grotesque*, the literary scholar Mary Russo offers
an extensive but inevitably incomplete list: 'the Medusa, the Crone,
the Bearded Woman, the Fat Lady, [...] the Hottentot Venus, [...] the
Hysteric'. But she also mentions bodily conditions that are perceived
differently in female bodies than in male ones, such as 'illness,
aging, reproduction, nonreproduction, secretions, lumps, [...], scars,
make-up, and prostheses'.[172]

All these conditions and bodies denote deviations from an ideal. But
at the same time they highlight the problematic nature of this ideal,
since nobody can really match up to it. The term 'body positivity' has
been used since the 2010s, especially in social media, to try to challenge
this. There have been intense discussions about how to achieve greater
acceptance of 'non-normative' bodies.[173] At the same time, however,
more and more critical voices have pointed out that efforts to develop
a 'positive' body image do not get to the heart of the problem, namely
'the positioning of certain bodies in a social "outside", including all the
associated discrimination', as Anna Klauke recently commented.[174] It
is not enough to assert the 'beauty' of all bodies, unless we simultaneously reflect on the political impact that the exclusion of certain
physicalities can have.

We all experience the world with and through our bodies, and each
of those bodies is presented and modified with reference to a gendered
normality, as the body of a 'man' or a 'woman'. Having our body at
our disposal, having it and being it simultaneously, is a 'contingent

dimension of our sociality', as emphasized by the sociologist Paula-Irene Villa. In other words, it is one of the things that makes people social beings or, in short, humans.[175] When a female bodybuilder is told that her muscles are too big and her breasts too small, and that she needs to affirm her 'true' gender in another way, e.g. with long hair, or when trans* men nursing their babies are denied the right to use different words for breasts and breast milk, these things make it clear how differently the technologies of the self are interpreted, demanded or suppressed.

This is why the 'technologies of the breast' that are needed to make breasts function as secondary sex characteristics are so diverse. They range from everyday items of clothing such as bras to breast operations. This is not to say that these two things are ultimately the same. There is a drastic difference, physically and economically, between wearing a bra and undergoing a potentially life-threatening operation. But the idea that the one is in harmony with the natural body, while the other is somehow 'artificial', is untenable.[176] Rather, the numerous interventions which humans have carried out and still carry out on the breasts – to enlarge them, reduce them, restore them, replace them, remove them, push them up, bind them, get rid of them and so on – are signs of people's need to continually prove their femininity, masculinity, or even humanity. While some people seem able to achieve this with ease, others face difficulties – and even legal obstacles.

4

'I AM GOD'
The breast as an organ of protest

Are breasts like swords? • Amazons as role models • 'Anarchic Amazons': the women of 1968 and their breasts • Burning bras: feminism as breast liberation? • 'Beautiful women': the limits of protest • Hysteria, ecstasy and the dance of the maenads: the naked breast as a sign of the 'other' • The two bodies of Angela Merkel: breasts and power

So far this book has considered paintings, photos, figures or statues which reveal, conceal, idealize or demonize the breast. All these things are directly linked to social and political conditions. As we have seen, the eighteenth-century fashion for pictures of breastfeeding mothers correlated with the propagation of a new approach to infant feeding, privileging the mother's own breast over that of a wet nurse. And the enduring impact of the classical figure of Venus/Aphrodite as a model for the female body and breasts – albeit one frequently overwritten and modernized – shows how images determine social reality and vice versa. Images influence the practices and politics of body perception, as well as what features are considered beautiful and what behaviour is seen as 'appropriate'. They are connected to ideas of sexuality, of femininity ('ours' and 'theirs'), and of the role that pregnancy, birth and child-raising (should) play in a woman's life. But one thing that has not yet been mentioned, in connection to all the images of ideal, sacred, covered and depraved breasts, is aggression.

At first glance, aggression seems to have nothing to do with the female breast, firmly established as an organ of care, of sexuality and of 'womanhood'. Amid the abundance of breastfeeding Madonnas, chastely seductive Venuses, racist representations of the 'Hottentot Venus', and pin-up girls with their fixed repertoire of poses, all the qualities attributed to the breast seem to relate more or less to sex, sin or motherhood. Now, however, we will turn to a new subject area: breasts as a means of attack. This is not about tasteless tales of 'a woman's weapons', based on the notion that women have no actual weapons and can only use their body, their sexuality and the associated power of seduction to reach their goals. Instead, this chapter will draw attention to the fact that the breast can literally embody protest and attack, because women with the power to control this body part signal a particularly obvious and effective break with the gender order – and the social order. If breasts become public at an 'inappropriate' moment because the woman in possession of those breasts wishes it to be so, then this stands for attack, aggression and a crossing of boundaries.

Are breasts like swords?

The idea of the breast as an organ of protest evokes events from relatively recent history, such as the 'breast attack' (*Busenattentat*, literally 'bosom assassination') on Theodor W. Adorno at the University of Frankfurt in 1969. Or, much more recently, a protest by Femen in the summer of 2022. During an open day in the garden of the Federal Chancellery in Berlin, two activists positioned themselves on either side of the German chancellor, Olaf Scholz, and took their tops off to reveal breasts daubed with 'Gas embargo now'. The aim of the protest was to demand a boycott on Russian gas.[1]

But these more recent examples have numerous precursors. The stories of people who have breasts and use them as weapons actually go back much further. The historian, archaeologist and Scandinavian studies scholar Heiko Hiltmann examined a thirteenth-century Icelandic narrative, the *Saga of Erik the Red*, about the conquest of Greenland and Newfoundland by Icelandic seafarers.[2] It tells of a woman who uses her breasts to actively intervene in a battle. Her story is less well known than that of the Amazons,[3] figures of the more familiar Greek mythology, who have been widely integrated into (pop-)cultural memory. And yet the breast-wielding Viking emerges from the battle victorious, unlike the Amazons. Freydís Eiríksdóttir, the heroine of the story, takes part in an expedition to Newfoundland by ship. Upon arrival, the explorers are attacked by natives. The men from the Icelandic group flee, but not the courageous Eiríksdóttir, as the saga tells. First she reprimands her male companions: 'Why, if I had a weapon, I think I could put up a better fight than any of you.' She then seizes a sword and takes a stand against the attackers. But she doesn't stop there. She 'pulled out her breasts from under her clothes and slapped the naked sword on them,'[4] whereupon the natives take fright and retreat. The battle is won.

In Western art, the female breast as a symbol of anger and aggression has its own iconography. In Giotto's fresco in the Arena Chapel in Padua, Temperantia (Temperance), in a high-cut dress and headscarf, is depicted next to Ira (Wrath), who tears open her dress with both hands and bares her chest (1305–7). Compared to other representations of female breasts in art, it is rare to see them used to illustrate the powerful feeling of anger, one of the seven deadly sins. But female personifications of anger, in which breasts play a prominent role, do exist.

Two centuries after Giotto, Georg Pencz equipped his Ira with a breastplate that strikingly emphasizes the figure's bosom (1539–43, Rijksmuseum, Amsterdam). Not only does the breastplate highlight the nipples, an arabesque decoration under the breasts increases their visibility. The figure's sword (recalling Eiríksdóttir) and brushwood torch, symbolizing easily inflamed anger, suggest readiness to attack. But the inscription ('Ira furor brevis sum') implies that wrath is just a brief moment of madness, which should be resisted.

Another sixteenth-century engraving shows Ira with bare breasts and a garment that looks as though – like Eiríksdóttir and Giotto's Ira – she has torn it from her body in rage (J. Matham, *Ira ferox*, 1585–9, Rijksmuseum, Amsterdam). This, too, is a warning against ferocious anger, which lashes out indiscriminately and sweeps away everything in its path. It should be noted, however, that, unlike Freydís

Eiríksdóttir, these 'strong women' going into battle with bared breasts were not positive role models, proving the existence of female strength. On the contrary, they were intended as visual warnings – as particularly frightening images of an emotion that was regarded as negative.

The research literature on the topic of breasts and aggression is not particularly extensive, and, as with the big-bosomed Stone Age figurines (Venus of Willendorf, etc. – see chapter 2), there is uncertainty about how this aggressive role of the breast should be interpreted. When interpreting the breast-baring of Eiríksdóttir, for example, researchers have repeatedly stressed that this was mainly about 'vilification, pacification, humiliation and deterrence'.[5] Yet none of these nouns actually fits the aggressive situation in which Eiríksdóttir decides to display her breasts. In response to these assumptions, the above-mentioned article by Hiltmann makes it very clear that the bared chest is actually being deployed here as a 'second weapon' alongside the sword. What the naked torso is intended to suggest to the enemy is 'boundless battle fury' and Eiríksdóttir's trust in her own invulnerability.[6]

The 'aggressive and warlike connotations of the naked breast'[7] are not only evident in the medieval saga and in the iconography of wrath personified; they are also found in many other images of and actions by people with breasts. Another example is the biblical story of Judith and Holofernes. The breasts of the protagonist do not actually play any particular part in this story, recorded in the Old Testament book of Judith, but they do feature prominently in the paintings and sculptures created by artists such as Artemisia Gentileschi, Donatello and Peter Paul Rubens. In the story, a widow named Judith, who 'was beautiful in appearance and was very lovely to behold' (Judith 8: 7) and 'feared God with great devotion' (Judith 8: 8), saves the inhabitants of the Jewish town of Bethulia, under siege by the cruel Assyrian general Holofernes. Judith sets out for Holofernes' tent with her maidservant and tells the gullible general that he will soon be victorious. He believes his visitor and allows her to stay with him for several days. In the end, however, he thinks: 'it would be a disgrace if we let such a woman go without being intimate with her. If we do not seduce her, she will laugh at us' (Judith 12: 12). He is very much mistaken, however: after consuming a large quantity of alcohol, he sinks onto his bed, defenceless, and is beheaded by the woman he had expected to rape without resistance. Judith and her servant pack up the severed head and deliver it to the grateful inhabitants of the besieged town. The Assyrians, now leaderless, flee, and Bethulia is freed. We learn nothing more about Judith, except that she remains extremely virtuous, frees her maidservant in gratitude, and lives to the blessed age of 105.

Given that this story combines women, sex and violence, thus evoking several motifs with great voyeuristic appeal, it comes as no surprise that it has inspired many artistic interpretations over the centuries.[8] Since it is about a woman who successfully kills a man with a sword, a weapon of war, it seems an obvious choice to draw on the iconography of Ira, which offered a ready-made template for the illustration of aggression and violence in the form of a female body. Scholars interpreting depictions of Judith and Holofernes often perceive the visibility of the breast as a reference to the situation of seduction that precedes the murder. However, it seems at least equally plausible that Judith's bared chest signals her strength, anger and aggressiveness. Incidentally, this subject was also occasionally used to present a supposedly appealing contrast between Judith's youthful body and that of her maid, who is drawn as an old woman – although her age is not actually mentioned in the biblical text. A drawing in red chalk by the Florentine artist Rosso Fiorentino takes the subject as an impetus (or pretext) to juxtapose female youth and beauty with age and decay, using the comparison to depict both states of the body extra vividly (*Judith with the Head of Holofernes*, 1540, Los Angeles County Museum of Art). A few lines indicating a headless body in the background are the only sign of Holofernes.

The juxtaposition of old and young, of 'beautiful' and 'ugly' bodies, has already been identified as an important element of the visual discourse on the breast in the preceding chapters, for example in Lucas Cranach the Elder's painting *The Fountain of Youth* (chapter 2, figure 15). However, it is not the 'old' bosom that is associated with aggression. It is (virtually) only young bodies that are permitted to enact aggression by exposing their breasts. In perfect harmony with this visual paradigm of Western art, the breasts that are shown as a symbol of attack largely correspond to the prevailing ideal of beauty (= youth).

Amazons as role models

Amazons, who evoke notions of transgression, wildness and female power even today, are also usually depicted as 'beautiful women'. Artists tend to portray them as young women with two breasts, one or both of them unclothed.[9] This is strange, since the Greek mythology where they first appeared associated these figures with a gruesome custom – one that is wholly at odds with the image of the 'beautiful savage'. Amazon mothers were said to mutilate the right breasts of their young daughters so they could learn to use a bow and arrow more easily. Boys were not raised at all, incidentally; they were either handed over to their fathers, who were not part of the community, or killed immediately. The plausible but false etymology of the word Amazon (*a-mazos*, 'breastless') was first proposed by Hippocrates and subsequently cited by other ancient and modern authors as proof of this practice of mutilation. Benjamin Hederich's *Gründliches mythologisches Lexicon* (In-depth dictionary of mythology, 1770), an important source for German-speaking scholars, writers and poets in the early nineteenth century, describes the different aspects of this practice:

> AMAZONES: [...] These warlike women are said to have got their name from the *alpha privativum* and *mazos*, the breast, because they burnt off the right breast of all girls immediately after their birth, so it would be no hindrance to them later in sword fighting. [...] They formed special kingdoms in Asia and Africa, where they had their own queens and, according to some sources, did not tolerate any men among them, but, to ensure that their race would not perish, would go to the borders of their countries at certain times, where the men from the neighbouring regions would come and serve them according to their will. When they subsequently gave birth, they kept the girls with them, burnt off their right breast in the way described above, and instructed them in running, hunting, riding, shooting and other such military exercises until they were skilled enough to handle weapons. [...] The boys, however, were killed immediately or, according to other sources, given back to their fathers [...].[10]

In 1971 bacteriologists pointed out that the story of the amputated breasts was extremely implausible.[11] Why should a woman with two breasts be unable to shoot a bow and arrow? And why should it be easier to fight with a maimed body? Furthermore, in a time without disinfectant this procedure would certainly have meant death for a large number of the girls subjected to it.

Another reason to doubt the story of the amputated breasts is that the ancient sources, such as Herodotus, Diodorus and Strabo, all based their accounts on hearsay.[12] None of the ancient historians had actually met these women without men who went to war against the Greeks. Such a meeting would probably not have been possible anyway, since it is more than questionable whether the Amazons ever existed. But this did not deter authors from giving precise descriptions of these fascinating female figures and their exploits. And the gruesome role of the breast in the creation of the Amazon myth fulfilled a purpose: the lives of the Amazons constituted an outrageous violation of conventional notions of gender, and the amputation of the breast was a vivid and memorable symbol of this violation. The killing of enemies fitted this image: 'The unnatural character of their activities is expressed in the symbolic reduction [of their body]', as the literary scholar Heinz-Peter Preußer puts it.[13] So all the evidence suggests that the story of the severed breast was intended to make the warlike deeds of the Amazons plausible. According to the ancient sources, this was what turned them into 'destroyers of men' (Hellanicus of Lesbos). Their actions inspired 'man-subjugating fear' (Pindar)[14] – and the myth of the severed breast fitted this narrative. Historians and archaeologists assume that the images, statues and accounts of Amazons in ancient Greece do not indicate that women's domination over men was seen as acceptable at the time. Instead, the amputation of the breast signalled that the Amazons were the antithesis of what was considered 'good' and 'normal' in patriarchal society.[15] The reason they were able to have the effect they did was that they were the 'other'. And they remained influential – as a simultaneously attractive and repellent 'vision of horror' – into the nineteenth century.[16] Hegel further intensified the dread associated with the idea of female domination in his *Lectures on the Philosophy of History* in 1837. Here an anecdote illustrates the supposed incapacity of Africans to establish an orderly state:[17]

Tradition alleges that in former times a state composed of women, at whose head was a woman, made itself famous by its conquests. She is said to have pounded her own son in a mortar, to have besmeared herself with the blood, and to have had the blood of pounded children constantly at hand. She is said to have driven away or put to death all the males, and commanded the death of all male children. These furies destroyed everything in their neighbourhood, and were driven to constant plunderings, because they did not cultivate the land. Captives in war were taken as husbands: pregnant women had to betake themselves outside the encampment; and if they had born a son, put him out of the way.[18]

It is worth noting that the Amazons appearing in classical myths are all eventually conquered by the Greek heroes. Or they kill themselves, like Heinrich von Kleist's *Penthesilea* (1808), and renounce the 'law of women'. Kleist's information, incidentally, came from the above-mentioned dictionary of mythology by Benjamin Hederich.[19] Kleist's drama marked an early peak in the nineteenth-century interest in Amazons, which was also manifested in ethnographic research.[20] British anthropologists such as Henry Sumner Maine, the author of *Ancient Law* (1861), and his adversary John Ferguson McLennan, the author of *Primitive Marriage* (1865), are just two examples of the great interest in the emergence of the patriarchy and in the role of the Amazons as evidence of matriarchal societies.

In feminist appropriations and reinterpretations of the myth, the Amazons became positive role models, 'strong women' to identify with. This shows the flexibility of myths: they are anything but closed, finalized narratives, whose 'real' meaning can be definitively deciphered. The idea of a female community independent of patriarchal domination was an extremely appealing feminist alternative over a surprisingly long period of time. Christine de Pizan's *Le Livre de la Cité des Dames* (The book of the city of ladies, 1405) is a fascinating early example and an influential contribution to the 'querelle des femmes', the centuries-long debate about the gender difference and women's rights. In her book, the author refers to the Amazons to prove that women can be independent of men and can fight.[21]

This was undoubtedly the aspect that, several hundred years later, made these mythical figures attractive to the West German women's movement in the 1960s and 1970s. The art historian Cillie Rentmeister calls these years 'the radical, Amazonian era, the era of female students, the era when women's centres and projects were founded'.[22] It was also the era of the labrys, the double-headed axe representing women's struggle.[23] Lesbians in particular wore this symbol demonstratively around their necks.[24] And there was a new interest in studying the history of matriarchies and rediscovering the forgotten research carried out in the early twentieth century. A pirated edition of Mathilde Vaerting's *Die weibliche Eigenart im Männerstaat und die männliche Eigenart im Frauenstaat* (Female character in a men's state and male character in a women's state, 1921) was published by a Berlin women's collective in 1974. It was advertised as an 'indispensable contribution [...] to the self-perception of the women's movement'.[25] The year 1975 saw a reprint of *Mütter und Amazonen: Ein Umriß weiblicher Reiche* (Mothers and Amazons: an outline of female empires), by the Austrian author Bertha Eckstein-Diener, originally published in 1932 under the pseudonym 'Sir Galahad'. There was also renewed interest in a book first published in 1861, *Das Mutterrecht: Eine Untersuchung über die Gynaikokratie der Alten Welt nach ihrer religiösen und rechtlichen Natur* (Matriarchy: a study on the gynocracy of the ancient world according to its religious and legal nature), by the Basel scholar Johann Jakob Bachofen. And women's bookshops took their names from Amazon queens. In Tübingen, for example, a store founded in 1979, with its roots in the autonomous women's movement, chose the name Thalestris, an Amazon queen described by the ancient historians Diodorus and Curtius Rufus. The bookshop still exists today.[26]

There is one thing that becomes very clear from these brief glimpses of Amazon fever, from classical antiquity to second-wave feminism. In the long history of images and stories of Amazons, there were major changes in what people saw in them, and in the hopes and fears they inspired. As a result, infatuation with the Amazons and the matriarchy associated with them could be cultivated in diametrically opposed systems of thought and antagonistic milieus. It was not just the feminists of the 1970s who found Amazons seductive, but also German fascists. Far from rejecting the idea of the matriarchy, they perceived it as compatible with their own ideology. This led to a dispute in the mid-1980s in the academic journal *Das Argument* about whether concepts of matriarchy were fascist.[27] Brita Rang denied this, pointing out the 'ambivalence, inconsistency, hetero-geneity of matriarchal approaches' and citing the diverse practices of the women's movement as proof.[28] Jost Hermand argued the opposite, quoting numerous texts that showed links between anti-emancipatory goals and an enthusiasm for Amazons. One example was the philosopher Alfred Baeumler, who co-founded the nation-alistic and antisemitic Kampfbund für deutsche Kultur (Militant league for German culture). In 1926 he wrote: 'The way of the people (*Volk*) is woman's way, anonymous, without a person, bringing forth unconsciously, working in silence like nature.'[29] The 'pre-fascist culti-fication of the mother' sought a matriarchy that was *deutschbewusst* (conscious of its Germanness). At the same time, this movement was strongly opposed to *Mannweiber* (mannish women), according to a contemporary source. Such women, it was argued, should be forcibly mated and thus coerced into motherhood.[30]

Between 1936 and 1939, the 'Night of the Amazons' took place annually in Munich. This was a pompous spectacle with thousands of actors, including more than a hundred 'Amazons' – women who were naked but for skimpy bikini bottoms. In the explan-atory brochure, they were described as follows: 'The "Night of the Amazons" seeks to reach back into the heroic greatness of a time unadorned by any glittering trumpery to the classical sagas of the gods. Forest deities awaken, Pan enters the park, and with him, lightly clothed, wild and noble: the Amazons, the ever-warlike horsewomen, resembling goddesses and yet so close to humans.'[31] In short, this performance of female independence and militance did nothing to counteract the misogynist and racist Nazi under-standing of gender, in which women's main role was to produce genetically healthy offspring and preserve the 'race'. Instead, the motif of the Amazons complemented this sinister role division, as the cultural studies scholar Doris Fuchsberger writes in her study on the 'Nights of the Amazons' in Munich.[32] In other words, Amazons are no guarantee of a subversive, revolutionary or progressive idea of femininity. Quite the contrary.

'Anarchic Amazons':
the women of 1968 and their breasts

While the Amazons were positive role models for second-wave feminism in the 1970s, and proof that a life beyond patriarchal domination was conceivable, 'Amazon' simultaneously acquired significance in a completely different area. For large parts of the German press at the time, it was a key word when it came to explaining a new phenomenon: women's capacity for political violence, as manifested by the emergence of the left-wing militant group Rote Armee Fraktion (Red Army Faction, abbreviated to RAF). Up to that point, such violence on the part of women had seemed unimaginable. In 1967 a plan was uncovered to disrupt the Berlin visit of the US vice president, Hubert H. Humphrey, with bombs filled with blancmange. Those involved in this *Pudding-Attentat* (pudding assassination) were arrested. The women in the group were released immediately, however, because they were seen as 'appendages' of the men and therefore not held responsible, as one of the women later recalled.[33] So when the topic of 'murderous women' arose, it was an obvious reflex to fall back on the Amazons, who represented something unthinkable and unimaginable. And this was also applicable – perhaps even more so – to emancipation and feminism. It became increasingly common to interpret the existence of female terrorists as evidence of emancipation that had got out of hand. And what is the culmination of women's emancipation? Women who kill!

In 1976, one German newspaper described the female members of the RAF as the 'Furies of terror'; another called them 'anarchist Amazons'.[34] The daily newspaper *Die Welt* talked about 'emancipation with bombs and pistols', while the weekly news magazine *Der Spiegel* reported that the women of the RAF were 'the dark side of the movement for full equality'.[35] The same magazine noted with astonishment, quoting the head of Hamburg's anti-terrorist intelligence agency, Hans Josef Horchem, that 'individual' women were 'man enough' not only to play an equal part, but to take a leading role. This was 'something irrational', the text continued. It quoted the former head of Germany's national domestic intelligence agency, Günther

Nollau, who castigated female violence as an 'excess of women's liberation'. *Der Spiegel* itself saw the group's actions as evidence of a 'romantic Amazonian understanding of equality of arms between the sexes in the underground'.[36] Thus the enthusiasm of second-wave feminists for matriarchy was perceived as a blueprint for terrorist acts. The psychologist Peter R. Hofstätter regarded it as 'highly likely, indeed almost certain' that 'the women in the terrorist movement take inspiration from the concept of matriarchy'. He assumed they would have encountered this concept in August Bebel's book *Die Frau und der Sozialismus* (Woman and socialism), if nowhere else.[37]

In actual fact, the connections between the feminist politics of the women's movement and the self-image of the RAF women were weak.[38] For the women of the RAF, explicitly feminist strategies such as those formulated in the second-wave women's movement played a subordinate role at best. This makes the conflation of emancipation and female terrorism in contemporary media reports – which were able to cite the views of the police and of government agencies – all the more striking.

Women such as Ulrike Meinhof or Gudrun Ensslin, who had helped to found the far-left terrorist organization, were simultaneously sexualized and demonized in the press. The magazine *Quick*, published in West Germany from 1949 to 1992, entertained its readership with titillating stories, attracting special attention in the 1960s and 1970s with advance publication of books by the German-Dutch sex educator Oswalt Kolle. In 1978 the magazine published a topless photo of Gudrun Ensslin with the caption 'The bride of terror'.[39] The Amazon had become a bride, a designation that was rehashed again and again for the women of 1968. As 'brides of the revolution',[40] they were not only forcibly heterosexualized but reduced completely to their relationship with male revolutionaries. RAF leader Andreas Baader, student activist Rudi Dutschke, or the men protesting against the Shah of Iran's visit to Germany on 2 June 1967 (during which student Benno Ohnesorg was shot dead by a policeman) were never called 'bridegrooms of the revolution'. They *were* the revolution.

In contrast, the subversive nature of the revolution was frequently illustrated with naked breasts. A photograph from 1968 shows members of Kommune 1, a radical commune in Berlin, sitting together on the ground, topless. The photo evoked mattresses, sit-ins and a new attitude to life. Sitting on the ground was a 'central element in the body code of the revolutionaries.'[41] So of course the communards, whose livelihood was partly dependent on the fees from such photo shoots, sat on the ground. Two prominent commune members, fashion model Uschi Obermaier and her lover Rainer Langhans, appear on the left-hand side. The naked chests seem to signal gender equality; all the communards are wearing jeans and no top. Their partial nudity is politically motivated: in the discourse of the 1960s, liberation from 'repressive' sexuality and body shame had been seen as the key to overcoming fascism. In 1962, the Frankfurt student newspaper *Diskurs* had argued along these lines, identifying 'repressed' sexuality as the source of racism: 'Without taboos, no renunciation of drives; without that, no pent-up aggression, which can at a given time be directed against minorities or external enemies – Jews, capitalists, communists.'[42]

But German fascism was not the only thing that could be explained by repressed sexuality. A monthly publication on sexual politics entitled *Sexpol Info*, the self-declared 'organ of the undogmatic and anti-authoritarian new left on the subject of sexuality and power', expanded this list in January 1973: 'Characteristics such as the patho-logical pursuit of achievement, aggressivity, brutality, exaggerated precision and punctuality, an excessive sense of duty and honour are to be explained by sexual repression.'[43] The images used to illus-trate the 'sexual revolution', however, were strikingly one-sided. The magazine *konkret* had close ties to the 1968 movement. In the 1960s and 1970s, nearly all its covers featured naked women and girls in playboy poses, with titles such as 'Beware: underage!' or 'Young love at 14' (this cover from 1970 showed a very young bare-breasted woman). Thus the liberating effect of sexuality 'without taboos' did not mean an end to the 'genitalization of sexuality, the heterosexual matrix of coercion' or the 'traditional active/passive attributions', which were all misogynistic. This is the conclusion reached by historian Pascal Eitler in his unsparing analysis of the body politics of the 1968 movement.[44] Practices within the West German student movement, as represented by the Socialist German Students' Union (SDS), were equally misogynistic. Dagmar Przytulla, a former member of Kommune 1, recalled in 2002: 'The attitude on the left was generally that women could be present, but were not expected to contribute.'[45]

This was one of the reasons for the founding of the Aktionsrat zur Befreiung der Frauen (Action Council on Women's Liberation) in West Berlin in 1968. This group was responsible for a particularly famous tomato-throwing incident. At the twenty-third delegates' conference of the SDS in September 1968, film-maker Helke Sanders, the spokeswoman of the Aktionsrat, gave a speech harshly criticizing her male comrades for failing to deal adequately – in either theoretical or practical terms – with the 'question of women'. This inspired another woman, Sigrid Rüger, to throw tomatoes at the male leaders of the SDS, signalling the beginning of West Germany's second-wave feminist movement.

In the photo of Kommune 1 mentioned above, Uschi Obermaier's breasts are more a symbol of revolutionary Bohemianism than of women's liberation. Obermaier, an 'icon of 68' (*Gala*) who still fascinates the tabloids today, is not actually the only (naked) woman in the picture. But it is her body, in its partial nudity, that most obviously demonstrates the revolutionary, unconventional nature of Kommune 1 and its realization of sexual 'liberation'. Only showing men with bare chests would not have worked. Female breasts signal resistance and serve to represent an overall 'performance of protest'.[46]

Since the breasts of the other two women in the photo are not visible, however, this falls into the category of a 'group portrait with a lady', a category cultivated in the revolutionary aesthetic of the early twentieth century. Revolution is both achieved and visualized via the female body. In a 1924 photograph by Man Ray, appearing on the cover of the first issue of the magazine *La Révolution surréaliste*, a group of (male) surrealist artists, including André Breton and Robert Desnos, surround Simone Breton. She sits at a typewriter, looking down at a small box which Desnos is holding open in his hands. This was about *écriture automatique*, automatic writing, and the surrealists' theory that it would give access to the unconscious and allow them to look into Pandora's box. Here the woman sitting at a typewriter symbolizes this process of automatic writing. She is, however, only the medium of this process, through which the male artists are revolutionizing art and life. They need the 'mythologized image of woman as the medium and instrument of [their] avant-garde artistic methods and objectives.'[47]

Just a few years later, a photo montage in *La Révolution surréaliste* took this to the extreme (1929). Sixteen passport photos of male surrealists frame a painting by René Magritte of a standing female nude with the words 'je ne vois pas la [femme] cachée dans la fôret' (I do not see the woman hidden in the forest) appearing above and below it. Logically, all the men in the photos have their eyes closed. 'Blind vision' enables the male art revolutionaries to receive inspiration. In combination with the naked female body, this refers to surrealists' ambition to create dangerous art that would overturn the bourgeois order.

The residue of this turn-of-the-century revolutionary aesthetic can still be found in the staged photo of Kommune 1. True, the visual language has been modernized: Obermaier is part of the commune, not just a nameless nude; the male communards have also removed parts of their clothing; and both the men and the women look out of the picture at the viewer. Yet there is still an imbalance. The removal of her jumper, blouse or shirt sexualizes Obermaier. The composition and perspective in the photo make her the only naked woman visible. And this means that she and her body stand for the ideals and aims of the men in the picture, embodying these in a way that is not reciprocated.

But what about the protests that women organized on their own? The power of naked breasts deliberately made visible in public by the women who possessed them was certainly recognized and used accordingly. Deploying one's own body as a means of protest was something that the student movement had learnt (in part) from performance artists, who, since the late 1950s, had moved outside museums and galleries and staged happenings on the street.[48] Valie Export's *Tapp- und Tastkino* (1968) is an example (see chapter 2). It is not known whether the three women who encircled Theodor W. Adorno in a lecture theatre at the University of Frankfurt in 1969 and exposed their breasts to him were aware of Export's performance. But theirs was just as sensational, if not more so. It went down in history as the *Busenattentat* (bosom assassination). In other words, an act of violence. This is partly because the famous philosopher's fatal heart attack just a few months later during a holiday in the mountains has repeatedly been interpreted as a belated consequence of the women's action. What actually happened? On 22 April 1969, Adorno had entered the auditorium to give a lecture entitled 'An introduction to dialectical thinking'. The atmosphere was heated, not least because Adorno, a few months earlier, had summoned the police to remove students who were occupying the Institute for Social Research. In the lecture theatre where he was about to speak, flyers had been distributed stating that 'Adorno as an institution is dead'. Shortly before the start of the lecture, three women stormed up to Adorno, bared their breasts, encircled him and threw flowers at him.

In 2003, the journalist Tanja Stelzer tried to speak about the event with the women involved, but met with silence and refusals.[49] None of those who had participated at the time wanted to talk about it. And the photographer who had taken the photo that was subsequently used by the press later took legal action to prevent its publication. The fact that there is only a single, very blurred picture of the event underlines a fundamental difference between that time and the era of the mobile phone: today there are countless pictures of Femen activists and their naked breasts. After a long search, Stelzer did finally succeed in speaking to one of the participants, the art historian Hannah Weitemeier. Thirty years after the attack, her predominant feeling was shame. Weitemeier, who died in 2013, even stated that she would have liked to ask for forgiveness from Adorno, a Holocaust survivor who had been exiled by the Nazis.

Other 'women of 1968' who helped to establish breast-baring as a form of protest have also expressed disillusionment. One such action took place at a court hearing against the student activist Ursula Seppel. She and eight other women activists bared their breasts and sang a protest song that they had composed themselves: 'Gentlemen, today you see us standing here naked, / And we're showing our breasts for everyone.' Yet those involved in the performance do not remember it as especially powerful. 'Nothing happened! We thought the judge would be scandalized and would call the police. But he didn't react! This man kept his cool, contrary to our expectations. We were helpless, we hadn't prepared anything else. So we sang the song again.'[50]

Both these recollections of breast-based protests of the late 1960s, concerned with liberation from repression, seem strangely subdued. Or, to put a positive spin on it, they are reflective rather than triumphant. It is therefore no wonder that Femen, in their quest for historical models for the use of breasts as weapons, ignore the activists of 1968, despite their temporal proximity and the similarity of their ideas. Instead they refer to the mythical Amazons, who were equally suited to the projections of Nazis and to the present-day protests of women who see themselves as feminists.

The retrospective view of the participants in the late-1960s protests contrasts vividly with public opinion at the time. The very use of the term *Attentat* (assassination) for the students' protest against Adorno is evidence of the heated atmosphere, which allowed naked breasts to be seen as weapons in an attempted murder.

Burning bras: feminism as breast liberation?

The mood was equally febrile in the US. Feminists who fought for women's rights in the women's liberation movement were celebrated – or ostracized – as 'bra-burners'. The narrative of the burning bras is fixed in the collective memory, with innumerable accounts of second-wave feminism claiming that 'burn your bras' was the movement's slogan. Thus feminists became women whose defining feature was that they not only refused to wear this central item of feminine clothing, but tossed it into the flames.[51] Not long ago, a text in *Der Spiegel* about the 'bra revolution' stated that the bra had been burnt as a 'symbol of oppression'.[52] Curiously, the article that follows admits that this isn't quite true – in fact, not a single bra was ever burnt. But the legend is so appealing that it has to be told again and again. What is the attraction of the story? It's worth taking a closer look at the historically verified events on which it is based. These did actually involve bras, among other things, but not in the way claimed by the bra-burning narrative.

It all started with a group of women who came together in New York at the end of the 1960s and engaged in feminist politics under the name 'New York Radical Women'.[53] Some of their members would go on to write fundamental texts of the women's movement: Kate Millett wrote *Sexual Politics* (1970); Anne Koedt, *The Myth of the Vaginal Orgasm* (1970); and Susan Brownmiller *Against Our Will: Men, Women, and Rape* (1975). The group decided to protest against the Miss America beauty pageant, which had been held since 1921. They travelled to Atlantic City, and Robin Morgan composed a press statement entitled 'No More Miss America!', denouncing the event as the celebration of a 'Degrading Mindless-Boob-Girlie-Symbol.'[54] The protest, held on 7 September 1968, was successful. Not only did some of the participants get into the convention hall and unfurl a banner with the words 'Women's Liberation'. The protest also inspired intense commentary and discussion in the press. This was partly due to the status of the event, which had a television audience of up to 17 million viewers, in addition to the nearly 25,000 present at the venue. It was an article in the *New York Post* by a 23-year-old reporter, Lindsy van Gelder, that had the most impact. She analysed her coverage of the events many years later:[55]

> But 'bra-burner', aside from being pleasingly alliterative, had a connotation that carried moral weight in 1968. At the height of the [Vietnam] war, thousands of young men had set fire to their draft cards in public demonstrations. It was an act associated with dignity, bravery, and impeccable politics. To talk about bras being burned was at one and the same time to speak in a language that the guys on the city desk could understand (i.e., tits) and to speak in code to the radicals of our generation. And so the lead of my article in the *Post* went: 'Lighting a match to a draft card or a flag has been a standard gambit of protest groups in recent years, but something new is due to go up in flames this Saturday. Would you believe a bra-burning?'[56]

From then on, the image of women burning their bras developed a life of its own, as a flexible, multi-purpose symbol of feminist activism. In an episode of *The Simpsons* from 1991, a young Marge Simpson sets fire to a bra to illustrate the feminist/rebellious phase of the now rather matronly heroine.

But the protesters threw many other objects besides bras into the 'Freedom Trash Can', including fake eyelashes, hair-curlers and *Playboy* magazines. So it remains puzzling why the idea of bra-burning became so entrenched. To find an answer, we have to consider two ideas in tandem: on the one hand, the clothing of the breast as a political issue in the fight for emancipation, and on the other hand, the history of the female breast as a weapon, which goes back much further than the debates over corsets and bras. These two ideas came together in the image of the putative bra-burners, creating an amalgam that revealed both the potentially revolutionary power of feminist protest and the recognition that the baring of breasts was linked to emancipation.

But the narrative about one of the starting points of Western feminism is not only based on an event that never took place (or not in the way reported). It also gives a distorted impression of the part played by Black women. The call to protest against the Miss America pageant in Atlantic City evokes the topic of racism. Not only had the competition never had a Black finalist in all its decades of existence, there had also never been a Hispanic winner, one from Hawaii or Alaska, or a representative of the Indigenous peoples of North America. The protest paper calls it 'racism with roses'.[57] In fact, the statutes of Miss America were racist: in the 1940s they had demanded that applicants be 'of the white race'.[58] Married women were not allowed to participate, and all applicants were intensively scrutinized for 'inappropriate' behaviour – including sex, drugs, and even rock 'n' roll. Although the passage excluding Black contestants was removed from the statutes in the 1950s, they were still excluded from the competition de facto until 1970. The American woman propagated as an ideal here was 'white, wealthy, virginal and apolitical'.[59]

While the New York Radical Women, who included Black feminists such as Bonnie Allen and the lawyer Florynce Kennedy, fundamentally rejected beauty pageants, this position was not shared by all Black people. Two men, J. Morris Anderson, a Black businessman, and Phillip H. Savage, a local representative of the NAACP (an organization founded in 1909 to advance Black civil rights and still in existence today), organized another pageant to crown a 'Miss Black America'. The contest was partly a protest against the purely white Miss America pageant and was held at the same time. A number of Black women took part, seeing their participation as a contribution to the Black civil rights movement. The finalists, including the winner, Saundra Williams, rode through the city in a motorcade, wearing evening dresses, highlighting the contrast with the discredited all-white pageant. It was not until 1977 that a national broadcaster deigned to televise this alternative contest.

Just as the Miss America pageant glossed over its racist rejection of non-white participants, simply claiming that the annual selection of a white woman embodied 'America', so also the narrative of the 'bra-burners' shows a tendency to ignore the role of Black women in the conception and execution of this protest. The artist and historian Georgia Paige Welch wrote an article examining the visual memory around the 'bra-burners', which is unduly dominated by white women.[60] One of the central figures of the protest, the above-mentioned Black lawyer Florynce Kennedy, was virtually never mentioned in connection to the protest in Atlantic City, although she later stated in an interview that she had been one of the driving forces behind it.[61]

'Beautiful women': the limits of protest

There is power and strength in the anger personified by a female figure who tears open her clothing and presents her naked breast. Aggressively confronting hostile warriors with this delicate and sensitive body part, as Eiríksdóttir does in the saga, turns weakness into strength. Femen, a group founded in Ukraine in 2008 and now active internationally, work on a similar principle. The protests they use to attract attention are based on the same assumption about the impact of the naked breast.[62] Femen fights for a number of worthy goals, including the abolition of the German law criminalizing abortion, and femicide education and prevention. Another campaign in Germany was the revision of a brochure distributed by the federal office for health education, the 'Little ABC of the body', which referred to the clitoris as a spot (*Stelle*) and the vagina as a tube (*Röhre*). But the group, which defines itself as feminist, wants more. It is all about perception and a very specific way of making female bodies visible in public: as female, courageous and combative. And it is about performance, a performance in which (according to Femen's own website), 'brave topless female activists [are] painted with [...] slogans and crowned with flowers'[63] – and then share photos of these protests.

In 2013 Josephine Witt, who was a Femen activist at the time, stormed into the Christmas service in Cologne Cathedral, jumped onto the altar topless, spread her arms wide in a crucifixion pose and revealed the words written on her torso: 'I am God.' The photo used repeatedly in reports about the event shows Witt at the climax of her protest. We look up to her as to an altarpiece. Her pose duplicates that of Christ on the cross. In this staged image, the bared breast does not conform to established Christian forms of representation for this body part, as either the motherly breast of Mary or a reference to vice. Instead, it serves as a protest against a male image of God and against the church's homophobia and misogyny – precisely because it runs counter to all known forms of representation. Witt subsequently appeared in court and was fined for disrupting the observance of religion.

Another spectacular protest took place on the square in front of Milan Cathedral, where Femen activists protested against Russia's annexation of the Crimea. There are still photos of this event on Femen's German-language Facebook page. But these photos are not just documentation: the production of images is a crucial component of the protest. The photos follow the choreography of the protests: arriving, shouting slogans, being arrested. All three stages generate effective photos, which are united by the same intention: the protesters' breasts must be readily visible. They constitute the visual and ideological centre. This is also reflected in the Femen logo, the small Cyrillic f (ф), which recalls two breasts.

Besides the breasts, another important element of the performance is the floral wreath, the Ukrainian *vinok*, which the protesters often wear on their heads. The group refers to this as a 'symbol of femininity' and a 'crown of heroism'.[64] The same pathos characterizes the activists' self-description as 'the special force of feminism, its spearhead militant unit, [the] modern incarnation of fearless and free Amazons'.[65] The activists united under the Femen logo argue for the 'weapon capability' of the breast as a natural strength of women: 'We do not use violence because our naked bodies speak for us: they are our manifesto and our battleground. Our breasts are our weapons because established power sees them as such. Nature gives us these weapons because the social, political and economic rules, all governed by a conventional morality, criminalize our attempt at liberation.'[66]

Inna Schewtschenko, one of the group's founders, states quite openly that 'classic feminism no longer works'. It has become 'impotent'.[67]

Femen's 'new' feminism is also advocated by Victor Svyatski, who appeared as the head of the group in its early days. In an interview he inadvertently revealed the backwardness of this supposedly new movement: 'The new feminism says: It is good that women are different from men. The woman is beautiful; her breasts are a symbol of femininity. That is why the women from Femen go topless on the streets. Only through differentiation can we truly reach equality.'[68]

In the same interview Svyatski also spoke of the 'grey jumpers' and 'armpit hair' of pre-Femen feminism, which he now considered to be outdated. Quite apart from the fact that this reduces the political dimension of second-wave feminist debates on clothing, fashion, make-up, hairstyles, etc. to an anti-feminist cliché, there is something strange here about the implied claim to sole representation of feminism. Feminism can only be had in the plural. And other feminist positions argue that the category 'woman', which Svyatski takes as a given, should be called into question. The gender studies scholar Paula-Irene Villa writes:

> Woman is a social construction. 'Woman' is one side of a gender difference that consists of both biological and cultural elements. Or, to frame it more in line with the research, 'woman' is embedded in a biosocial differentiation [...], which is itself culturally interpreted and historically constituted. A differentiation that is continually being put into practice but is institutionally framed and is also the object of ongoing political, legal and cultural debates. Sounds complicated? It is.[69]

Even if Femen now claims to have parted ways with Svyatski, the talk of 'women' using their breasts for political activism suggests a diversity that is not present in the group's protests. True, Femen's public proclamations no longer repeat the unrestrainedly sexist dictum 'woman is beautiful', but street protests and their visual documentation continue to follow this principle. The group, which considers itself 'the most influential and battle-ready women's organization in the world', is aiming for a 'new aesthetic of the women's revolution'. The result, however, is indistinguishable from the object of its critique.[70] It must be asked whether the rhetoric and the visual performance of Femen, with its extreme focus on the breasts, does not in fact keep alive a well and truly patriarchal narrative. When beautiful young women activists kneel in front of the cathedral of Milan, pelvis pushed forward and legs spread, in ultra-short black miniskirts, this doesn't merely look like a pin-up pose, it is one. Of course, taking up such a pose doesn't necessarily exclude one from feminist activism. This is shown by the performances of feminist burlesque, that is, those practices in the late twentieth century and the present in which striptease and critique of patriarchal culture are combined.[71] Here too, however, as pointed out by Kay Siebler, Professor of English at Missouri Western State University, the rule is: 'As with many things [...], something does not automatically become feminist simply because it is delivered, written and/or performed by a feminist.'[72] A further problem is that the topless protesters are almost always people who correspond to prevailing ideas of what constitutes a 'beautiful woman'. What about the protests of those who do not fit this pattern, or who do not correspond to the category referred to here as 'woman'? Breasts exposed in public as a signal of protest always embody a breach of the rules, but this performance remains within quite narrowly defined boundaries (of beauty).

One of these boundaries arises from the medium that Femen relies on: the internet. On many social media platforms, one part of the female breast is not allowed to be visible: the nipple. The revolution that Femen protesters seek to initiate by baring their breasts thus loses much of its revolutionary impact. The activists' nipples are pixellated so that their actions can be documented visually on social media – a core aspect of the 'new aesthetic' envisaged by Femen. This is problematic, given that the rules rigorously applied by Instagram and co. can unquestionably be called misogynistic. Another example is an Instagram post by the writer Rupi Kaur, who opposes the taboo imposed on anything to do with menstruation. A photo series developed with her sister included a rear view of the artist lying in bed, with a small spot of blood on her grey joggers and on the sheet. A sight that could hardly be more unremarkable, and is surely familiar to all (menstruating) people and their partners and children.[73] Nonetheless, Instagram deleted the photo twice with reference to its rules, which prohibit images that are 'violent, nude, partially nude, discriminatory, unlawful, infringing, hateful, pornographic or sexually suggestive'. None of this applies to Kaur's photographs. Clearly, however, the reference to this bodily function has the potential to be all of these things – even if Instagram did eventually allow the photos after a widespread protest. The strange rule that the nipple must never, under any circumstances, be visible in the visual worlds of social networks functions in a similar way.[74]

The reactions of the powerful men who are generally the target of Femen's protests also help to ensure that the usual boundaries are preserved, despite the protesters' efforts. The activists only meet with limited indignation and resistance: bodyguards deal with them while the actual targets of the performance often smile indulgently or even give a thumbs up. The latter was Putin's response to a protest at the Hanover trade fair on 8 April 2013, a gesture that affirmed his role as a man entitled to appraise women's bodies. This was reinforced by smug comments in the press, such as the observation that Putin was not terribly appalled.[75] This corresponds to the legal situation in Germany: according to paragraph 183 in the German criminal code, exhibitionism is an offence that can only be committed by a 'man who harasses another person by an exhibitionist act'. The reasoning behind this is interesting. The paragraph was only written in the 1970s and was intended to replace the previous gender-neutral expression 'unzüchtige Handlungen' (lewd/indecent acts). The explanation of the reform was that such acts by women 'hardly ever had the negative effects typically caused by exhibitionist acts by men'.[76] In other words, naked female bodies are not, in legal terms, seen as having the same power as male bodies. In terms of punishable offences against others, they are harmless. People with female bodies who expose themselves in public can therefore not be charged with anything worse than 'Erregung öffentlichen Ärgernisses' (literally 'causing a public nuisance', usually used for sexual acts performed in public). This negates both male vulnerability and the female capacity for aggression.[77]

Hysteria, ecstasy and the dance of the maenads: the naked breast as a sign of the 'other'

In the visual logic of the mass media, a crucial part of the topless protest is its forcible repression. It is not only the performance itself that finds its way into the newspapers and visual worlds of the internet, but its ending, the moment when the women are seized and removed from the scene. The preference is for photos in which the drama of the political conflict finds both its climax and its finale in the naked female body. The following ingredients are crucial: the naked breasts must be visible, flowing hair signals wildness, and a female body writhing in male arms signifies (futile) resistance to the powerful.

Thus, the illustration of breast-based protest does not escape established visual formulae: the overpowering of the naked female

Figure 23 Peter Paul Rubens, *The Rape of the Daughters of Leucippus*, around 1616.

body by men, who wrench and tug on it until its defences are broken down. This follows the tradition of earlier images such as Rubens's oil painting *The Rape of the Daughters of Leucippus* ('rape' in the archaic sense of abduction). Painted between 1615 and 1618, this has been described by art historian Margaret D. Carroll as a 'celebratory depiction of sexual violence' (figure 23).[78] Rubens's scene shows the story of the twins Castor and Pollux (known as the Dioscuri), who abducted and then married Phoibe und Hilaeira, the daughters of King Leucippus. The interpretations put forward by some art historians actually perpetuate male violence. They claim, for example, that Phoibe experiences her 'destiny as a woman' through the rape, and that the battle of the sexes is a 'necessity of nature'.[79] This misogynist notion that women secretly long to be raped was propagated in early-twentieth-century caricatures based on Rubens's painting. One such caricature (*Fliegende Blätter*, 1906) shows a solitary woman, not in the first flush of youth, visiting a museum. Standing in front of Rubens's painting, she longs for the 'good old days', according to the caption. In the painting, the bodies of the horses and those of the men – as they overpower the naked female bodies – are full of strength and purposeful movement. The caricaturist contrasts this with the static pose, drooping shoulders, downturned mouth and sagging cheeks of the woman in the foreground. She represents femininity in stasis, yearning – according to the reading proposed by the caricature – for wildness, physicality and sexuality, while embodying the exact opposite in attitude, clothing and habitus.

The planning of the bare-breasted protests, then, always includes their media publicization. The protests are held at times when the cameras are already in position, for example during appearances by politicians. The naked breasts ensure maximum attention. But the kind of pictures that are ultimately circulated, and that largely determine how the activists' performance is perceived, play out in a thoroughly conventional visual arena. Wildness, difference, disruption of order – all these things, in various historical and cultural constellations, have been represented again and again by female bodies with naked breasts and unfastened hair. Nearly untameable, and yet tamed in the end. Several of these iconographic strategies are woven into the photographs of protesting women who end up being physically overpowered.

There is, for example, the figure of the maenad or bacchante, companion of the god Dionysus/Bacchus. 'Maenad' is more a state of being than a designation of character. The name is derived from the Greek word *mainas*, meaning mad or demented (it is also the origin of 'mania' and 'maniac'), and the figure is a visual emblem of female wildness and threat.[80] This 'transgressive figure' (*Übertretungsfigur*)[81] from classical antiquity enables us to envision how the motifs associated with it – ecstasy, women's capacity for violence and the disruption of male order – have been renegotiated and modified over the centuries. One of the works of literature that presents the classical myth is Euripides' tragedy *The Bacchae*. The story is somewhat complicated, as is often the case in the world of Graeco-Roman gods and goddesses, but the key dramatic points are as follows. The bacchantes, companions of the god Dionysus (also known as Bacchus), follow an ecstatic cult, which displeases those in power. The king of Thebes, Pentheus, dismisses the cult as barbaric. The maenads' ability to terrify men into flight, armed only with a *thyrsus* (a staff of fennel), is certainly a contributing factor. Secretly, however, the critical king is attracted to the activity he wishes to prohibit. Simultaneously fascinated and repelled, he allows himself to be persuaded to watch the Bacchanalia in secret. But he is discovered and eventually killed by the frenzied maenads – led by his mother, who doesn't recognize him at first. They don't stop there, however: in their frenzy, they prepare to eat their victim. The practice, known as *omophagia*, had an established place in the cult of Dionysus and referred to the consumption of the raw meat of the animals killed during their rites.

The classical myth of the frenzied, ecstatic dancers who become cannibals can be found in transmuted form in the post-classical era. The art historian Ines Lindner has described this aptly as the 'injection of the mythical material into the biblical text'. One of the examples she cites is the description, by a Greek church father in the early Middle Ages, of Salome's dance (which of course led to the beheading of John the Baptist):[82] '[...] and she danced like a Bacchante, shaking her hair, turning in an unseemly way, raising her arms, baring her breasts, [...], revealing her body through the rapidity of her whirling movement [...]'. The alluring way the maenads moved and revealed their bodies, condemned by the Christian church fathers, also attracted particular attention in the classical representations found on vases from around 500 BC. A transparent chiton (tunic), clinging closely to the dancers' bodies, identifies the maenads as graceful and desirable. This threatening and simultaneously seductive female figure not only featured as a haunting presence throughout antiquity and the Middle Ages, but was also relevant for a much later type of out-of-control woman: the hysteric.

Hysteria, whose name derives from the Greek word for womb, *hystera*, was one of the key topics in medicine around 1900. Instead of vase paintings, there were now photographs of hysterical women. The aim was to use this ultramodern medium to better understand the illness (which, incidentally, was not removed from the influential *Diagnostic and Statistic Manual of Mental Disorders* until 1980). The images created at the time had much in common with those of the maenads: 'The head thrown back, the unfastened hair, the clothing in disarray and other markers of the hysteric are borrowed from the iconography of the maenad. This also implies an aestheticization of the images of illness. Once again, woman is reduced to her "status as image".'[83]

This is especially the case for the Paris doctor Jean Martin Charcot, who had countless photos taken of the patients he had diagnosed with hysteria. The photos show the women's bodies in the different phases of an attack of hysteria, as described by Charcot. It was only in these attacks – transformed into images – that the phenomenon perceived by the medical world as hysteria first became visible and describable. Charcot developed methods that reliably triggered hysterical attacks in patients, such as pressing on their ovaries or conducting other similarly painful procedures. This then enabled him to present his patients to an audience. In 1885 Sigmund Freud used a travel scholarship to spend several months in the Salpêtrière, the Paris clinic where Charcot worked. Freud's research on hysteria was linked to his experiences in Paris.[84] Every week, Charcot would exhibit female patients in his lectures. The audience included artists and actors attracted by the spectacle. One of these patients, named Augustine, became particularly famous and was referred to by Charcot as the 'ideal patient'.

Augustine had been admitted to the hospital in 1873, at the age of fifteen. She was one of over 4,000 women incarcerated in the clinic, which has been described as 'a kind of feminine inferno'.[85] Many patients died there. Augustine escaped after a number of years in the hospital, and her subsequent fate is unknown. What remains are the photographs, the *Iconographie photographique de la Salpêtrière*, in which Augustine gave a perfect demonstration of all the phases of a hysterical attack: the 'portents', the 'epileptoid phase', the 'passionate postures' (*attitudes passionnelles*), the ecstasies. Charcot's colleague, Paul Richer, a professor of artistic anatomy, systematized these phases in concentrated line drawings on a panel. The French art historian Georges Didi-Huberman describes the process:

> A reciprocity of charm was instituted between physicians, with their insatiable desire for images of Hysteria, and hysterics, who willingly participated and actually raised the stakes through their increasingly theatricalized bodies. In this way, hysteria in the clinic became the spectacle, the invention of hysteria. Indeed, hysteria was covertly identified with something like an art, close to theater or painting.[86]

The surrealists were fascinated by these ecstatic female figures. In 1928, on what they called the 'fiftieth birthday' of hysteria, Louis Aragon and André Breton published a selection of photos of Augustine in *La Révolution surréaliste*. They saw her as the embodiment of an ideal they themselves had conceived, that of the 'convulsive beauty'. The spasmodic seizures of the hysteric and her frantic or delirious state were idealized as the 'discharging of non-adapted emotional forces'.[87] In 1938, at Dalí's suggestion, the dancer and visual artist Hélène Vanel performed at the opening of the Exposition internationale du surréalisme, scantily clad in a torn dress. Those involved in the event perceived the performance as 'an only too realistic presentation of a hysterical attack'.[88]

Cultural studies research on Charcot's hysteria has shown how much his medical practice – which was primarily based on the production of images – depended on the use of models from art history.[89] In a book published by Charcot and Richer in 1887, *Les démoniaques dans l'art* (Demonic possession in art), the authors saw artworks such as Rubens's *Miracles of Saint Ignatius* (which include the healing of a possessed woman) as proof that the pathology they were describing had 'always' existed. They, however, were the first to discover it scientifically. They could then use this knowledge to comb through art history in search of new evidence of the supposed timelessness of hysteria. A perfect example of circular reasoning. The visual presentation of hysterics in medicine and art became a picture puzzle, in which the 'illness' and its representations, inspired by older visual models, were indistinguishable.

Similarly, Femen's use of public breast-baring as a signal of protest is firmly tied to the past 'pathos formulae' (*Pathosformeln*) associated with female power and powerlessness.[90] This means that the photos of the activists being dragged away by mainly male security forces, pictures that are shown repeatedly in the media, are not random snapshots. The photos of the protests reactivate much older images, and it is this schema that is used to select them. But the 'old' ideas do not simply disappear. On the contrary, they contribute to people's understanding of the photos.[91] So what Femen exalts as a violation of the patriarchal order is actually a very traditional association between irrationality, transgression and the female body. The protesters' naked breasts serve as a symbol for the proximity between the maenad (= wild woman) and nature, in which 'nudity and nature are equated' – a proximity that has been presented in visual form at least since the nineteenth century. 'In this way', art historian Alexandra Karentzos argues, 'the depiction of maenads makes it possible to see the affinity between women and madness as unalterably "natural".'[92]

In the pictures of female activists being overpowered and dragged away, this idea of wild, sexual, natural femaleness is coupled with a modernized restoration of order. The women turn up, disrupt proceedings, and are then made to disappear.

The two bodies of Angela Merkel: breasts and power

'How much cleavage is a chancellor allowed to show?' This was the question asked by the daily newspaper *Die Welt* on 14 April 2008, after Angela Merkel had appeared in a low-cut evening dress at the opening of the Oslo opera house. It is difficult to say whether such a strange question would still be asked today, but it seems quite possible given the debates about the high heels (too high, supposedly) of the German minister of defence, Christine Lambrecht, who resigned in 2023 (*Bild*, April 2022: 'minister in stilettos').[93] If both serious media and tabloids still focus on the way powerful female politicians dress, and on their use of items of clothing regarded specifically as 'feminine' (high heels, low-cut dresses), this confirms that clothing is 'not just an identifying mark, but also an arena for political battles.'[94] And that items of clothing are places where power and powerfulness become visible.

Who is allowed to wear what? The question of whether Merkel is *allowed* to wear something evokes laws and prohibitions, yet such things seem a relic of the distant past. The first written dress codes appeared at the beginning of the thirteenth century;[95] the last Bavarian dress code was published in 1730.[96] Such codes strictly regulated the use of certain fabrics, furs, buttons, head coverings etc.[97] Today it might be assumed that anyone can wear what they want – but this is evidently not the case. Male dress is regulated to some extent: male politicians are still largely expected to wear 'uniform', and the Green politician Joschka Fischer caused a stir by wearing trainers to his investiture as a minister in the 1980s.[98] The vast majority of today's debates about clothing, however, are concerned with women (cleavage, high heels, headscarf, burkini).

This connects them to the long-forgotten dress codes of the Middle Ages and early modern period. These focused partly on class differences: in Leipzig in 1550, for example, it was a punishable offence for 'common tradespeople' to wear silk clothing or golden bracelets or necklaces. But their other focus was on upholding the gender difference in clothing.[99] Careful distinctions were made between what was 'seemly' for a woman and for a man. In Speyer in 1365, women were forbidden to wear men's coats.[100] So clothing not only showed gender difference, it also produced it. A violation of these dress norms could have terrible consequences, as shown by historical cases such as that of Catherina Link, who wore male clothing and married a woman in 1717. She was betrayed, charged with sodomy and executed in 1721.[101] The production of gender difference can also be seen in the fact that the Hamburg dress code of 7 September 1500 links dress rules for women with the tax paid by their husbands. In the case of unmarried women, the permission to wear 'braided trim or stomachers' or 'gold clasps with gemstones and pearls' depended on their parents' wealth. In any case, this dress code was only issued to 'moderate women's adornment and finery'.[102]

So while the historical dress codes concentrated on the costliness of the fabrics and the decorative elements used, such as clasps, bonnets, trims or buttons, questions about the covering of individual body parts played a comparatively small role. This is also a major difference from the current debates about 'dress codes' – for example, the code that was designed to stop women from wearing burkinis at French beaches (see chapter 1), or the endless debates about the headscarf.[103] Excessive freedom or licence, in men and women, seems to have been part of the rationale for such dress codes – that is, the question of *why* they were necessary – rather than an issue that needed to be resolved in itself. For example, a chronicle from the town of Limburg, following an outbreak of plague, notes that people 'were beginning to live and be happy again' after months of hardship.[104] This text does in fact explicitly criticize the cut of the women's new clothing, which uncovered the breasts; another passage mentions the excessively low necklines of their dresses.[105] But the magistrates and territorial lords who issued these dress codes[106] were much more interested in things like the colours of people's clothing. The reason for this was that colours, because of their very different production costs, indicated wealth, modest resources or outright poverty, and were therefore an important contribution to social differentiation. Regal purple could be distinguished from grey-brown, undyed wool at a glance.

These legally enforced dress codes seem very distant today, and most of their provisions are obsolete. Yet their core element, gender segregation, remains relevant. In German schools, girls were still forbidden to wear trousers in the 1950s and 1960s.[107] The ban on toplessness, which keeps coming before the courts today, is one of the last gender-specific clothing rules.[108] But even if there are generally no more trials or fines, the fuss made about Merkel's cleavage shows that dress codes do still exist, in the form of other types of discipline. These particularly affect women in politics. An older example is the famous trouser suit worn by Lenelotte von Bothmer, a member of the West German parliament, on 14 October 1970. The vice-president of the Bundestag at the time, Richard Jäger, had proclaimed that he would not allow a woman in trousers to step up to the lectern. This awakened von Bothmer's spirit of rebellion, so she bought an elegant, light-coloured trouser suit with a long blazer and wore it to address the plenary. This not only made the evening news, but also inspired a flood of insulting letters – long before Twitter and co. One letter-writer called the politician a 'swine'; another suggested: 'Next time you'll probably come topless!'[109] Thus the trouser suit leads – horror of horrors – straight to the bare bosom.

Over thirty years later, the question is still: is she allowed? Is it acceptable for Angela Merkel to show her cleavage? The majority of commentators seemed to think not, and the debate made it more than clear that the breasts still play a significant role when it comes to power and politics. In the German press, the tabloid *Bild* described the chancellor's décolletage as a 'different way of doing politics' ('Politik mal anders'), and the news magazine *Focus* took the event as an excuse to rehash the *Mutti* ('mum') topos that had accom-panied Merkel throughout her time in office. This topos formed the conceptual substrate for the debate about Merkel's cleavage: the term *Mutti*, which refers to a bodily function (giving birth to children), not only foregrounds the gender of the person designated in this way but immediately links this femaleness with motherliness. In the same article, *Focus* calls Merkel the 'Queen Mother', and an '*alma mater* who not only tames quarrelling politicians and saves Tibet, but wants to press the whole nation to her breast'[110] In nearly all media outlets, including the more respectable newspapers, the breasts served as a welcome cue for various puns. *Die Zeit* spoke of 'Wettbrüsten', a play on words combining *Brüste* (breasts) and *Wettrüsten* (arms race), and the *Frankfurter Allgemeine Sonntagszeitung* suspected that Merkel's partially naked bosom was motivated by naked calculation. The celebrity gossip magazine *Bunte* made the patronizing obser-vation that Merkel's cleavage 'is in fact a political matter, albeit a very charming one'. In the UK, the *Daily Mail* published a photo of the outfit under the headline 'Weapons of mass distraction'.

The politicization of the chancellor's breasts – even her press officer was asked to comment on his boss's cleavage – explains once again why the breast functions as an organ of protest. True, it was not being used in this way here. Merkel was keeping an official appointment in her capacity as the German chancellor, not protesting against anything. But the excitement over her breasts shows that their exposure – which owed a great deal to the photos chosen for publication – clashed with the power of the person to whose body they belonged. This goes far beyond tabloid scrutiny of the outfits of stars and starlets. As the headlines and slogans quoted above show, it's all about politics.

This becomes obvious in a painting of another powerful woman showing her breasts: Eugène Delacroix's *Liberty Leading the People*, painted in 1830. This famous painting has perhaps done more than any other artwork to link politics, power/powerlessness and protest in the collective visual memory of Western (and non-Western) societies. It was inspired by the three-day July Revolution of 1830, which led to the overthrow of Charles X. Shortly after it was first exhibited in the Paris Salon of 1831, the painting disappeared into storage and was not officially displayed again until more than twenty years later. The artist had experienced the uprising in Paris at first hand, and his work shows moments of high drama. The fighting on the barricades has already claimed the lives of some of the rebels. Dead bodies lie in the foreground. On the left-hand side lies a man who is naked except for a bloody shirt and a sock rolled down to the ankle. Led by a female figure, the street fighters storm forward over the victims. Who is this solitary woman amidst the otherwise purely male revolutionaries? In the literature on Delacroix's painting – which would fill many metres of bookshelves – she was once rather aptly described as a 'creature from the world of ideas'.[111] She is not really present; she is not in the same space as the people surrounding her. Nobody seems to notice her, nobody looks at her – except for the dying man who kneels among the dead and looks up to her. Perhaps, as researchers have also suggested, she is a vision, only visible in the imagination of the dying man.[112]

It is no coincidence that the allegory or personification of freedom is female. Aleida Assmann sees the female body as the 'matrix of the invisible', the necessary precondition for embodying abstract values such as freedom, the nation, justice or peace.[113] In patriarchal societies which restrict women's scope for political influence, female bodies appear as an ideal surface for projections, because 'they have neither name, nor character, nor history'.[114] This is in line with the specific form of corporeality shown by the personification of freedom in Delacroix's painting, which differs from that of the men who are actually fighting and dying. The almost entirely bare-breasted Liberty has a young, attractive body, corresponding to conventional ideas of beauty. Allegories are only 'ugly' when they embody negative things, such as avarice, envy or illegitimate sexuality.[115]

'Liberty', who, as the title of the painting states, is 'leading the people', waves the tricolour flag of the revolution, wears the Phrygian cap of liberty, and holds a bayonetted musket in her left hand. She is clearly ready to fight for her goals and convictions. Her classicizing dress is fastened at the waist by a red sash, its loose ends flying out behind her, and is soiled at the bottom by the dust of the barricades. The events depicted offer a plausible explanation of why the chiton, which perhaps once covered her breasts completely, has slipped to the side, revealing all of the right-hand side of her torso and most of her left breast. The right arm, thrust aloft, seems to have freed itself from the constricting clothing. Liberty storms ahead, indifferent to decorum. Incidentally, the asymmetrical exposure of the breasts may sound familiar to attentive readers of this book. Around 1800, the French painter Marie-Guillemine Benoist had included a half-exposed bosom in both her portrait of a Black woman and her self-portrait (hinted at rather than explicit in the latter case) (chapter 2, p. 52, figures 12 and 13).

The male artists painting Amazons also presented their heroines in this way. Johann Heinrich Wilhelm Tischbein's *Amazons*, an oil painting from 1788 (Landesmuseum Oldenburg), shows the female fighters armed with lances, bows and arrows. All wear a short chiton, which is only gathered at the left shoulder and leaves the right breast fully unclothed. Hederich's 1770 dictionary of mythology offers a similar description: 'They went with the right side naked to below the breast.'[116] In other words, what looks like disarray, the product of momentary negligence, is in fact more a type than a coincidence. As Anne Hollander argues, with reference to Delacroix's Liberty: 'Her exposed bosom could never have been denuded by the exertions of the moment; rather, the exposure itself, built into the costume, is an original part of her essence – at once holy, desirable, and fierce.'[117] This means that the seemingly fortuitous style of dress, signalling total physical involvement, is in reality anything but fortuitous. The multilayered associations that the half-bared breast could awaken in contemporaries are quite calculated.

The link between the battles of the French Revolution and the Amazons was firmly established in the art and literature of eighteenth-century France. Prudhomme called the female revolutionaries of 1789 'our valiant Amazons'. This, however, did not stop him from opining in 1791 that 'civic and political freedom is unnecessary for women'. This was his response to demands for equality such as those made in the same year by Olympe de Gouges (who was guillotined in 1793) with her *Déclaration des droits de la femme et de la citoyenne* (Declaration of the rights of woman and the female citizen).[118] Those women who took an active part in the revolutionary struggle, for example by discussing republican ideals in women's clubs, were told that they were incapable of political activity. This was justified by reference to the breast as the physical sign of their 'nature'. In the words of a representative of the city of Paris in 1793: 'Since when is it customary for women to abandon their sacred family duties, their children's cradle, to enter the solemn speakers' rostrum on the public square? Has not nature given them breasts to feed our children? Nature has told women: be women.'[119] In the same year, the women's clubs mentioned above were prohibited.

In 1985 the British literary scholar Marina Warner published a study on allegories, asking why these nearly always appear in female form. She describes the effect of this association between breasts, wildness, Amazons and politics:

> In its nineteenth-century form, the figure of Liberty reveals that the female who enjoyed and suffered the special stigma which associated her with the wild, could exercise in a time of ferment a positively perceived and desirable potency. The breast of a woman as distinct from the generic human bosom acts as a sign of nature and its wild connotations in visual imagery that complements and reinforces the magic outsider status of the Amazon.[120]

Here too, it could be objected that 'magic outsiders' might be quite appealing as an identificatory ideal of rebellious women. But ascribing women this kind of 'wild' status, associated with nature and the dissolving of boundaries, is also a trap. As the exclusion of French women from the revolutionary ideals of liberty, equality and fraternity(!) proves, such an ideal can readily be combined with the oppression of those whose bodies are imagined as idealizations of liberty – the liberty that needs to be protected by men. Or to put it in Warner's words, 'Otherness is a source of potential and power; but it cannot occupy the centre.'[121]

And this brings us back to the beginning of this section, to Angela Merkel and the question of why her cleavage provoked such a scandal. To use Warner's expression, the German chancellor occupied the 'centre'. Her body did not reference *imaginary* female power in the sense of otherness, wildness and liberation from traditional limitations; instead, it was *real*. It was the body of a leader in office. This meant that she did not represent power and freedom as an abstract concept, but actually possessed them as an individual, historical person. This is why the excited debates, in which new photos kept being found to offer further 'proof' of the shocking décolletage, should not be confused with a strange relapse into prudish times, or a reversion to early modern dress codes. Instead, the reactions to an event that actually wasn't one (a woman goes to the opera in an evening dress) show the persistent incongruence between femininity and power. Not because Merkel's clothing was too 'feminine', but because the image of the female bosom is an extremely effective body metaphor for the modern self-reflection of liberal societies. The first illustration in chapter 1 (figure 3) is a picture of a young woman whose clothing has been pulled open to expose both breasts. The caption reads: 'La France républicaine ouvrant son sein à tous les Français' (Republican France opening her breast to all the French people). The magazine *Focus*, in response to the pictures from Oslo, wrote that Merkel wanted to 'press the whole nation to her breast'.[122] This seems a little forced, a little too desperate to be funny, but ultimately it confirms the persistent association between breasts and the nation – an association that has close historical links to the exclusion of real women from republican freedoms and thus lays the foundation for the scandalized politicization of Merkel's (almost) naked bosom. The exposed cleavage calls into question the politician's authority, since female breasts, in the political sphere, turn the female body into an allegory. This is irreconcilable with the 'individualization and self-determination of women.'[123] Angela Merkel was not an allegory, but a politician who held democratic power.

The immediate reactions to the figure of Liberty marching over the barricades were also negative. Delacroix's contemporaries saw her as repulsive, a 'courtesan from the lowest class', a 'slovenly harlot' or a 'dirty, disreputable streetwalker'.[124] These are associations that the figure no longer evokes for modern viewers. Art historian Monika Wagner interprets them in the context of the ideas of femininity prevailing at the time, and the (im)possibility of women's participation in the political struggle. Holding a modern musket, her dirty feet planted firmly on the barricade, Delacroix's Liberty breaks with the conventional 'visual propaganda of the revolutionary years', Wagner argues, because she is 'active herself and thus no longer available'.[125] She is neither an unarmed *femme fragile*, who has to be protected by Hercules and other armed male freedom fighters, nor a mythical Amazon. In the eyes of contemporary critics, this lowered her to the most depraved form of femininity, a whore, and rendered her unsuitable for the projection of ideals. In short, Liberty presents a clash between images of femininity which contemporary reviewers found irreconcilable. She was therefore not 'allowed' to appear as she was.

Today things have changed: the painting, which has been in the Louvre's collection since 1874, has lost its terror. *Liberté* on the barricades of the July Revolution – seen as a whore just under 200 years ago – has now become a role model. Among other things, she has served as a reference for protest art in Arab and African countries.[126] Nowadays she is sold as a fridge magnet.[127] The once reviled allegory is now courted. Her revival as a figure who stands for freedom proves that the female body can still function as an allegorical space for projections, even for today's viewers, who know nothing of the original political circumstances or the concepts of allegory and allegoresis. The same cannot be said of Hercules, who played an important role in revolutionary iconography as the protector of Liberty. In 1793 a competition was announced for a 15-metre-tall bronze statue of Hercules, who was to hold his omnipresent club in one hand, and two comparatively tiny figures, *Liberté* and *Fraternité*, in the other.[128] Hercules has vanished completely from the present-day imagery of 'freedom', while Delacroix's figure, painted in 1830, has become an all-purpose symbol for this abstract concept.

Surprisingly, the conflicts once triggered by the painting and the desire to project ideas onto a female body can still be reanimated today by the image of a chancellor's (excessively) daring show of cleavage. A new old quarrel, ignited by a naked bosom. It seems that here, as in Delacroix's painting, the idealized allegory of freedom is incompatible with the gun-toting female (*Flintenweib*)[129] fighting alongside the mortal revolutionaries. The powerful (= masculine) woman clashes with the disconcerting sight of the breasts, which evokes the allegorization of women and the associated exclusion of real women from power.

In 1957 the historian Ernst Kantorowicz developed a concept that was to become influential in cultural studies: 'the king's two bodies'.[130] It states that, in medieval political theology, the political body of a deceased king lived on in the form of the institutionalized office. This is the idea behind the proclamation made in France (up to the death of Louis XVII) to confirm the continuity of royal rule: 'The king is dead, long live the king.' Merkel was not a queen, of course, but a democratically elected representative of the people, whose power derived not from her body, but from her office. Nonetheless, the dispute over her breasts also involves an interaction between two bodies, in a metaphorical sense. On the one hand, there is Merkel's body, read as female, the visible breasts aggressively highlighted in the photos of her visit to the Oslo opera house. And on the other hand, there is the body of the officeholder, which always reflects the political power it represents. These two bodies, which otherwise coexist peace-fully, collide irreconcilably in the image of Merkel's bosom. Seen in this way, the cleavage revealed by the chancellor in Oslo was political dynamite – much more so than the naked breasts of the Femen street protests. In the latter case, the impact of the constantly reproduced photo sequences is restricted by the existing discourses. As maenads, hysterics and overpowered Amazons, their rebellion plays out from a position marked as exclusively feminine, and follows a script written by others.

Merkel's plunging neckline, on the other hand, produced images that the chancellor did *not* wish to repeat. As the newspapers relate, she never again wore such a low-cut dress in public.

Breasts and power – clearly an uncontrollable combination even today.

CONCLUSION
Weighty breasts

The breast seems harmless, yet it has the power to provoke. It is multifunctional and ambiguous, variously seen over the course of history as sinful, attractive, sacred, liberating, repulsive or heroic. Its status and meaning are ostensibly determined by nature, divine providence or science. As the object of moral, scientific, artistic and feminist debates, it is unquestionably political. In all these constellations, the image of the breast has exposed prevailing gender relations, but has also shown its potential to powerfully disrupt them.

Its potential to disturb is obvious. On the one hand, it is regarded as the embodiment of femininity, even of gender difference per se; on the other hand, it disrupts clear classifications. This is why it remains disconcerting, even today. The previous chapters have shown the potential masculinity of breasts and their ability to illustrate the uncertainty of gender classifications, as in depictions of 'bearded ladies'. The supposedly unique function and ability of the female breast to nurse babies has also been relativized again and again. Some authors, for example, advocated the use of goat udders to feed infants; sometimes these were even seen as a better alternative to human breasts, destabilizing the opposition between natural and artificial. Today there are still arguments about naked breasts in parks or swimming pools, and both the covering and uncovering of the female chest are the object of legal disputes – further evidence of the transgressive potential of this underestimated body part. Its visibility can be upsetting and requires regulation. In short: even now, the breast highlights the limitations of Western promises of freedom.

It is therefore both necessary and illuminating to examine the political effects of its various dimensions – as the embodiment of supposedly asexual motherhood, a national symbol, a weapon of attack, an object of lust, or a target of medical scrutiny and intervention. This includes clarifying to what extent cultural attributions are connected to societal differences and hierarchies, and therefore result in exclusions and inequalities. One example is the racism that is indelibly inscribed into the history of the breast; another is the patriarchal obsession with perfect breasts, which leads to the invisibility and denigration of bodies that do not meet this norm.

This ambiguous and contradictory body part can inspire a desire for clear messages and simple slogans. For someone to blame, for a lifeline to cling to. But this book offers neither a rhetoric of liberation nor essentialist statements on what the breast 'actually' is. The final insight is this: there is no escaping the bewildering flood of claims, projections and ideals which, to this day, play a greater role in shaping the breast than push-up bras and cosmetic surgery. Time and again, too many people have been far too certain about the nature, purpose and ideal appearance of the breast. It is, as ever, a multitool of the patriarchy.

Sometimes, however, all it takes is a small but radical change to disrupt the master narrative. Recently, for example, a tiny amendment to the regulations of many parks and swimming pools in Germany has ended the differentiation between male and female breasts. This can be read as a progressive sign, affirming equality across multiple genders and the right to bodily autonomy. There are elegant and witty ways to circumvent attributions, deflect identity-based ascriptions, and formulate objections that are both exuberant and funny. Not to offer a new concept of what the breast should be, but to understand how such concepts are developed. A work by the Hamburg-based artist Evgenia Tsanana shows the charm and the political potency of such a detached and down-to-earth approach to the overcrowded discourse on the breast (figure 24).

Tsanana writes: 'I will treat the breasts as neither symbolic nor erotic, not from a medical and hardly from an aesthetic point of view. I will rather treat them as the first thing I sense from them: as

Figure 24 Not books on breasts, but breasts on books. Photo from Evgenia
Tsanana's long-term project *Weighted Body Parts* (part of a series of four
photos), 1996.

weight.'[1] This is a highly effective rejection of the continuing efforts to
explain, discipline or idealize the breast. Instead, she asks humorously
whether 'weighted body parts' can be used 'in the household and even
for education'. In the photos she puts various objects underneath her
breasts: a brush and dustpan, plates, books. So what would happen
if breasts stopped performing the many complicated tasks that are
constantly being imposed on them by society, politics and art? What
would happen if, regardless of who they were attached to, they could
just hang around for a change?

Notes

The Politics of the Breast

1 'Free the Nipple v. City of Fort Collins 17-1103 (10th Circuit 2019)', *Justia*, https://law.justia.com/cases/federal/appellate-courts/ca10/17 -1103/17-1103-2019-02-15.html#:~:text=Fort%20Collins%2C%20No .-,17%2D1103%20(10th%20Cir.,2019)&text=The%20city%20of%20Fort %20Collins,their%20breasts%20below%20the%20areola.

2 Gabriela Dimova, 'Free the Nipple', *Oklahoma Intercollegiate Legislature*, 19 October 2023, https://okoil.org/free-the-nipple.

3 Another court case in which women sued for their right to bare their breasts at the beach – just as men are allowed to – took place in the US in 2019. Three women from New Hampshire who had been arrested at the beach for exposing their nipples appealed to the US Supreme Court to overturn their convictions for public nudity. See 'Justices Turn Away Appeal of Women Who Went Topless at Beach', *AP News*, 13 January 2020, https://apnews.com/justices-turn-away-appeal-of-women-who -went-topless-at-beach-87c04c3cbcd3072a92f52d2e43ee316a.

4 Benthien and Wulf 2001, 'Einleitung' [Introduction], p. 17.

5 These were the words of the early medieval scholar Isidore of Seville, quoted in Lange 1966, p. 98.

6 www.wired.com/story/politics-sexism-google-search-jo-swinson.

7 This imbalance in access to political power can still be found today in all Western democracies. For example, the 118th US Congress (2023–5)

has 151 women among its 535 members (https://cawp.rutgers.edu/facts
/levels-office/congress/women-serving-118th-congress-2023-2025).   In
the twentieth German Bundestag (2021 to the present), 256 out of a
total of 736 members of parliament are female.

8 Warnke 1992; Forschungsstelle Politische Ikonographie 1996; Fleckner,
   Warnke and Ziegler 2011.

9 Urte Krass, 'Politische Ikonographie', pp. 345–6, here p. 346. English-
   speaking readers can find out more here: www.warburg-haus.de/en
   /forschungsprojekte/forschungsstelle-politische-ikonographie;   Bertoli
   et al. 2023.

10 Herrmann and Wienand 2017.

11 Kohout 2019.

12 Kaufmann 1995, p. 101.

13 www.statista.com/statistics/281321/breast-augmentation-procedures
    -among-us-adults-by-age;   https://torontoplasticsurgeon.com/blog
    /breast-augmentation-implants-statistics-2023#:~:text=In%20the%20
    United%20States%20alone,of%20breast%20augmentations
    %20performed%20worldwide.

14 www.jkrowling.com/opinions/j-k-rowling-writes-about-her-reasons-for
    -speaking-out-on-sex-and-gender-issues.

15 Klees 1806, p. 30.

16 'Von der schönen Frauen Brust und Taille' [On the breast and waist of
    beautiful women], in Krauss 1904, pp. 286–300.

17 Ibid., p. 291.

18 Ibid., p. 292.

19 Gilman 1999.

20 Ibid., p. 221.

21 Freeman 2020; on the subject of advertising, see Emilia Roig's analysis
    of an Instagram post from the German health and beauty retailer
    Rossmann during the first Covid lockdown. Here a picture of a Black
    woman with a well-tended Afro appears as an illustration of neglected,
    'ugly' hair, under the hashtag #badhair: Roig 2021, pp. 176f.

22 Criado-Perez 2019.

23 Bischoff 2001, p. 293.

24 Young 2005 [first published 1990], p. 88.

25 For these topics, see the following chapters and also, for example,
    Bynum 1977; Fildes 1986; Sykora 1994; Gilman 1999.

26 Jan Kedves, 'Haut Couture' [Skin couture], 5 June 2020, www
.sueddeutsche.de/stil/mode-haut-couture-1.4924561.

1 Tops On! Tops Off!

1 Angelique Chrisafis, 'French PM Suggests Naked Breasts Represent
France Better than a Headscarf', *Guardian*, 30 August 2016, www
.theguardian.com/world/2016/aug/30/france-manuel-valls-breasts
-headscarf-burkini-ban-row.

2 Hark and Villa 2017.

3 Peters 2021.

4 Letters to the editor, *Die Zeit*, no. 19, 6 May 2021, p. 19.

5 Schmincke 2019 offers an overview of the field.

6 Sanyal 2020 [2009].

7 Laqueur 1990.

8 Irigaray 1985, p. 133.

9 Kohl 1934.

10 Hammer-Tugendhat 1987, p. 29.

11 Quoted in Bologne 1986, p. 54.

12 Bonetti 2020.

13 'Katholische Kirche: Hut ab vor der Heiligkeit' [Catholic church: hats
off in the presence of holiness], *Kölner Stadt-Anzeiger*, 27 June 2014,
www.ksta.de/ratgeber/heiliger-knigge-katholische-kirche-hut-ab-vor
-der-heiligkeit-144041.

14 Kania 2010; Thesander 1997, p. 57.

15 Quoted in Bologne 1986, p. 54.

16 Ibid., pp. 55–6.

17 Barbe 2012.

18 Junker and Stille 1988, p. 109.

19 Thesander 1997, pp. 83 and 36ff. for the remarks above.

20 Ibid.

21 See for example Junker and Stille 1988; Steele 2001; Ober 2005; Härtel
2020.

22 Quoted in Bologne 1986, p. 57.

23 Quoted in ibid., p. 66.

24 Quoted in Kunzle 1982.

25 Juvernay 1637.

26 Quoted in Bologne 1986, p. 69.

27 Duerr 1997, pp. 48f.

28 Christian Tobias Ephraim Reinhard, *Satyrische Abhandlung von den Krankheiten der Frauenspersonen [...]* [Satirical essay on the diseases of females [...]], part 2, Berlin and Leipzig, 1757, pp. 12ff., quoted in Junker and Stille 1988, pp. 39f.

29 Schade 1994.

30 Wenk 1987, p. 224.

31 Quoted in Junker and Stille 1988, p. 61.

32 This expression comes from Johanna Schaffer 2008.

33 The following sections are largely based on the remarks of Barta 1987.

34 Ibid., p. 94.

35 Thesander 1997, pp. 36–8.

36 Barta 1987, p. 101.

37 Rousseau 1979 [first published 1762], p. 46.

38 Badinter 1981.

39 Duncan 1973.

40 Schiebinger 1993, p. 40.

41 Feher 1989, p. 11.

42 See also the overview in Lorenz 2000.

43 For the relationship between seeing and thinking with regard to changing worldviews, see the works of science historian Ludwik Fleck (1979; first published in 1935 but still fundamental today) and Zimmermann 2009.

44 Bonnaud 1770.

45 Ibid., p. xvi.

46 Quoted in Junker and Stille 1988, p. 43; the note about the use of the corset as a means of birth control is also found here.

47 Sömmerring 1793, p. 8.

48 Ibid., p. 11.

49 Further examples of the adoption of the illustration from Sömmerring can be found in *Das Pfennig-Magazin der Gesellschaft zur Verbreitung gemeinnütziger Kenntnisse* [Society's penny magazine for the dissemination of knowledge of public utility], vol. 1, section 1, Leipzig, 1833 (no. 12, 20 July 1833, p. 92), and J. F. Albrecht, *Heimlichkeiten der Frauenzimmer oder die Geheimnisse der Natur hinsichtlich der Fortpflanzung des Menschen* [Secrets of women or the mysteries of nature with regard to human reproduction], Quedlinburg/Leipzig, 1851.

50 Richter-Wittenfeld 2006, p. 301.

51 Diers 1997.
52 Schultze-Naumburg 1901, p. 6.
53 For modernity, seeing and the invention of the viewer, see Crary 1990.
54 Ibid.
55 Welsch 1996 uses the term 'Ausstieg aus dem Korsett', which has connotations of phasing out, opting out, escaping or withdrawing from something.
56 Bruns 1901, p. 378.
57 Ibid.
58 Junker and Stille 1988, p. 152.
59 Schultze-Naumburg 1901, p. 55.
60 'dirnenhafte Aufdringlichkeit': ibid., p. 142.
61 Anon. [Minna Cauer / Maria Lischnewska] 1904.
62 Thomas Theodor Heine, *Simplicissimus* 1902 (vol. 7), issue 36, p. 288.
63 Quoted in Ewers-Schultz 2018, p. 148.
64 Belting 2010.
65 Ewers-Schultz 2018, p. 148.
66 Schäfer 1902/3, p. 193.
67 Diederichs 2014, p. 50.
68 Ober 2005, p. 59.
69 Stratz 1904a, p. 23.
70 Stratz 1904b, p. 42.
71 Ibid., p. 62.
72 Ibid., p. 2.
73 Said 1978; Nochlin 1989.
74 Stratz 1904a, p. 238.
75 Stratz 1904b, pp. 366f.
76 Rulffes 2023, p. 218.
77 Schmidt-Linsenhoff 2010.
78 Ibid., vol. 1, p. 179.
79 Ibid., p. 168.
80 Ibid., p. 162.
81 'In Paris sind die Neger große Mode' [In Paris Negroes are the height of fashion], in *Die Bühne*, issue 52 (5 November 1925), p. 21, quoted in Horncastle 2020, p. 63.
82 Horncastle 2020, p. 125.
83 Sweeney-Risko 2018.

2 From Venus to Pin-Up and Back

1 Sanyal 2020 [2009], pp. 137–51.
2 Hinz 1998, p. 183.
3 Shaw 2000, p. 91.
4 Ibid., p. 90.
5 Venturi 2019, p. 266.
6 Sanyal 2020 [2009]; Gsell 2001.
7 Hammer-Tugendhat 2006, p. 77.
8 Mulvey 1975.
9 Schade and Wenk 1995, p. 384.
10 Klinger 1995, p. 39.
11 'Venus-Forschung' [Venus Research], Naturhistorisches Museum Wien, www.nhm-wien.ac.at/forschung/praehistorie/forschungen/venus -forschung.
12 Krammer 1963, p. 7.
13 Lösch 2014, p. 7.
14 Kampmann 2020. This also applies to other groups of motifs, e.g. images of the scholar, almost always represented as male – cf. Haug 2021.
15 Hartlaub 1943, p. 10.
16 Ibid., p. 5.
17 Walkowitz 1993, p. 370.
18 Gilman 1999, p. 232.
19 Lewis Page, 'Archaeologists Unearth Oldest Known 3D Pornography', *The Register*, 15 May 2009, www.theregister.com/2009/05/15/german _stone_age_3d_smut_figurine.
20 Nowell and Chang 2014, p. 564.
21 Collins and Onians 1978, quoted in Stannard and Langley 2021, p. 29.
22 Quoted in Stannard and Langley 2021, p. 29.
23 Quoted in Hinz 1989, p. 51.
24 Lewis Page, see n. 19.
25 Quoted in Stannard and Langley 2021, p. 29.
26 McDermott 1996, p. 227.
27 El Ouassil and Karig 2022, p. 14.
28 Bahn, in McDermott 1996, pp. 248f.
29 Elkins, in McDermott 1996, pp. 255–8; Joan Semmel is also discussed here, but not in relation to the representation of the female body in the self-portrait.

30 Here and below I draw on the summaries in Ritter 2010.
31 Quoted in ibid., p. 29.
32 Ibid., p. 44.
33 A summary of this debate can be found in Schiebinger 1993, pp. 160–72. The sections in the text above are a summary of Schiebinger's arguments.
34 Ibid., p. 163.
35 Förschler 2011.
36 Schiebinger 1993, p. 163.
37 Sharpley-Whiting 1999.
38 Zöllner 1998, p. 39.
39 Lessing 1890, p. 162.
40 Rosenkranz 2015, p. 28.
41 hooks 1992.
42 Davis 2009.
43 Quoted in Heinz 2006, p. 45.
44 Ibid.
45 Pfisterer 2014.
46 Blanchard et al. 2018.
47 Aristotle 1943, p. 11. For form and material, see Wagner 2001.
48 Clark 1956, p. 27.
49 Nead 1992, p. 85.
50 Williams 1993, p. 176.
51 Sprinkle 1997, p. 69.
52 Bourdieu 1984.
53 Jarrett 1997.
54 Kris and Kurz 1995.
55 Dilly 1979; Christadler 2000.
56 Herber 2009.
57 Nochlin 2021.
58 Jahn 2019.
59 Meyer 2019, p. 111.
60 Ibid.
61 Koos 2015 offers a brilliant interpretation of the work of Mendieta against the background of nineteenth-century painting.
62 www.das-waren-noch-zeiten.de/img/filmhits_30_1969.jpg.
63 www.historische-magazine.de/der-stern-archiv-titelbilder.
64 Moral 2014, p. 64; cf. Zimmermann 2017, p. 87.

65 Schor 2015.
66 Ibid., p. 63.
67 Weibel 1984, p. 50.
68 Schade 2006.
69 Hausbichler 2021.
70 Samira El Ouassil, 'Freiheit den Brüsten!' [Freedom for the breasts!], *SPIEGEL Kultur*, 12 May 2022, www.spiegel.de/kultur/soziale-kontrolle -freiheit-den-bruesten-a-959f5bef-e8ed-49f0-9d5c-3882f4287143.
71 Quoted in Schor 2015, p. 192.
72 Dyer 1997.
73 Zimmermann 2007.
74 Cf. Fletcher 2016.
75 'Differential treatment based on skin color, especially favoritism toward those with a lighter skin tone and mistreatment or exclusion of those with a darker skin tone, typically among those of the same racial group or ethnicity' (www.dictionary.com/browse/colorism). The videos can be found at www.youtube.com/watch?v=QcVGXElLjL0.

3 Breasts and Other Illusions of the Natural

1 Osthus 2022, p. XI.
2 Krauss 1904, p. 287.
3 Honegger 1996 [first published 1991], p. ix.
4 Schiebinger 1993, p. 225. The following examples are also from Schiebinger.
5 Orland 2013.
6 Isidore of Seville, *Encyclopaedia*, quoted in Laqueur 1990, p. 36.
7 Neugebauer 1908, p. 194.
8 Duden 1991, p. 105.
9 Fildes 1986, p. 100.
10 Klees 1806, p. 37.
11 Bynum 1977.
12 Ibid., p. 263.
13 Lifshitz 2004; DeVun 2021, p. 191.
14 Duden 1991, p. 114.
15 Thiemann 2006, p. 50.
16 Francis (François) Mauriceau, *The accomplisht midwife*, London, 1673, quoted in Fildes 1986, p. 139.

17 For example, Seichter 2014.

18 Fildes 1986, p. 115.

19 Ibid., p. 116.

20 Quinlan 2004, p. 139.

21 Yalom 1997, p. 117.

22 Hunt 1992.

23 Honegger 1996, p. 58.

24 Seichter 2014, p. 57.

25 Fildes 1986, p. 104.

26 Schütze 1988, pp. 119–20.

27 Quinlan 2004, p. 147.

28 The following remarks are mainly based on the insights of Londa Schiebinger; see Schiebinger 1993, pp. 40–74.

29 Milam 2015, p. 192.

30 Ibid., p. 193.

31 Liharžik 1839, p. 27.

32 Klees 1806, p. 32.

33 Ibid., p. 9.

34 Ibid., p. 33.

35 Ibid., p. 49.

36 Wierrer 1870, p. 29.

37 Hyrtl 1847, p. 402.

38 Klees 1806, pp. 16f. (emphasis added).

39 Ibid., S. 38.

40 Gilman 1999, p. 228.

41 Strahsen 1831, p. 11.

42 Ibid., pp. 9 and 10.

43 The book was dedicated to 'All mothers who are unable to breastfeed for natural reasons'.

44 Klees 1806, p. 36.

45 Ibid., pp. 36 and 37.

46 Strahsen 1831, p. 10.

47 Ibid., p. 14.

48 Ibid., p. 15.

49 Ibid., p. 14.

50 Klees 1806, p. 24.

51 Zwierlein 1816, p. 2.

52 Fildes 1986, p. 269.

53 *Neue Jugend-Zeitung* [New youth newspaper] (Leipzig), no. 83, 17 July 1819, column 657.

54 Zwierlein 1816, p. vi.

55 Cf. the 'figure of the third' as a paradigm in cultural studies: 'a third [element] that makes binary codings possible, while, as a constituting mechanism, it generally remains hidden itself' – Eßlinger et al. 2010, p. 11.

56 Zwierlein 1816, p. 29 (emphasis added).

57 Ibid., p. 8.

58 Ibid., pp. 27–9.

59 Ibid., p. 8.

60 Ibid., p. 47.

61 Ibid., p. 94.

62 Fildes 1986, p. 270.

63 Klencke 1870, p. 45.

64 Haarer 1941, p. 115.

65 Ibid., p. 271.

66 Ibid., p. 168.

67 Ibid., p. 168 (printed in spaced type for emphasis in the original). For more on Haarer, see Chamberlain 2010.

68 Haarer 1941, p. 174.

69 The examples and remarks are based on DeVun 2021, pp. 46–63.

70 Pliny, *Natural History*, VII, II, 15–16, www.attalus.org/translate/pliny_hn7a.html.

71 DeVun 2021, p. 62

72 The following remarks are largely based on Thiemann 2006.

73 Tunbridge 2011.

74 Thiemann 2006 with reference to Tönz 2000.

75 Jalilipour 2023.

76 Johnston 2007.

77 DeVun 2021, p. 46. The Hamburg-based art historian and artist Silke Büttner contributed a seminal article on 'visual othering' in the Middle Ages: Büttner 2013.

78 Clavigero 1780/1, vol. IV, Dissertazione V, p. 169.

79 Humboldt and Bonpland 1907 [1852].

80 Ibid.

81 Franklin 1823, p. 157.

82 *Medicinische Jahrbücher des kaiserl. königl. Österreichischen Staates* [Medical yearbooks of the imperial-royal Austrian state] (Vienna), vol. 30 / new series vol. 21 (1840), p. 144.

83 Humboldt and Bonpland 1818, p. 44.

84 Hyrtl 1847, p. 380.

85 Burdach 1819, p. 49.

86 Brooks 2022, p. 21.

87 Hunter 1780, p. 530.

88 *Sibylle. Unterhaltungsblatt zum Würzburger Journal* [Sibylle: entertainment supplement to the Würzburg journal], no. 152, 19 December 1867, p. 608.

89 Gruber 1866.

90 Ibid., p. 1.

91 Ibid., p. 5.

92 Ibid., p. 16.

93 Zimmermann 2009, p. 159.

94 Kurella 1893, p. 85.

95 Adler 1912, p. 90.

96 Gilman 1999, pp. 264f.

97 Emmert 1862, p. 39.

98 Krieg 1877, p. 75.

99 'Verteilung von Brustvergrößerungen nach Ländern mit den häufigsten Eingriffen im Jahr 2023' [Distribution of breast augmentations by countries with the most frequent procedures in 2023], Statista, June 2024, de.statista.com/statistik/daten/studie/449423/umfrage/verteilung -von-brustvergroesserungen-nach-laendern-mit-den-haeufigsten -eingriffen.

100 Benedikt Hollenstein, 'Darum sind Schönheits-OPs für Kinder in Brasilien neu kostenlos' [This is why cosmetic operations for children in Brazil are now free], *20 Minuten*, 11 June 2023, www.20min.ch/story /darum-sind-schoenheits-ops-fuer-kinder-in-brasilien-neu-kostenlos -604137841123 [5.7.2023].

101 For this connection, see Gilman 1999, pp. 225–7.

102 Edmonds 2007, p. 373.

103 VDÄPC, *Behandlungsstatistik 2023: Mitgliederbefragung* [Treatment statistics 2023: survey of members],vdaepc.de/wp-content/uploads /2023/04/2023_VDAEPC_Behandlungsstatistik_2023.pdf, p. 5.

104 *DGÄPC-Statistik 2020–2021*, p. 3.

105 Gersuny 1903, column 2257.

106 Gilman 1999, p. 229.

107 Hyrtl 1847, p. 401.

108 Gilman 1999, pp. 227 and 238.

109 Zeis 1838, p. 2.

110 Gilman 1999, p. 228.

111 Czerny 1895.

112 Gilman 1999, p. 252.

113 Cooper 2014, p. 250.

114 Genevieve Gluck, 'Sex Trafficked Women First Victims of Silicone Injections', 28 December 2021, *Women's Voices*, genevievegluck.substack .com/p/sex-trafficked-women-first-victims.

115 Leonardi et al. 2016.

116 'San Francisco's Topless Dancing Pioneer, Carol Doda, Dead at 78', Reuters, 12 November 2015, www.reuters.com/article/us-people-doda -idCNKCN0T107X20151112.

117 Zimmermann 1998, p. 27.

118 Ibid.

119 Gilman 1999, pp. 243f.; Fardo et al. 2022.

120 Fitts 1999, p. 5.

121 Coll-Planas et al. 2017, p. 186.

122 Jones 2008, p. 90.

123 Ibid., p. 90.

124 At the same time, the political debates on the new law were accompanied by a broad discussion in the media. This contributed to the inclusion of a few points that are problematic from the point of view of those affected. One is the addition of a passage limiting trans* women's access to, for example, saunas or changing rooms, with reference to *Hausrecht* (the right of the proprietor to determine who is allowed entry). Another is the rule that trans* women are not exempt from conscription to the armed forces if their application to change their gender is made shortly before the country needs to defend itself against attack.

125 'Was bedeutet das Selbstbestimmungsgesetz?' [What does the Self-Determination Act mean?], *Tagesschau*, 23 August 2023, www .tagesschau.de/inland/innenpolitik/selbstbestimmungsgesetz-106.html entwurf-100.html.

126 Bullion 2023.

127 Pearce et al. 2020.

128 Abby Gardner, 'A Complete Breakdown of the J. K. Rowling Transgender Comments Controversy', *Glamour*, 3 September 2024, www.glamour .com/story/a-complete-breakdown-of-the-jk-rowling-transgender -comments-controversy.

129 E.g. in Ewert 2021.

130 Sciuto 2022, pp. 164f.

131 Louis 2022, pp. 50f.

132 Ibid., p. 51.

133 'Chestfeeding If You're Trans or Non-binary', NHS, last reviewed January 2025, www.nhs.uk/pregnancy/having-a-baby-if-you-are-lgbt-plus/chest feeding-if-youre-trans-or-non-binary.

134 Fitts 1999, p. 5.

135 MacDonald et al. 2016.

136 LSVD, '9 Kritikpunkte an Alice Schwarzers gefährlichen und falschen Thesen zu "Transsexualität"' [9 criticisms of Alice Schwarzer's dangerous and false theses on 'transsexuality'], www.lsvd.de/de/ct/6772-alice-schwarzer-transsexualitaet?gclid=Cj0KCQjw6cKiBhD5ARIsAKXU dybKo TCkb3J71sGZQObX_exrWJ_Kik4QyMZeYpr3 -snZ3EjoI3RTQZEaAvz7EALw_wcB.

137 Limper 2021, pp. 455 and 386.

138 Schwarzer and Louis 2022, p. 10.

139 Ewert 2021, pp. 125f.

140 Hoenes 2014, pp. 54f.

141 Sobiech and Gentile 2012, p. 171.

142 Patrick Krull, 'Diese wackeligen Busen sind eine schwere Sünde' [Those bobbing breasts are a mortal sin], *Welt*, 30 July 2015, www.welt.de/sport /article144620097/Diese-wackeligen-Busen-sind-eine-schwere-Suende .html.

143 Ibid.

144 Heckemeyer 2018, p. 163.

145 www.ran.de/fussball/bildergalerien/die-schoensten-fussballerinnen-der -welt-morgan-ekroth-ertz.

146 Düntzer and Hellendall 1929, pp. 1835–8.

147 Westmann 1930, pp. 2f.

148 Ibid., p. 6.

149 Ibid., p. 36.

150 Ibid.

151 Ibid., p. 47.

152 Bergmann 1925, p. 19.

153 Ibid., p. 85.

154 Gutsmuths 1793, pp. 19f.

155 Solomon-Godeau 1997; Fend 2003.

156 Gilman 1999, p. 262.

157 Toney 1999, p. 166.

158 Ibid., p. 166.

159 Jörg Scheller has coined the term 'body-bilding' – combining 'body-building' with the German word for image, *Bild* (Scheller 2021, pp. 61–6).

160 Sciuto 2022, p. 163.

161 Website of Netzwerk Männer mit Brustkrebs [Network for men with breast cancer], www.brustkrebs-beim-mann.de.

162 Zeis 1838, p. 472.

163 Lorde 1980; Ehlers 2012, p. 122.

164 Kubitza 1994, p. 77.

165 Spence 1986, pp. 156 and 152.

166 Ibid., p. 153.

167 Peterson 2018.

168 In 2018 it was reported that Matuschka had opted for a surgical reconstruction of the breast around twenty years after her illness. The reason she gave was that she finally wanted to be able to appear incognito.

169 Fitts 1999, p. 4.

170 Ibid., p. 6.

171 Meskimmon 1996, p. 6.

172 Russo 1995, p. 14.

173 Hauke 2022, p. 71.

174 Klauke 2022, p. 51.

175 Villa 2008, p. 252.

176 Ibid.

4 'I Am God'

1 'Busen-Protest im Kanzleramt: DAS forderten die Oben-ohne-Aktivistinnen von Olaf Scholz' [Breast protest in the Chancellery: THIS is what the topless activists demanded from Olaf Scholz], *Berliner Kurier*, 21

August 2022, www.berliner-kurier.de/politik-wirtschaft/busen-protest-oben-ohne-aktivistinnen-fordern-gas-embargo-von-scholz-li.258813.

2 The following remarks and some of the examples are based on Hiltmann 2008.

3 Except to viewers of the Netflix series *Vikings: Valhalla*. The second season has been out since January 2023.

4 *Eirik the Red and Other Icelandic Sagas*, trans. Gwyn Jones, Oxford: Oxford University Press, 1961, pp. 152–3.

5 See Hiltmann 2008, p. 427.

6 Ibid.

7 Ibid.

8 Kobelt-Groch 2005

9 Wagner-Hasel 2010, p. 32.

10 Hederich 1967 [1770], columns 203 and 205, quoted in Scheifele 1992, p. 38.

11 Bisset 1971.

12 Wagner-Hasel 2010, p. 19. The following remarks are based on Wagner-Hasel 2010.

13 Preußer 2010, p. 36.

14 Wagner-Hasel 2010, p. 23.

15 Eller 2011, p. 17. I cannot go into the nuanced research positions on this topic, for example objections such as that raised by Wagner-Hasel, that 'all [...] interpretations that draw attention to the gender of the Amazons [...] are referring to an idea of the oppressed and subordinated life of Attic women, which was developed at the end of the eighteenth century and was fed by both European fantasies about harems and ideal images of the bourgeois housewife. But a society that uses images of a female community of warriors to reassure itself of its identity cannot be conceived of as having a purely masculine orientation': Wagner-Hasel 2010, p. 28.

16 Scheifele 1992, p. 48.

17 For the connection with the myth of the Amazons and the idea of female rule, see Gilman 1980, pp. 144f.

18 Hegel 2011, p. 90. See also Gilman 1980, pp. 48f.

19 Hederich 1967 [1770].

20 Eller 2011, pp. 65–99.

21 Ibid., pp. 18f.; Kelly 1982.

22 Rentmeister 1988, p. 443.

23 Ibid.

24 Ibid., p. 449.

25 Ibid., p. 446.

26 It can only be viewed as a sad irony that the online retailer making life difficult for many bookshops refers to the Amazons in its name.

27 Hermand 1984; Rang 1984.

28 Rang 1984, p. 556.

29 Quoted in Hermand 1984, p. 544.

30 Ibid., pp. 547f.

31 Quoted in Jooss 2006, p. 282.

32 Fuchsberger 2017, p. 199.

33 Kätzel 2002, p. 207.

34 Quoted in Rosenfeld 2010, p. 351.

35 Quoted in Bandhauser-Schöffmann 2009, p. 68.

36 'Frauen im Untergrund: "Etwas Irrationales"' [Women in the underground: 'Something irrational'], *Der Spiegel*, no. 33, 7 August 1977, pp. 22–33.

37 Quoted in Wagner-Hasel 1991, p. 80.

38 Rosenfeld 2010, pp. 370f.

39 Duerr 1995, p. 70.

40 For example in Michael Ruetz's book of photographs: 1997, p. 202.

41 Linke 2012, p. 209.

42 Quoted in Herzog 2008, p. 77.

43 Projektgruppe Sexualität und Politik 1988 [1973], p. 99.

44 Eitler 2007, p. 239.

45 Kätzel 2002, p. 205.

46 Fahlenbrach 2002.

47 Eiblmayr 1993, p. 85.

48 Papenbrock 2007.

49 Stelzer 2003.

50 Helene Heise, 'Aktion blanker Busen' [Bare-breasted protest], *Spiegel Geschichte*, 16 October 2007, www.spiegel.de/geschichte/achtundsechzig-aktion-blanker-busen-a-949905.html.

51 For example, in Warner 2000, p. 286.

52 Katja Iken, 'Er hebe hoch!' [Long lift the bra], *Spiegel Geschichte*, 5 July 2012, www.spiegel.de/geschichte/bh-revolution-befreiung-vom-korsett-a-947632.html.

53 Joy Press, 'The Life and Death of a Radical Sisterhood', *The Cut*, www.thecut.com/2017/11/an-oral-history-of-feminist-group-new-york -radical-women.html.

54 'No More Miss America', *Redstockings*, www.redstockings.org/index.php /no-more-miss-america.

55 Lindsy van Gelder, 'How We Got There: The Truth about Bra-Burners', *Ms.*, September/October 1992, gradschool.wayne.edu/news/the_truth _about_bra_burners.pdf.

56 Ibid.

57 www.redstockings.org/index.php/no-more-miss-america.

58 Kreydatus 2018, p. 22.

59 Ibid.

60 Welch 2015.

61 Ibid., p. 81.

62 The founders were Oksana Shachko, Inna Shevchenko, Sasha Shevchenko and Anna Hutsol.

63 femen.org/about-us.

64 www.facebook.com/femengermany/?locale=de_DE.

65 Ibid.

66 Quoted in Baldauf 2015, p. 60.

67 Quoted in O'Keefe 2014, p. 11.

68 Quoted in ibid., p. 12.

69 Villa 2022, p. 254.

70 www.facebook.com/femengermany [13 January 2023].

71 Siebler 2015.

72 Ibid., p. 562.

73 Zing Tsjeng, 'Why Instagram Censored This Image of an Artist on Her Period', *Dazed*, 27 March 2015, www.dazeddigital.com/artsandculture /article/24258/1/why-instagram-censored-this-image-of-an-artist-on -her-period.

74 Cf. Faust 2017.

75 'Nackte Tatsachen gegen Putin und Merkel' [Naked facts against Putin and Merkel], *Spiegel Politik*, 8 April 2013, www.spiegel.de/fotostrecke /messe-protest-femen-aktivistinnen-stoeren-merkel-und-putin -fotostrecke-95267.html.

76 Julia Rohnau, 'Ungerecht? Warum Frauen keine Exhibitionisten sein können' [Unjust? Why women cannot be exhibitionists], *Nordbayern*,

6 September 2021, www.nordbayern.de/region/ungerecht-warum
-frauen-keine-exhibitionisten-sein-konnen-1.9273481. This regulation
is also criticized by legal experts. For example, the rationale that
the vast majority of exhibitionist acts are committed by men is not
tenable because offences are also not restricted to a certain age, even
if 93-year-old exhibitionists may be a rarity. See also Gereon Wolters,
'Der kleine Unterschied und seine strafrechtlichen Folgen' [The small
difference and its penal consequences], in *Golddammer's Archiv für
Strafrecht*, vol. 161, no. 10 (2014), pp. 556–71.

77 With disastrous consequences, as shown by the prevailing tendency
to ignore violence against men in the public discourse on domestic
violence, for example. According to police statistics, around 19 per cent
of the victims of domestic violence are men (www.maennergewaltschutz
.de/event/hospitation-msw-leipzig).

78 Carroll 1989, p. 3.

79 Ibid., p. 5.

80 Schneider and Seifert 2010.

81 Lindner 1987, p. 301.

82 Ibid., p. 296.

83 Karentzos 2005, p. 158.

84 Zenaty 2022.

85 Didi-Huberman 2003, p. xi.

86 Ibid.

87 Peter Gorsen, quoted in Schneede 2006, p. 51.

88 Schneede 2006, p. 211.

89 Schade 1993; Didi-Huberman 2003; Charcot and Richer 1887.

90 For Aby Warburg's concept of the *Pathosformel*, which has been influential in art and cultural studies, see Baumgart et al. 1993; Pfisterer 2003;
Hurttig 2012.

91 For the persistence and impact of the maenad motif, see Lindner 1987,
p. 302.

92 Karentzos 2005, pp. 99f.

93 Lydia Rosenfelder and Angelika Hellemann, 'Soldaten sauer auf
Stöckelschuh-Ministerin' [Soldiers angry at high-heeled minister], *Bild*,
13 April 2022, www.bild.de/bild-plus/politik/ausland/politik-ausland
/lambrecht-traegt-bei-truppenbesuch-pumps-soldaten-sauer-auf
-stoeckelschuh-minist-79758704.bild.html.

94 Hofmann 2014, p. 34.

95 Bulst 1988, p. 29.

96 Dinges 1992, p. 74

97 Rublack 2022, p. 400.

98 Unlike Lambrecht's high heels, however, which diminished the politician's reputation rather than boosting it, Fischer's legendary choice of footwear helped to create a positive myth around him.

99 Rublack 2022, p. 400.

100 Bulst 1988, p. 43.

101 Steidele 2021.

102 'Hamburger Kleiderordnung vom 7. September 1500' [Hamburg dress code of 7 September 1500], in Quellenpaket [Source pack] 27, ed. Susanne Grünewald, Universität Hamburg, www.spaetmittelalter.uni-hamburg.de /spaetmittelalter/Lehre/Ergebnisse/Hamburg/quellen/Paket Siebenundzwanzig.html.

103 Thüsing 2006.

104 Quoted in Bulst 1988, p. 39.

105 Ibid., and p. 43.

106 Bulst 1988.

107 For more on this see e.g. Byer 2022, p. 142.

108 For the case of the Berlin woman Gabrielle Lebreton, see the introduction to this book (www.berliner-zeitung.de/mensch-metropole/oben -ohne-auf-dem-wasserspielplatz-berliner-gericht-prueft-heute-klage-li .266815).

109 Lenelotte von Bothmer, 'Meine Hosenanzurg' [My trouser suit], *Die Zeit*, 30 August 1996, www.zeit.de/1996/36/Mein_Hosenanzug /komplettansicht.

110 Quoted in Lünenborg et al. 2009, p. 86. For the following press quotations, see pp. 86–90.

111 Rohlmann 2009, p. 226.

112 Ibid.

113 Assmann 1994, p. 25.

114 Ibid.

115 Warner 1994.

116 Hederich 1967 [1770], column 206, quoted in Scheifele 1992, p. 38.

117 Hollander, quoted in Warner 2000, p. 272.

118 Grubitzsch 2020, p. 244.

119 Quoted in Wagner 1989, p. 17.
120 Warner 2000, p. 276.
121 Ibid., p. 287.
122 Quoted in Lünenborg et al. 2009, p. 86. The following press quotations are from the same source, pp. 86–90.
123 Assmann 1994, p. 25.
124 Wagner 1989, p. 8.
125 Ibid., pp. 23 and 24.
126 Bogerts 2016; Maltz-Leca 2013.
127 www.museion-versand.de/alte-kategorien/THEMEN/Special--Klassiker-der-Kunstgeschichte/Delacroix--Die-Freiheit-fuehrt-das-Volk.html.
128 Wagner 1989, p. 19.
129 Ibid., p. 23.
130 Kantorowicz 1957. More recent studies have transferred Kantorowicz's concept to questions of gender difference: see for example Banakas 2018.

Conclusion

1 Evgenia Tsanana, 'Weighted Body Parts', 1996, https://evgeniatsanana.com/works-bodyparts.html.

Bibliography

Adler, Alfred, *Über den nervösen Charakter* [On the nervous character], Wiesbaden, 1912.

Allen, Regulus, '"The Sable Venus" and Desire for the Undesirable', *Studies in English Literature, 1500–1900*, vol. 51, no. 3 (summer 2011): 667–91.

Anon. [Minna Cauer / Maria Lischnewska], 'Eingabe des Verbandes Fortschrittlicher Frauenvereine an Seine Exzellenz den Herrn Minister der geistlichen Schul- und Medizinalangelegenheiten in Preußen, Verbot des Korsetts in der Schule betreffend' [Submission from the Federation of Progressive Women's associations to His Excellence the Minister of Spiritual, Educational and Medical Affairs in Prussia, regarding the prohibition of the corset in schools], *Die Frauenbewegung*, vol. 10, no. 22 (15 November 1904): 64–5.

Aristotle, *Generation of Animals*, with an English translation by A. L. Peck, London: Heinemann, 1943.

Assmann, Aleida, 'Der Wissende und die Weisheit' [The knower and wisdom], in Sigrid Schade et al. (eds.), *Allegorien und Geschlechterdifferenz*, Cologne/Weimar/Vienna: Böhlau, 1994, pp. 11–25.

Bader, Lena, et al. (eds.), *Vergleichendes Sehen* [Comparative seeing], Paderborn: Fink, 2010.

Badinter, Elisabeth, *Mother Love: Myth and Reality. Motherhood in Modern History*, New York: Macmillan, 1981.

Baldauf, Anette, 'Girl Aktivismus' [Girl activism], in Alexander Fleischmann and Doris Guth (eds.), *Kunst. Theorie. Aktivismus. Emanzipatorische*

Perspektiven auf Ungleichheit und Diskriminierung, Bielefeld: transcript, 2015, pp. 59–89.

Banakas, Anne-Sophie, 'Die zwei Körper der Herrscherin: Der politische und der natürliche Körper in den Porträts von Maria Theresia (1740–1780)' [The two bodies of the sovereign: the political and natural body in the portraits of Maria Theresa (1740–1780)], *Mitteilungen des Instituts für Österreichische Geschichtsforschung*, vol. 126, no. 1 (May 2018): 73–109.

Bandhauser-Schöffmann, Irene, '"Emanzipation mit Bomben und Pistolen"? Feministinnen und Terroristinnen in deutschsprachigen Sicherheitsdiskursen der 1970er Jahre' ['Emancipation with bombs and pistols'? Feminists and female terrorists in German-language security discourses in the 1970s], *L'homme: Zeitschrift für feministische Geschichtswissenschaft*, vol. 20, no. 2 (2009): 65–84.

Barbe, Josephine, *Figur in Form: Geschichte des Korsetts* [Figure in form: history of the corset], Bern/Stuttgart/Vienna: Haupt, 2012.

Barta, Ilsebill, 'Der disziplinierte Körper: Bürgerliche Körpersprache und ihre geschlechtsspezifische Differenzierung am Ende des 18. Jahrhunderts' [The disciplined body: bourgeois body language and its gender-specific differentiation at the end of the eighteenth century], in Barta et al. (eds.), *Frauen, Bilder, Männer, Mythen. Kunsthistorische Beiträge*, Berlin: Reimer, 1987, pp. 84–106.

Baumgart, Silvia, et al. (eds.), *Denkräume zwischen Kunst und Wissenschaft* [Spaces for thought between art and science], Berlin: Reimer, 1993.

Belting, Isabella, *Mode sprengt Mieder: Silhouettenwechsel* [Fashion bursts bodices: change of silhouette], catalogue Münchner Stadtmuseum, Munich: Hirmer, 2010.

Benthien, Claudia, and Christoph Wulf (eds.), *Körperteile: Eine kulturelle Anatomie* [Body parts: a cultural anatomy], Reinbek b. Hamburg: Rowohlt, 2001.

Bergmann, Walter, *Die Frau und der Sport* [Woman and sport], Oldenburg: Walter Bergmann, 1925.

Bertoli, Angelica, Giulia Gelmi, Andrea Missagia and Maria Novella Tavano (eds.), *A Driving Force: On the Rhetoric of Images and Power*, Venice: Edizioni Ca' Foscari, 2023.

Bischoff, Doerte, 'Körperteil und Zeichenordnung: Der Phallus zwischen Materialität und Bedeutung' [Body part and order of signs: the phallus between materiality and meaning], in Claudia Benthien and Christoph

Wulf (eds.), *Körperteile: Eine kulturelle Anatomie*, Reinbek b. Hamburg: Rowohlt, 2001, pp. 293–315.

Bisset, K. A., 'Who Were the Amazons?' *Greece & Rome*, vol. 18, no. 2 (October 1971): 150–1.

Blanchard, Pascal, et al., *Sexe, race et colonies: La domination des corps du XVe siècle à nos jours* [Sex, race and colonies: the domination of bodies from the fifteenth century to our days], Paris: La Découverte, 2018.

Bogerts, Lisa Katharina, 'Die "Responsibility to Protest": Street Art als "Waffe" des Widerstands?' [The 'responsibility to protest': street art as a 'weapon' of resistance?], *Zeitschrift für Außen- und Sicherheitspolitik*, vol. 9, no. 4 (2016): 503–29.

Bologne, Jean-Claude, *Histoire de la pudeur* [History of modesty], Paris: Olivier Orban, 1986.

Bonetti, Tiziana, 'Aufs Wohl der Gemeinschaft! Marienmilch als Heilmittel: Eine historisch-anthropologische Annäherung' [To the health of the community! Mary's milk as a cure: a historical-anthropological approach], *Geschichte in Wissenschaft und Unterricht*, vol. 71, issues 11/12 (2020): 620–34.

Bonnaud, Jacques, *Dégradation de l'éspece humaine par l'usage des corps a baleine [...]* [The degradation of the human race through the use of the whalebone corset [...]], Paris: Hérissant, 1770.

Bourdieu, Pierre, *Distinction: A Social Critique of the Judgement of Taste*, trans. Richard Nice, Cambridge, MA: Harvard University Press, 1984.

Brandes, Kerstin, 'Portrait, Travelogues und Weblogs – zu visuellen Migrationen der Hottentotten-Venus' [Portraits, travelogues and weblogs – on visual migrations of the Hottentot Venus], *FKW: Zeitschrift für Geschlechterforschung und visuelle Kultur*, issue 51 (June 2011): 73–87, doi .org/10.57871/fkw5120111205.

Brooks, Ross, 'Bounds of Diversity: Queer Zoology in Europe from Aristotle to John Hunter', *Zoological Journal of Linnean Society*, vol. 195, no. 1 (May 2022): 1–32.

Bruns, Margarete, 'Der Stil der modernen Kleidung' [The style of modern clothing], *Deutsche Kunst und Dekoration*, vol. 4, issue 7 (April 1901): 374–88 and 458–78.

Bullion, Constanze von, 'In der Zwickmühle' [In a quandary], *Süddeutsche Zeitung*, 31 May 2023, p. 5.

Bulst, Neithard, 'Zum Problem städtischer und territorialer Kleider-,

Aufwands- und Luxusgesetzgebung in Deutschland (13.–Mitte 16. Jahrhundert)' [On the problem of urban and territorial legislation on dress, expenditure and luxury in Germany (thirteenth to mid-sixteenth century)], in André Gouron and Albert Riggaudière (eds.), *Renaissance du pouvoir législatif et genèse de l'Etat*, Montpellier: Société d'histoire du droit et des institutions des anciens pays de droit écrit, 1988, pp. 29–57.

Burdach, Karl Friedrich, *Vom Baue und Leben des Gehirns* [On the structure and life of the brain], vol. I, Leipzig: Dyk, 1819.

Büttner, Frank, and Andrea Gottdang, *Einführung in die Ikonographie: Wege zur Deutung von Bildinhalten* [Introduction to iconography: paths to the interpretation of image content], Munich: Beck, 2006.

Büttner, Silke (ed.), 'Visual Othering 1100–1200', special issue of *FKW: Zeitschrift für Geschlechterfoschung und visuelle Kultur*, no. 54 (May 2013), doi.org/10.57871/fkw542013.

Byer, Doris, *Weiße Haut, Schwarze Seele* [White skin, Black soul], Berlin: Matthes & Seitz, 2022.

Bynum, Caroline Walker, 'Jesus as Mother and Abbot as Mother: Some Themes in Twelfth-Century Cistercian Writing', *Harvard Theological Review*, vol. 70, no. 3/4 (October 1977): 257–84.

Carroll, Margaret D., 'The Erotics of Absolutism: Rubens and the Mystification of Sexual Violence', *Representations*, no. 25 (winter 1989): 3–30.

Chamberlain, Sigrid, *Adolf Hitler, die deutsche Mutter und ihr erstes Kind* [Adolf Hitler, the German mother and her first child], 5th edn, Gießen: Psychosozial-Verlag 2010.

Charcot, Jean Martin, and Paul Richer, *Les démoniaques dans l'art* [Demonic possession in art], Paris: Delahaye et Lecrosnier, 1887.

Christadler, Maike, *Kreativität und Geschlecht: Giorgio Vasaris 'Vite' und Sofonisba Anguissolas Selbst-Bilder* [Creativity and gender: Giorgio Vasari's Vite and Sofonisba Anguissola's self-portraits], Berlin: Reimer, 2000.

Clark, Kenneth, *The Nude: A Study of Ideal Art*, London: J. Murray, 1956.

Clavigero, Francisco Saverio, *Storia antica del Messico* [Ancient history of Mexico], 4 vols., Cesena: Gregorio Biasini, 1780/1.

Collins, Desmond, and John Onians, 'The Origins of Art, Part 2: Commentary', *Art History*, vol. 1, no. 1 (1978): 11–25.

Coll-Planas, Gerard, et al., 'Breast Surgery as a Gender Technology: Analyzing Plastic Surgeons' Discourses', *Studies in Gender and Sexuality*, vol. 18, no. 3 (2017): 178–89.

Cooper, Katherine Cohen, 'Injecting Caution: A Need for Enhanced State-Level Enforcement Tactics Targeting the Cosmetic Use of Liquid Silicone Products', *Journal of Contemporary Health Law & Policy*, vol. 30, no. 2 (2014): 249–78.

Crary, Jonathan, *Techniques of the Observer: On Vision and Modernity in the Nineteenth Century*, Cambridge, MA: MIT Press, 1990.

Criado-Perez, Caroline, *Invisible Women: Exposing Data Bias in a World Designed for Men*, London: Chatto & Windus, 2019.

Czerny, Vincenz, 'Plastischer Ersatz der Brustdrüse durch ein Lipom' [Plastic replacement of the mammary gland with a lipoma], *Zentralblatt für Chirurgie*, vol. 22 (1895): 544–50.

Davis, Kathy, 'Editorial: "Black is Beautiful" in European Perspective', *European Journal of Women's Studies*, vol. 16, no. 2 (May 2009): 99–101.

DeVun, Leah, *The Shape of Sex: Nonbinary Gender from Genesis to the Renaissance*, New York: Columbia University Press, 2021.

DGÄPC (Deutsche Gesellschaft für Ästhetisch-Plastische Chirurgie), *DGÄPC-Statistik 2020–2021. Zahlen, Fakten und Trends der Ästhetisch-Plastischen Chirurgie* [Statistics of the German Society for Aesthetic-Plastic Surgery 2020–21: figures, facts and trends in aesthetic-plastic surgery], Berlin 2021, www.dgaepc.de/wp-content/uploads/2021/10/DGAePC_Statistik-2021.pdf.

Didi-Huberman, Georges, *Invention of Hysteria: Charcot and the Photographic Iconography of Salpêtrière*, trans. Alisa Hartz, Cambridge, MA: MIT Press, 2003.

Diederichs, Ulf, *Eugen Diederichs und sein Verlag: Bibliographie und Buchgeschichte 1896 bis 1931* [Eugen Diederichs and his publishing house: bibliography and history of books *1896 to 1931*], Göttingen: Wallstein, 2014.

Diers, Michael, *Schlagbilder: Zur politischen Ikonographie der Gegenwart* [Striking images: on the political iconography of the present], Frankfurt am Main: Fischer-Taschenbuch-Verlag, 1997.

Dietze, Gabriele, 'Okzidentalismuskritik: Möglichkeiten und Grenzen einer Forschungsperspektivierung' [Critique of Orientalism: possibilities and limitations of a perspectivization of research], in Dietze et al. (eds.), *Kritik des Okzidentalismus. Transdisziplinäre Beiträge zu (Neo-)Orientalismus und Geschlecht*, Bielefeld: transcript, 2009, pp. 23–54.

Dietze, Gabriele, 'Sexueller Exzeptionalismus als Kulturalisierung von

Geschlecht und Sexualität' [Sexual exceptionalism as a culturalization of gender and sexuality], *Freiburger Zeitschrift für Geschlechterstudien*, vol. 23, issue 2 (2017): 21–36.

Dilly, Heinrich, *Kunstgeschichte als Institution: Studien zur Geschichte einer Disziplin* [Art history as an institution: studies on the history of a discipline], Frankfurt am Main: Suhrkamp, 1979.

Dinges, Martin, 'Der "feine Unterschied": Die soziale Funktion der Kleidung in der höfischen Gesellschaft' [The 'fine distinction': the social function of clothing in courtly society], *Zeitschrift für Historische Forschung*, vol. 19, no. 1 (1992): 49–76.

Duden, Barbara, 'Geschlecht, Biologie, Körpergeschichte: Bemerkungen zu neuer Literatur in der Körpergeschichte' [Gender, biology, body history: remarks on recent literature on body history], *Feministische Studien*, vol. 9, issue 2 (1991): 105–22.

Duerr, Hans-Peter, *Der Mythos vom Zivilisationsprozeß* [The myth of the civilization process], vol. III: *Obszönität und Gewalt* [Obscenity and violence], Frankfurt am Main: Suhrkamp, 1995.

Duerr, Hans-Peter, *Der Mythos vom Zivilisationsprozeß* [The myth of the civilization process], vol. IV: *Der erotische Leib* [The erotic body], Frankfurt am Main: Suhrkamp, 1997.

Duncan, Carol, 'Happy Mothers and Other New Ideas in French Art', *Art Bulletin*, vol. 55, no. 4 (December 1973): 570–83.

Düntzer, Emilie, and Martha Hellendall, 'Einwirkungen der Leibesübungen auf weibliche Konstitution, Geburt und Menstruation' [Effects of physical exercise on the female constitution, birth and menstruation], *Münchener medizinische Wochenschrift*, vol. 71, no. 44 (1929): 1835–8.

Dyer, Richard, *White*, London: Routledge, 1997.

Edmonds, Alexander, '"The Poor Have the Right to Be Beautiful": Cosmetic Surgery in Neoliberal Brazil', *Journal of the Royal Anthropological Institute*, vol. 13, no. 2 (June 2007): 363–81.

Ehlers, Nadine, '*Tekhnē* of Reconstruction: Breast Cancer, Norms, and Fleshy Rearrangements', *Social Semiotics*, vol. 22, no. 1 (February 2012): 121–41.

Eiblmayr, Silvia, *Die Frau als Bild: Der weibliche Körper in der Kunst des 20. Jahrhunderts* [Woman as image: the female body in twentieth-century art], Berlin: Reimer, 1993.

Eitler, Pascal, 'Die "sexuelle Revolution": Körperpolitik um "1968"' [The 'sexual revolution': body politics around '1968'], in Martin Klimke and Joachim

Scharloth (eds.), *1968: Handbuch zur Kultur- und Mediengeschichte der Studentenbewegung*, Stuttgart/Weimar: Metzler, 2007, pp. 235–46.

El Ouassil, Samira, and Friedemann Karig, *Erzählende Affen: Mythen, Lügen, Utopien: Wie Geschichten unser Leben bestimmen* [Monkeys telling stories: myths, lies, utopias. How stories determine our lives], Berlin: Ullstein, 2022.

Eller, Cynthia, *Gentlemen and Amazons: The Myth of Matriarchal Prehistory, 1861–1900*, Berkeley: University of California Press, 2011.

Emmert, Carl, *Lehrbuch der Chirurgie* [Textbook of surgery], part 3: *Lehrbuch der speciellen Chirurgie* [Textbook of specialist surgery], vol. II: *Chirurgische Krankheiten der Brust, des Bauches und Beckens* [Surgical diseases of the breast, abdomen and pelvis], Stuttgart: Rud. Dann, 1862.

Eßlinger, Eva, et al. (eds.), *Die Figur des Dritten: Ein kulturwissenschaftliches Paradigma* [The figure of the third: a cultural studies paradigm], Frankfurt am Main: Suhrkamp, 2010.

Ewers-Schultz, Ina, '"Das Wesentliche ist die individuelle Anpassung an die Trägerin". Anna Muthesius' Eigenkleid der Frau' ['The essential thing is the individual adaptation to the wearer': Anna Muthesius's 'woman's own' dress], in Ewers-Schultz and Magdalena Holzhey (eds.), *Auf Freiheit zugeschnitten: Das Künstlerkleid um 1900 in Mode, Kunst und Gesellschaft*, exhibition catalogue, Kunstmuseen Krefeld, Kaiser Wilhelm Museum, Munich: Hirmer, 2018, pp. 146–51.

Ewert, Felicia, *Trans. Frau. Sein. Aspekte geschlechtlicher Marginalisierung* [Trans. Woman. Being. Aspects of social marginalization], 3rd edn, Münster: edition assemblage, 2021.

Fahlenbrach, Kathrin, *Protest-Inszenierungen: Visuelle Kommunikation und kollektive Identitäten in Protestbewegungen* [Protest performances: visual communication and collective identities], Wiesbaden: Westdeutscher Verlag, 2002.

Fardo, Dean, et al., 'Breast Augmentation', *StatPearls*, 26 September 2022, pubmed.ncbi.nlm.nih.gov/29489168.

'Father's Milk', *Bio Science*, vol. 44, no. 6 (June 1994): 439.

Faust, Gretchen, 'Hair, Blood and the Nipple: *Instagram* Censorship and the Female Body', in Urte Undine Frömming et al. (eds.), *Digital Environments: Ethnographic Perspectives across Global Online and Offline Spaces*, Bielefeld: transcript, 2017, pp. 159–70.

Feher, Michel, with Ramona Naddaff and Nadia Tazi (eds.), *Fragments for a History of the Human Body*, vol. III, New York: Urzone Inc., 1989.

Fend, Mechthild, *Grenzen der Männlichkeit: Der Androgyn in der franzö-sischen Kunst und Kunsttheorie 1750–1830* [Limits of masculinity: the androgyne in French art and art theory 1750–1830], Berlin: Reimer, 2003.

Fildes, Valerie A., *Breasts, Bottles and Babies: A History of Infant Feeding*, Edinburgh University Press, 1986.

Fitts, Karen, 'The Pathology and Erotics of Breast Cancer', *Discourse*, vol. 21, no. 2 (spring 1999): 3–20.

Fleck, Ludwik, *Genesis and Development of a Scientific Fact*, trans. Frederick Bradley and Thaddeus J. Trenn, University of Chicago Press, 1979 [first published in German in 1935].

Fleckner, Uwe, Martin Warnke and Hendrik Ziegler (eds.), *Handbuch der politischen Ikonographie* [Handbook of political iconography], 2 vols., Munich: C. H. Beck, 2011.

Fletcher, Kanitra, 'No Body's Perfect', *NKA: Journal of Contemporary African Art*, vol. 2016, issues 38–39 (November 2016): 142–51, read.dukeupress .edu/nka/article-abstract/2016/38-39/142/2091/No-Body-s-Perfect.

Förschler, Silke, 'Ikonografie der kleinen Unterschiede: Chardins malender Affe und Menschenaffen in naturhistorischen Illustrationen' [Iconography of small differences: Chardin's drawing monkey and great apes in natural history illustrations], in Elisabeth Johanna Koehn et al. (eds.), *Andersheit um 1800: Figuren – Theorien – Darstellungsformen*, Munich: Brill/Fink, 2011, pp. 249–63.

Forschungsstelle Politische Ikonographie (ed.), *Bildindex zur politischen Ikonographie* [Visual index of political iconography], Hamburg, 1996.

Franklin, John, *Narrative of a Journey to the Shores of the Polar Sea in the Years 1819, 20, 21 and 22*, London: John Murray, 1823.

Freeman, Andrea, *Skimmed: Breastfeeding, Race, and Injustice*, Stanford University Press, 2020.

Frietsch, Elke, 'Kulturalisierung und Geschlecht' [Culturalization and gender], *Freiburger Zeitschrift für Geschlechterstudien*, vol. 23, no. 2 (2017): 5–18.

Fuchsberger, Doris, *Nacht der Amazonen: Eine Münchner Festreihe zwischen NS-Propaganda und Tourismusattraktion* [Night of the Amazons: a Munich celebration between Nazi propaganda and tourist attraction], Munich: Allitera, 2017.

Gersuny, Robert, 'Über einige kosmetische Operationen' [About some cosmetic operations], *Wiener medizinische Wochenschrift*, vol. 53, no. 48 (28 November 1903), columns 2253–7.

Gilman, Sander L., 'The Figure of the Black in the Thought of Hegel and Nietzsche', *German Quarterly*, vol. 53, no. 2 (March 1980): 141–58.

Gilman, Sander L., *Making the Body Beautiful: A Cultural History of Aesthetic Surgery*, Princeton University Press, 1999.

Gruber, Wenzel, *Über die männliche Brustdrüse und über die Gynaecomastie* [On the male mammary gland and gynaecomasty], St Petersburg, 1866.

Grubitzsch, Helga, 'Mit Piken, Säbeln und Pistolen … "Amazonen" der Französischen Revolution' [With pikes, sabres and pistols … 'Amazons' of the French Revolution], in Historisches Museum der Pfalz Speyer (ed.), *Amazonen: Geheimnisvolle Kriegerinnen*, exhibition catalogue, Munich: Edition Minerva, 2010, pp. 242–9.

Gsell, Monika, *Die Bedeutung der Baubo: Kulturgeschichtliche Studien zur Repräsentation des weiblichen Genitales* [The meaning of the Baubo: studies in cultural history on the representation of the female genitals], Frankfurt am Main: Stroemfeld/Nexus, 2001.

'Gutachten von Ärzten über das Miedertragen' [Expert opinions by doctors about the wearing of corsets], *Frauen-Rundschau*, vol. 6, issue 23 (1 March 1902): 667–75.

Guth, Doris, 'Das Bildnis *Gabrielle d'Estrées und ihre Schwester*' [The portrait *Gabrielle d'Estrées and her sister*], in Doris Guth and Elisabeth Priedl (eds.), *Bilder der Liebe: Liebe, Begehren und Geschlechterverhältnisse in der Kunst der Frühen Neuzeit*, Bielefeld: transcript, 2012, pp. 301–32.

Gutsmuths, J. C. F., *Gymnastik für die Jugend, enthaltend eine praktische Anweisung zu Leibesübungen: Ein Beytrag zur nöthigsten Verbesserung der körperlichen Erziehung* [Gymnastics for youth, containing practical instructions on physical exercises: a contribution to the very necessary improvement of physical education], Schnepfenthal: Buchhandel der Erziehungsanstalt, 1793.

Haarer, Johanna, *Die deutsche Mutter und ihr erstes Kind* [The German mother and her first child], Munich/Berlin: Lehmann, 1941.

Hammer-Tugendhat, Daniela, 'Venus und Luxuria: Zum Verhältnis von Kunst und Ideologie im Hochmittelalter' [Venus and Luxuria: on the relationship between art and ideology in the high Middle Ages], in Ilsebill Barta et al. (eds.), *Frauen, Bilder, Männer, Mythen: Kunsthistorische Beiträge*, Berlin: Reimer, 1987, pp. 13–34.

Hammer-Tugendhat, Daniela, 'Jan van Eyck: Autonomisierung des Aktbildes und Geschlechterdifferenz' [Jan van Eyck: autonomization of the nude and gender difference], in Anja Zimmermann (ed.), *Kunstgeschichte und Gender: Eine Einführung*, Berlin: Reimer, 2006, pp. 73–97.

Hark, Sabine, and Paula-Irene Villa, *Unterscheiden und herrschen: Ein Essay zu den ambivalenten Verflechtungen von Rassismus, Sexismus und Feminismus in der Gegenwart* [Differentiate and rule: an essay on the ambivalent interconnections between racism, sexism and feminism in the present], Bielefeld: transcript, 2017.

Härtel, Maren C., et al. (eds.), *Kleider in Bewegung: Frauenmode seit 1850* [Clothes in motion: women's fashion since 1850], catalogue, Historisches Museum Frankfurt am Main, Petersberg: Michael Imhof, 2020.

Hartlaub, Gustav Friedrich, *Lucas Cranach d. Ä.: Der Jungbrunnen, 1549* [Lucas Cranach the Elder: the Fountain of Youth, 1549], Der Kunstbrief 4, Berlin: Mann, 1943.

Haug, Henrike, 'Zur Un/Möglichkeit des Gelehrtinnenbildes' [On the im/possibility of the image of a female scholar], *kritische berichte*, vol. 49, issue 4 (2021; *Die Kunsthistorikerin? Bilder und Images*, ed. Brigitte Sölch et al.): 37–49.

Hauke, Alexandra, 'Body Positivity', in Anja Herrmann et al. (eds.), *Fat Studies: Ein Glossar*, Bielefeld: transcript, 2022, pp. 71–4.

Hausbichler, Beate, *Der verkaufte Feminismus: Wie aus einer politischen Bewegung ein profitables Label wurde* [Sell-out feminism: how a political movement turned into a profitable label], Salzburg/Vienna: Residenz, 2021.

Heckemeyer, Karolin, *Leistungsklassen und Geschlechtertests: Die heteronormative Logik des Sports* [Performance classes and sex testing: the heteronormative logic of sport], Bielefeld: transcript, 2018.

Hederich, Benjamin, *Gründliches mythologisches Lexikon* [In-depth dictionary of mythology], reprint of the expanded edition of 1770, Darmstadt: Wissenschaftliche Buchgesellschaft, 1967.

Hegel, G. W. F., *Lectures on the Philosophy of History*, trans. Ruben Alvarado, Aalten: Wordbridge Publishing, 2011.

Heinz, Kathrin, 'Der Drachenkämpfer Wassily Kandinsky: Über Helden und ihre Verbindungen' [The dragon-fighter Wassily Kandinsky: on heroes and their connections], *Frauen, Kunst, Wissenschaft*, issue 41 (2006): 35–50.

Heinze, Anna, 'Die Amazonen – Zur Flexibilität eines Mythos' [The Amazons: on the flexibility of a myth], in Michail Chatzidakis et al. (eds.), *Con bella maniera: Festgabe für Peter Seiler zum 65. Geburtstag*, Heidelberg: arthistoricum.net, 2021, pp. 253–66.

Herber, Anne-Kathrin, *Frauen an deutschen Kunstakademien im 20. Jahrhundert* [Women at German art academies in the twentieth century], University of Heidelberg, unpublished dissertation, 2009, archiv .ub.uni-heidelberg.de/volltextserver/11048.

Hermand, Jost, 'Alle Macht den Frauen: Faschistische Matriarchatskonzepte' [All power to the women: fascist concepts of matriarchy], *Das Argument*, 146 (1984): 539–54.

Herrmann, Anja, and Kea Wienand (eds.), *FKW: Zeitschrift für Geschlechterforschung und visuelle Kultur* [FKW: journal for gender studies and visual culture], no. 62 (August 2017; *Visual Fat Studies*), www .fkw-journal.de/index.php/fkw/issue/view/74.

Herzog, Dagmar, '"Orgasmen wie Chinaböller": Sexualität zwischen Politik und Kommerz' ['Orgasms like firecrackers': sexuality between politics and commerce], in Andreas Schwab et al. (eds.), *Die 68er: Kurzer Sommer – lange Wirkung*, exhibition catalogue, Historisches Museum, Frankfurt am Main, Essen: Klartext, 2008, pp. 76–85.

Hiltmann, Heiko, 'Von nackten Brüsten und blanken Schwertern: Offensive Formen der weiblichen Brustentblößung am Beispiel der "Eiríks saga rauða", K11' [On bare breasts and naked swords: aggressive forms of female breast-baring using the example of *Eiríks saga rauða*, K11], in Stefan Bießenecker (ed.), *'Und sie erkannten, dass sie nackt waren': Nacktheit im Mittelalter*, University of Bamberg Press, 2008, pp. 413–36.

Hinz, Berthold, 'Knidia, oder: Des Aktes erster Akt' [Knidia, or: the nude's first act], *kritische berichte*, vol. 17, no. 3 (1989): 49–77.

Hinz, Berthold, *Aphrodite: Geschichte einer abendländischen Passion* [Aphrodite: history of a Western passion], Munich: Hanser, 1998.

Hirschauer, Stefan, *Die soziale Konstruktion der Transsexualität – Über die Medizin und den Geschlechtswechsel* [The social construction of trans-sexuality: On medicine and gender reassignment], Frankfurt am Main: Suhrkamp, 1993.

Hoenes, Josch, *Nicht Frosch – nicht Laborratte: Transmännlichkeiten im Bild. Eine kunst- und kulturwissenschaftliche Analyse visueller Politiken* [Not frog – not lab rat: trans masculinities in the picture. An analysis of visual politics from the perspective of art studies and cultural studies], Bielefeld: transcript, 2014.

Hoenes, Josch, and Utan Schirmer, 'Transgender/Transsexualität: Forschungsperspektiven und Herausforderungen' [Transgender/

transsexuality: research perspectives and challenges], in Beate Kortendieck et al. (eds.), *Handbuch interdisziplinäre Geschlechterforschung*, Wiesbaden: Springer VS, 2019, pp. 1203–12, doi.org/10.1007/978-3-658-12496-0_77.

Hofmann, Viola, *Das Kostüm der Macht: Das Erscheinungsbild von Politikern und Politikerinnen von 1949 bis 2013 im Magazin 'Der Spiegel'* [The costume of power: the appearance of male and female politicians from 1949 to 2013 in the magazine *Der Spiegel*], Berlin: edition ebersbach, 2014.

Honegger, Claudia, *Die Ordnung der Geschlechter: Die Wissenschaften vom Menschen und das Weib, 1750–1850* [The order of the sexes: the human sciences and women, 1750–1850], Munich: Deutscher Taschenbuch Verlag, 1996.

hooks, bell, 'Eating the Other: Desire and Resistance', in hooks, *Black Looks: Race and Representation*, Boston, MA: South End Press, 1992, pp. 21–39.

Horncastle, Mona, *Josephine Baker: Weltstar, Freiheitskämpferin, Ikone: Die Biografie* [Josephine Baker: global star, freedom fighter, icon. The biography], Vienna/Graz: Molden, 2020.

Humboldt, Alexander von, and Aimé Bonpland, *Reise in die Aequinoctial-Gegenden des neuen Continents in den Jahren 1799, 1800, 1801, 1802, 1803 und 1804* [Journey into the equinoctial regions of the new continent in the years 1799, 1800, 1801, 1802, 1803 and 1804], part 2, Stuttgart/Tübingen: Cotta, 1818.

Humboldt, Alexander von, and Aimé Bonpland, *Personal Narrative of Travels to the Equinoctial Regions of America During the Years 1799–1804*, trans. Thomasina Ross, London: George Bell & Sons, 1907 [1852]. The Project Gutenberg eBook, www.gutenberg.org/cache/epub/6322/pg6322-images .html.

Hunt, Lynn, *The Family Romance of the French Revolution*, Berkeley / Los Angeles: University of California Press, 1992.

Hunter, John, 'Account of an Extraordinary Pheasant', *Philosophical Transactions of the Royal Society of London*, vol. 70 (1780): 527–35.

Hurttig, Marcus Andrew, in collaboration with Thomas Ketelsen, *Die entfesselte Antike: Aby Warburg und die Geburt der Pathosformel* [Antiquity unleashed: Aby Warburg and the birth of the pathos formula], exhibition catalogue, Cologne: Verlag der Buchhandlung Walther König, 2012.

Hyrtl, Joseph, *Handbuch der topographischen Anatomie und ihrer praktisch medizinisch-chirurgischen Anwendungen* [Handbook of topographical anatomy and its practical medical–surgical applications], vol. I: *Enthält die topographische Anatomie des Kopfes, des Halses, der Brust und des Unterleibes* [Contains the topographical anatomy of the head, the neck, the chest and the abdomen), Vienna: Wallishausser, 1847.

Irigaray, Luce, *Speculum of the Other Woman*, trans. Gillian C. Gill, Ithaca, NY: Cornell University Press, 1985.

Jahn, Andrea (ed.), *In the Cut: Der männliche Körper in der feministischen Kunst* [In the cut: the male body in feminist art], exhibition catalogue, Stadtgalerie Saarbrücken, Bielefeld/Berlin: Kerber Verlag, 2019.

Jalilipour, Katayoun, 'Saint Agatha as a Boy: Katayoun Jalilipour in Conversation with D Mortimer', *Texte zur Kunst*, 17 May 2023, www.textezurkunst.de/de /articles/katayoun-jalilipour-d-mortimer-saint-agatha-as-a-boy.

Jarrett, Lucinda, *Stripping in Time: A History of Erotic Dancing*, London: Pandora, 1997.

Johnston, Mark Albert, 'Bearded Women in Early Modern England', *Studies in English Literature, 1500–1900*, vol. 47, no. 1 (December 2007): 1–28.

Jones, Meredith, 'Makeover Culture's Dark Side: Breasts, Death and Lolo Ferrari', *Body & Society*, vol. 14, no. 1 (2008): 89–104, doi.org/10.1177 /1357034X07087532.

Jooss, Birgit, 'Die Stucksche Amazone – Eine "wehrhafte bronzene Jungfrau in kühner Pose"' [The Stuck Amazon – a 'warlike bronze maiden in a bold pose'], in Jo-Anne Birnie Danzker (ed.), *Villa Stuck*, Ostfildern: Hatje Cantz, 2006, pp. 273–83.

Junker, Almut, and Eva Stille, *Zur Geschichte der Unterwäsche 1700–1960* [On the history of underwear 1700–1960], exhibition catalogue, Frankfurt am Main: Historisches Museum Frankfurt, 1988.

Juvernay, Pierre, *Discours particulier contre les femmes desbraillées de ce temps* [Special discourse against the slovenly women of this time], Paris, 1637, gallica.bnf.fr/ark:/12148/bpt6k1511780d/f7.item.

Kampmann, Sabine, *Bilder des Alterns: Greise Körper in Kunst und visueller Kultur* [Images of ageing: aged bodies in art and visual culture], Berlin: Reimer, 2020.

Kania, Katrin, *Kleidung im Mittelalter: Materialien – Konstruktion – Nähtechnik: Ein Handbuch* [Clothing in the Middle Ages: materials – construction – sewing technique. A handbook], Cologne/Weimar/Vienna: Böhlau, 2010.

Kantorowicz, Ernst H., *The King's Two Bodies: A Study in Mediaeval Political Theology*, Princeton University Press, 1957.

Karentzos, Alexandra, *Kunstgöttinnen: Mythische Weiblichkeit zwischen Historismus und Secessionen* [Art goddesses: mythical femininity between historicism and secessions], Marburg: Jonas-Verlag, 2005.

Kätzel, Ute, *Die 68erinnen: Porträt einer rebellischen Frauengeneration*, Berlin: Rowohlt, 2002, pp. 201–19.

Kaufmann, Jean-Claude, *Corps de femmes, regards d'hommes: Sociologie des seins nus* [Women's bodies, men's gazes: the sociology of naked breasts], Paris: Éditions Nathan, 1995.

Kelly, Joan, 'Early Feminist Theory and the "Querelle des Femmes", 1400–1789', *Signs*, vol. 8, no. 1 (autumn 1982): 4–28.

Klauke, Anna, '#Bodypositivity', *FKW: Zeitschrift für Geschlechterforschung und visuelle Kultur*, no. 70 (February 2022): 50f., doi.org/10.57871/fkw7020221586.

Klees, Johann Georg, *Über die weiblichen Brüste* [On the female breasts], 3rd edn, Frankfurt am Main: Andreäische Buchhandlung, 1806.

Klencke, Hermann, *Die Mutter als Erzieherin ihrer Töchter und Söhne zur physischen und sittlichen Gesundheit vom ersten Kindesalter bis zur Reife* [The mother as the educator of her daughters and sons to physical and moral health from earliest childhood to maturity], Leipzig: Kummer, 1870.

Klinger, Cornelia, 'Beredtes Schweigen und verschwiegenes Sprechen: Genus im Diskurs der Philosophie' [Eloquent silence and reticent speaking: gender in the discourse of philosophy], in Hadumod Bußmann and Renate Hof (eds.), *Genus: Zur Geschlechterdifferenz in den Kulturwissenschaften*, Stuttgart: Kröner, 1995, pp. 34–59.

Kobelt-Groch, Marion, *Judith macht Geschichte: Zur Rezeption einer mythischen Gestalt vom 16. bis 19. Jahrhundert* [Judith makes history: on the reception of a mythical figure from the sixteenth to the nineteenth century], Paderborn/Munich: Fink, 2005.

Kohl, Richard, *Das Melusinenmotiv: Eine symbolgeschichtliche Studie zur Sirenen-, Erd- und Sündendarstellung* [The motif of Melusine: a study in the history of symbols on the representation of sirens, earth and sin], Bremen: Winter, 1934.

Kohout, Annekathrin, *Netzfeminismus: Strategien weiblicher Bildpolitik* [Online feminism: strategies of female image politics], Berlin: Klaus Wagenbach, 2019.

Koos, Marianne, 'Sur/face: Manet malt Mlle E. G.' [Sur/face: Manet paints Mlle E. G.], *Zeitschrift für Kunstgeschichte*, vol. 78, issue 2 (2015): 239–76.

Krammer, Hanns, *Das entblösste Frauen-Zimmer: Die Geschichte des*

Dekolletés [The bared broad / the uncovered woman: the history of the décolleté], Gütersloh: Signum Verlag, 1963.

Krass, Urte, 'Politische Ikonographie' [Political iconography], in Ulrich Pfisterer, ed., *Metzler Lexikon Kunstwissenschaft* [Metzler dictionary of art science], Heidelberg: Metzler Verlag, 2019, pp. 345–6.

Krauss, Friedrich Salomo, *Die Anmut des Frauenleibes* [The grace of the female body], Leipzig: A. Schumann's Verlag, 1904.

Kreydatus, Beth, 'Contesting Miss America: The Boardwalk Protests of 1968', *Pennsylvania Legacies*, vol. 18, no. 2 (Autumn 2018): 20–5.

Krieg, 'Ein Fall von Gynäkomastie' [A case of gynaecomasty], *Medicinisches Correspondenz-Blatt des Württembergischen Ärztlichen Vereins*, vol. 47, no. 10 (18 March 1877): 75.

Kris, Ernst, and Otto Kurz, *Die Legende vom Künstler: Ein geschichtlicher Versuch* [The legend of the artist: a historical experiment], Frankfurt am Main: Suhrkamp, 1995 [first published 1934].

Kubitza, Anette, 'Hannah Wilke: Bilder vollständiger und unvollständiger Schönheit' [Hanna Willke: images of complete and incomplete beauty], *Frauen, Kunst, Wissenschaft*, issue 17 (1994): 72–84.

Kunzle, David, *Fashion and Fetishism: A Social History of the Corset, Tight-Lacing and Other Forms of Body Sculpture*, Totowa, NJ: Rowman and Littlefield, 1982.

Kurella, Hans, *Naturgeschichte des Verbrechers. Grundzüge der criminellen Anthropologie* [Natural history of the criminal: fundamentals of criminal anthropology], Stuttgart: Ferdinand Enke, 1893.

Lange, Klaus, 'Geistliche Speise: Untersuchungen zur Metaphorik der Bibelhermeneutik' [Spiritual food: studies on the imagery of Bible hermeneutics], *Zeitschrift für deutsches Altertum und deutsche Literatur*, vol. 95, issue 2 (May 1966): 81–122.

Laqueur, Thomas, *Making Sex: Body and Gender from the Greeks to Freud*, Cambridge, MA: Harvard University Press, 1990.

Leonardi, Nicholas R., et al., 'Illicit Cosmetic Silicone Injection: A Recent Reiteration of History', *Annals of Plastic Surgery*, vol. 77, no. 4 (October 2016): 485–90.

Lessing, Gotthold Ephraim, *Laocoon: An Essay upon the Limits of Painting and Poetry, with Remarks Illustrative of Various Points in the History of Ancient Art*, trans. Ellen Frothingham. Boston: Robert Brothers, 1890, www.gutenberg.org/cache/epub/73078/pg73078-images.html.

Lifshitz, Felice, 'The Persistence of Late Antiquity: Christ as Man and Woman in an Eighth-Century Miniature', *Medieval Feminist Forum*, vol. 38, no. 1 (2004): 18–27.

Liharžik, Franz, *Inaugural-Dissertation über die natürliche und künstliche Ernährung der Kinder* [Inaugural dissertation on the natural and artificial feeding of children], Vienna, 1839.

Limper, Verena, *Flaschenkinder: Säuglingsernährung und Familienbeziehungen in Deutschland und Schweden im 20. Jahrhundert* [Bottle babies: infant nutrition and family relationships in Germany and Sweden in the twentieth century], Vienna/Cologne/Weimar: Böhlau, 2021.

Lindner, Ines, 'Die rasenden Mänaden: Zur Mythologie weiblicher Unterwerfungsmacht' [The frenzied maenads: on the mythology of the female power of subjugation], in Ilsebill Barta et al. (eds.), *Frauen, Bilder, Männer, Mythen: Kunsthistorische Beiträge*, Berlin: Reimer, 1987, pp. 282–303.

Linke, Angelika, 'Unordentlich, langhaarig und mit der Matratze auf dem Boden: Zur Protestsemiotik von Körper und Raum in den 1968er Jahren' [Untidy, long-haired and with the mattress on the floor: on the protest semiotics of body and space in 1968 and the years that followed], in Heidrun Kämper et al. (eds.), *1968: Eine sprachwissenschaftliche Zwischenbilanz*, Berlin / Boston, MA: De Gruyter, 2012, pp. 201–26.

Lorde, Audre, *The Cancer Journals*, Argyle, NY: Spinsters Ink, 1980.

Lorenz, Maren, *Leibhaftige Vergangenheit: Einführung in die Körpergeschichte* [Bodily past: introduction to body history], Tübingen: Edition discord, 2000.

Lösch, Günter Maria, *Plastische Chirurgie: Ästhetik – Ethik – Geschichte: Kulturgeschichte eines medizinischen Fachgebiets* [Plastic surgery: aesthetics – ethics – history. Cultural history of a field of medicine], Berlin/Heidelberg: Springer, 2014.

Louis, Chantal, 'Das Verschwinden der Frauen', in Alice Schwarzer and Chantal Louis (eds.), *Transsexualität: Was ist eine Frau? Was ist ein Mann? Eine Streitschrift* [Transsexuality: What is a woman? What is a man? A polemic], Cologne: Kiepenheuer & Witsch, 2022, pp. 45–61.

Lünenborg, Margreth, et al., '"Merkels Dekolleté" als Mediendiskurs: Eine Bild-, Text- und Rezeptionsanalyse zur Vergeschlechtlichung einer Kanzlerin' ['Merkel's décolleté' as a media discourse: an analysis of images, tests and reception on the gendering of a chancellor], in Lünenborg (ed.),

Politik auf dem Boulevard? Die Neuordnung der Geschlechter in der Politik der Mediengesellschaft, Bielefeld: transcript, 2009, pp. 73–102.

MacDonald, Trevor, et al., 'Transmasculine Individuals' Experiences with Lactation, Chestfeeding, and Gender Identity: A Qualitative Study', *BMC Pregnancy and Childbirth*, vol. 16, no. 106 (2016), www.researchgate .net/publication/303291109_Transmasculine_individuals%27_experiences _with_lactation_chestfeeding_and_gender_identity_A_qualitative_study.

Maltz-Leca, Leora, 'Spectres of the Original and the Liberties of Repetition', *African Arts*, vol. 46, no. 4 (winter 2013): 32–45.

McDermott, LeRoy, 'Self-Representation in Upper Paleolithic Female Figurines', *Current Anthropology*, vol. 37, no. 2 (April 1996): 227–75.

Meskimmon, Marsha, 'The Monstrous and the Grotesque', *MAKE: The Magazine of Women's Art*, no. 72 (1996): 6–12.

Meyer, Richard, 'Harte Ziele: Feministische Kunst, männliche Akte und die Macht der Zensur in den 1970er Jahren' [Hard targets: feminist art, male nudes and the power of censorship in the 1970s], in Andrea Jahn (ed.), *In the Cut: der männliche Körper in der feministischen Kunst*, exhibition catalogue, Stadtgalerie Saarbrücken, Bielefeld/Berlin: Kerber, 2019, pp. 104–26.

Milam, Jennifer, 'Rococo Representations of Interspecies Sensuality and the Pursuit of "Volupté"', *Art Bulletin*, vol. 97, no. 2 (June 2015): 192–209.

Miles, Margaret R., 'The Virgin's One Bare Breast: Female Nudity and Religious Meaning in Tuscan Early Renaissance Culture', in Susan Rubin Suleiman (ed.), *The Female Body in Western Culture*, Cambridge, MA: Harvard University Press, 1986, pp. 193–208.

Miles, Margaret R., *A Complex Delight: The Secularization of the Breast, 1350–1750*, Berkeley: University of California Press, 2008.

Moral, Şükran, *B[r]yzanz*, exhibition catalogue, Edith Russ-Haus für Medienkunst, Oldenburg: Edith-Russ-Haus für Medienkunst, 2014.

Mulvey, Laura, 'Visual Pleasure and Narrative Cinema', *Screen*, vol. 16, issue 3 (autumn 1975): 6–18.

Nead, Lynda, *The Female Nude: Art, Obscenity, and Sexuality*, London / New York: Routledge, 1992.

Neugebauer, Franz Ludwig von, *Hermaphroditismus beim Menschen* [Hermaphroditism in humans], Leipzig: Klinkhardt, 1908.

Nochlin, Linda, 'The Imaginary Orient', in Nochlin, *The Politics of Vision: Essays on Nineteenth-Century Art and Society*, New York: Harper & Row, 1989, pp. 33–59.

Nochlin, Linda, *Why Have There Been No Great Women Artists?* 50th anniversary edition, London: Thames & Hudson, 2021.

Nowell, April, and Melanie L. Chang, 'Science, the Media, and Interpretations of Upper Paleolithic Figurines', *American Anthropologist*, vol. 116, no. 3 (September 2014): 562–77.

Ober, Patricia, *Der Frauen neue Kleider: Das Reformkleid und die Konstruktion des modernen Frauenkörpers* [The women's new clothes: the reform dress and the construction of the modern female body], Berlin: Schiler, 2005.

O'Keefe, Theresa, 'my body is my manifesto! SlutWalk, FEMEN and Femmenist Protest', *Feminist Review*, no. 107 (2014): 1–19.

Orland, Barbara, 'Why Could Early Modern Men Lactate? Gender Identity and Metabolic Narrations in Humoral Medicine', in Jutta Gisela Sperling (ed.), *Medieval and Renaissance Lactations*, Farnham/Burlington: Ashgate, 2013, pp. 37–54.

Osthus, Holger, *Herzenswunsch Brustvergrößerung: Der Ratgeber für Ihre Entscheidung* [Heart's desire: breast augmentation. The guidebook for your decision], Berlin: Springer, 2022.

Papenbrock, Martin, 'Happening, Fluxus, Performance: Aktionskünste in den 1960er Jahren' [Happening, Fluxus, performance: action arts in the 1960s], in Martin Klimke and Joachim Scharloth (eds.), *1968: Handbuch zur Kultur- und Mediengeschichte der Studentenbewegung*, Stuttgart/Weimar: Metzler, 2007, pp. 137–49.

Pearce, Ruth, et al., 'TERF Wars: An Introduction', *Sociological Review*, vol. 68, no. 4 (July 2020; TERF Wars: Feminism and the Fight for Transgender Futures), doi.org/10.1177/0038026120934713.

Peters, Lisa Marie, 'Brust raus!' [Chest out!], *Die Zeit*, no. 17, 2 April 2021, p. 65.

Peterson, Pia, 'The Times Magazine Cover That Beamed a Light on a Movement', *New York Times*, 15 August 2018, www.nytimes.com/2018/08/15/insider/breast-cancer-mastectomy-photo.html.

Pfisterer, Ulrich, '"Die Bilderwissenschaft ist mühelos": Topos, Typus und Pathosformel als methodische Herausforderung der Kunstgeschichte' ['The science of images is effortless': topos, type and pathos formula as methodological challenge of art history], in Pfisterer and Max Seidel, *Visuelle Topoi: Erfindung und tradiertes Wissen in den Künsten der italienischen Renaissance*, Munich/Berlin: Deutscher Kunstverlag, 2003, pp. 21–47.

Pfisterer, Ulrich, *Kunst-Geburten: Kreativität, Erotik, Körper in der Frühen*

Neuzeit [Art(ificial) births: creativity, eroticism, bodies in the early modern era], Berlin: Wagenbach, 2014.

Pliny the Elder, *Natural History, Volume II: Books 3–7*, trans. H. Rackham, Loeb Classical Library 352, Cambridge, MA: Harvard University Press, 1942, www.attalus.org/translate/pliny_hn7a.html.

Preußer, Heinz-Peter, 'Der Mythos der Amazonen: Eine männliche Konstruktion und ihre feministischen Fehldeutungen' [The myth of the Amazons: a male construction and its feminist misinterpretations], in Udo Franke-Penski and Preußer (eds)., *Amazonen – Kriegerische Frauen*, Würzburg: Königshausen & Neumann, 2010, pp. 35–48.

Projektgruppe Sexualität und Politik, *Sexpol-Info* 3 [vol. 2, no. 3, January 1973], in Carsten Seibold (ed.), *Die 68er: Das Fest der Rebellion*, Munich: Droemer Knaur, 1988, pp. 98–101.

Quinlan, Sean M., 'Physical and Moral Regeneration after the Terror: Medical Culture, Sensibility and Family Politics in France, 1794–1804', *Social History*, vol. 29, no. 2 (May 2004): 139–64.

Rang, Brita, 'Sind Matriarchatskonzepte faschistisch? Zu Jost Hermand' [Are concepts of matriarchy fascist? On Jost Hermand], *Das Argument*, 146 (1984): 555–8.

Rentmeister, Cillie, 'Frauenwelten – fern, vergangen, fremd? Die Matriarchatsdebatte und die Neue Frauenbewegung' [Women's worlds – remote, past, foreign? The matriarchy debate and the New Women's Movement], in Ina-Maria Greverus (ed.), *Kulturkontakt – Kulturkonflikt: Zur Erfahrung des Fremden, Beiträge zum 26. Deutschen Volkskundekongreß 1987*, part 2, Frankfurt am Main: Institut für Kulturanthropologie und europäische Ethnologie, 1988, pp. 443–60, www.cillie-rentmeister.de /download/frauenwelten_fern443-460.pdf.

Richter-Wittenfeld, Daniela, *Die Arbeit des Verbandes für Deutsche Frauenkleidung und Frauenkultur auf dem Gebiet der Frauenkleidung von 1896 bis 1935* [The work of the Association for German Women's Clothing and Women's Culture in the area of women's clothing from 1896 to 1935], Hamburg: Kovač, 2006.

Ritter, Sabine, *Facetten der Sarah Baartman: Repräsentationen und Rekonstruktionen der 'Hottentottenvenus'* [Facets of Sarah Baartman: representations and reconstructions of the 'Hottentot Venus'], Münster: Lit, 2010.

Rohlmann, Michael, 'Delacroix' *Liberté*: Die Erlösung der Bilder' [Delacroix's

Liberty: the salvation of images], *WallrafRichartz-Jahrbuch*, vol. 70 (2009): 223–44.

Roig, Emilia, *Why We Matter: Das Ende der Unterdrückung* [Why we matter: the end of oppression], Berlin: Aufbau, 2021.

Rosenfeld, Alan, '"Anarchist Amazons": The Gendering of Radicalism in 1970s West Germany', *Contemporary European History*, vol. 19, no. 4 (November 2010): 351–74.

Rosenkranz, Karl, *Aesthetics of Ugliness*, trans. Andrei Popp and Mechtild Widrich, New York: Bloomsbury, 2015 [first published in German in 1853].

Rousseau, *Emile or On Education*, trans. Allan Bloom, New York: Basic Books, 1979.

Rublack, Ulinka, *Die Geburt der Mode: Eine Kulturgeschichte der Renaissance* [The birth of fashion: a cultural history of the Renaissance], Stuttgart: Klett-Cotta, 2022.

Ruetz, Michael, *1968: Ein Zeitalter wird besichtigt* [1968: surveying an era], Frankfurt am Main: Zweitausendeins, 1997.

Rulffes, Evke, 'Geschnürte Körper: Vom Korsett und der Schwierigkeit, es nicht mehr zu tragen' [Laced bodies: on the corset and the difficulty of not wearing it any more], in Jasmin Mersmann and Evke Rulffes (eds.), *unBinding Bodies: Zur Geschichte des Füßebindens in China*, Bielefeld: transcript, 2023, pp. 218–33.

Russo, Mary, *The Female Grotesque: Risk, Excess, and Modernity*, New York / London: Routledge, 1995.

Said, Edward, *Orientalism*, New York: Pantheon Books, 1978.

Sanyal, Mithu, *Vulva: Die Enthüllung des unsichtbaren Geschlechts* [Vulva: the unveiling of the invisible sex], Berlin: Wagenbach 2020 [first published 2009].

Schade, Sigrid, 'Charcot und das Schauspiel des hysterischen Körpers: Die "Pathosformel" als ästhetische Inszenierung des psychiatrischen Diskurses – Ein blinder Fleck in der Warburg-Rezeption' [Charcot and the spectacle of the hysterical body: the 'pathos formula' as an aesthetic staging of the psychiatric discourse. A blind spot in the reception of Warburg], in Silvia Baumgart et al. (eds.), *Denkräume zwischen Kunst und Wissenschaft*, Berlin: Reimer, 1993, pp. 461–84.

Schade, Sigrid (ed.), *Allegorien und Geschlechterdifferenz* [Allegories and gender difference], Cologne/Weimar/Vienna: Böhlau, 1994.

Schade, Sigrid, 'Körper und Körpertheorien in der Kunstgeschichte' [Bodies and theories of the body in art history], in Anja Zimmermann (ed.), *Kunstgeschichte und Gender: Eine Einführung*, Berlin: Reimer, 2006, pp. 61–72.

Schade, Sigrid, and Silke Wenk, 'Inszenierungen des Sehens: Kunst, Geschichte und Geschlechterdifferenz' [Performances of seeing: art, history and gender difference], in Hadumod Bußmann and Renate Hof (eds.), *Genus: Zur Geschlechterdifferenz in den Kulturwissenschaften*, Stuttgart: Kröner, 1995, pp. 340–407.

Schäfer, Wilhelm, 'Das Eigenkleid der Frau: Vortrag der Frau Muthesius in der Handelskammer zu Krefeld' [Woman's own dress: lecture by Frau Muthesius in the chamber of commerce in Krefeld], *Die Rheinlande: Vierteljahrsschrift des Verbandes der Kunstfreunde in den Ländern am Rhein*, vol. 5, issue 4/5 (1902/3): 193f.

Schaffer, Johanna, *Ambivalenzen der Sichtbarkeit: Über die visuellen Strukturen der Anerkennung* [Ambivalences of visibility: on the visual structures of recognition], Bielefeld: transcript, 2008.

Scheifele, Sigrid, *Projektionen des Weiblichen: Lebensentwürfe in Kleists Penthesilea* [Projections of the feminine: models of life in Kleist's *Penthesilea*], Würzburg: Königshausen & Neumann, 1992.

Scheller, Jörg, *Body-Bilder, Körperkultur, Digitalisierung und Soziale Netzwerke* [Body images, body culture, digitalization and social networks], Berlin: Wagenbach, 2021.

Schiebinger, Londa, *Nature's Body: Gender in the Making of Modern Science*, Boston, MA: Beacon Press, 1993.

Schmidt-Linsenhoff, Viktoria, *Ästhetik der Differenz: Postkoloniale Perspektiven vom 16. bis 21. Jahrhundert* [Aesthetics of difference: postcolonial perspectives from the sixteenth to the twenty-first century], 2 vols., Marburg: Jonas, 2010.

Schmincke, Imke, 'Body Politic – Biopolitik – Körperpolitik: Eine begriffsgeschichtliche Rekonstruktion der Body Politics' [Body politic – biopolitics – body politics: a reconstruction of body politics in terms of conceptual history], *Body Politics*, vol. 7, issue 11 (2019): 15–40.

Schneede, Uwe M., *Die Kunst des Surrealismus: Malerei, Skulptur, Dichtung, Fotografie, Film* [The art of surrealism: painting, sculpture, poetry, photography, film], Munich: Beck, 2006.

Schneider, Lambert, and Martina Seifert, *Sphinx, Amazone, Mänade: Bedrohliche Frauenbilder im antiken Mythos* [Sphinx, Amazon, maenad:

threatening images of women in ancient myths], special issue of *Archäologie in Deutschland*, Stuttgart: Theiss, 2010.

Schor, Gabriele (ed.), *Feministische Avantgarde: Kunst der 1970er Jahre* [Feminist avant-garde: art of the 1970s], exhibition catalogue, Sammlung Verbund, Vienna / Munich / London / New York: Prestel, 2015.

Schultze-Naumburg, Paul, *Die Kultur des weiblichen Körpers als Grundlage der Frauenkleidung* [The culture of the female body as the basis for women's clothing], Leipzig: Diederichs, 1901.

Schultze-Naumburg, Paul, 'Die Ausstellung "Neue Frauentracht" in Berlin' [The exhihibition 'New Female Dress' in Berlin], *Der Kunstwart: Rundschau über alle Gebiete des Schönen. Monatshefte für Kunst, Literatur und Leben*, vol. 16, issue 2 (second October issue 1902): 60–2.

Schütze, Yvonne, 'Mutterliebe – Vaterliebe. Elternrollen in der bürgerlichen Familie des 19. Jahrhunderts' [Motherly love – fatherly love: parental roles in the nineteenth-century bourgeois family], in Ute Frevert (ed.), *Bürgerinnen und Bürger: Geschlechterverhältnisse im 19. Jahrhundert*, Göttingen: Vandenhoeck & Ruprecht, 1988, pp. 118–33.

Schwarzer, Alice, and Chantal Louis (eds.), *Transsexualität: Was ist eine Frau? Was ist ein Mann? Eine Streitschrift* [Transsexuality: What is a woman? What is a man? A polemic], Cologne: Kiepenheuer & Witsch, 2022.

Sciuto, Cinzia, 'Auf der Suche nach der Identität' [In search of identity], in Alice Schwarzer and Chantal Louis (eds.), *Transsexualität. Was ist eine Frau? Was ist ein Mann? Eine Streitschrift*, Cologne: Kiepenheuer & Witsch, 2022, pp. 158–67.

Seichter, Sabine, *Erziehung an der Mutterbrust: Eine kritische Kulturgeschichte des Stillens* [Education at the mother's breast: a critical cultural history of breastfeeding], Weinheim/Basel: Beltz Juventa, 2014.

Sharpley-Whiting, Tracy Denean, *Black Venus: Sexualized Savages, Primal Fears, and Primitive Narratives in French*, Durham, NC: Duke University Press, 1999.

Shaw, Jennifer L., 'The Figure of Venus: Rhetoric of the Ideal and the Salon of 1863', in Caroline Arscott and Katie Scott (eds.), *Manifestations of Venus: Art and Sexuality*, Manchester / New York: Manchester University Press, 2000, pp. 90–108.

Shaw, Rhonda, 'Performing Breastfeeding: Embodiment, Ethics and the Maternal Subject', *Feminist Review*, vol. 78, no. 1 (2004): 99–116.

Siebler, Kay, 'What's So Feminist about Garters and Bustiers? Neo-burlesque as Post-feminist Sexual Liberation', *Journal of Gender Studies*, vol. 24, no. 5 (2015): 561–73.

Sobiech, Gabriele, and Gian-Claudio Gentile, 'Die Logik der Praxis: Frauenfußball zwischen symbolischer Emanzipation und männlicher Herrschaft' [The logic of practice: women's football between symbolic emancipation and male domination], in Sobiech and Andrea Ochsner (eds.), *Spielen Frauen ein anderes Spiel? Geschichte, Organisation, Repräsentationen und kulturelle Praxen im Frauenfußball*, Wiesbaden: Springer, 2012, pp. 171–94, doi.org/10.1007/978-3-531-19133-1_10.

Solomon-Godeau, Abigail, *Male Trouble: A Crisis in Representation*. London: Thames and Hudson, 1997.

Sömmerring, Samuel Thomas, *Über die Wirkungen der Schnürbrüste* [On the effects of corsets], Berlin: Voß, 1793, www.digitale-sammlungen.de/de/view/bsb10474772?page=1.

Spence, Jo, *Putting Myself in the Picture: A Political, Personal and Photographic Autobiography*, London: Camden Press, 1986.

Sprinkle, Annie, 'Some of My Performances in Retrospect', *Art Journal*, vol. 56, no. 4 (winter 1997): 68–70.

Stannard, Melissa K., and Michelle C. Langley, 'The 40,000-Year-Old Female Figurine of Hohle Fels: Previous Assumptions and New Perspectives', *Cambridge Archaeological Journal*, vol. 31, no. 1 (February 2021): 21–33.

Steele, Valerie, *The Corset: A Cultural History*, New Haven, CT / London: Yale University Press, 2001.

Steidele, Angela, *In Männerkleidern: Das verwegene Leben der Catharina Margaretha Linck alias Anastasius Lagrantinus Rosenstengel, hingerichtet 1721* [In men's clothing: the venturesome life of Catharina Margaretha Linck alias Anastasius Lagrantinus Rosenstengel, executed in 1721], Berlin: Insel Verlag, 2021.

Stelzer, Tanja, 'Die Zumutung des Fleisches' [The impertinence of the flesh], *Tagesspiegel*, 7 December 2003, web.archive.org/web/20210302055306, www.tagesspiegel.de/zeitung/die-zumutung-des-fleisches/471728.html.

Strahsen, Friedrich Christian, *Ueber die Eigenschaften, welche eine gute Amme besitzen muss, und über das Verhalten derselben beim Stillen* [On the qualities a good wet nurse must possess, and on her behaviour while breastfeeding], Riga: Häcker, 1831.

Stratz, Carl Heinrich, *Die Frauenkleidung und ihre natürliche Entwicklung*

[Women's clothing and its natural development], 3rd edn, Stuttgart: Enke, 1904a.

Stratz, Carl Heinrich, *Die Rassenschönheit des Weibes* [The racial beauty of woman], 5th edn, Stuttgart: Ferdinand Enke, 1904b.

Stratz, Carl Heinrich, *Die Rassenschönheit des Weibes* [The racial beauty of woman], 16th and 17th edns, Stuttgart: Enke, 1922.

Sweeney-Risko, Jennifer, 'Fashionable "Formation": Reclaiming the Sartorial Politics of Josephine Baker', *Australian Feminist Studies*, vol. 33, no. 98 (2018): 498–514.

Sykora, Katharina, 'Vom Korsett zum Body-Shaping – Von den Bloomers zu den Jeans. Zum Verhältnis von Mode und Emanzipation' [From corset to body-shaping – from bloomers to jeans: on the relationship between fashion and emancipation], *Frauen, Kunst, Wissenschaft*, issue 17 (May 1994): 30–41, doi.org/10.57871/fkw171994.

Thesander, Marianne, *The Feminine Ideal*, New York: Reaktion Books, 1997.

Thiemann, Susanne, '*Sex trouble*: Die bärtige Frau bei Jusepe de Ribera, Luis Vélez de Guevara und Huarte de San Juan' [Sex trouble: the bearded woman in the work of Jusepe de Ribera, Luis Vélez de Guevara and Huarte de San Juan], in Judith Klinger and Susanne Thiemann (eds.), *Geschlechtervariationen: Gender-Konzepte im Übergang zur Neuzeit*, Universitätsverlag Potsdam, 2006, pp. 47–82.

Thüsing, Gregor, 'Kleiderordnungen' [Dress codes], *JuristenZeitung*, vol. 61, no. 5 (3 March 2006): 223–30.

Toney, René [Joanna Frueh: Interviews with Women Bodybuilders], in Joanna Frueh et al. (eds.), *Picturing the Modern Amazon*, exhibition catalogue, New Museum of Contemporary Art, New York: Rizzoli, 1999, pp. 164–8.

Tönz, Otmar, 'Curiosa zum Thema Brusternährung: Von stillenden Vätern, bärtigen Frauen und saugenden Greisen' [Curiosities on the subject of breastfeeding: on breastfeeding fathers, bearded women and old men sucking on the breast], *Schweizerische Ärztezeitung*, vol. 81, no. 20 (2000): 1058–63.

Tsanana, Evgenia, *Weighted Body Parts*, https://evgeniatsanana.com/works-bodyparts.html.

Tunbridge, W. Michael G., 'La Mujer Barbuda by Ribera, 1631: A Gender Bender', *QJM: An International Journal of Medicine*, vol. 104, no. 8 (August 2011): 733–6, academic.oup.com/qjmed/article/104/8/733/1581997.

Venturi, Riccardo, 'Into the Abyss: On Salvador Dalí's *Dream of Venus*', in

Ana Debenedetti and Caroline Elam (eds.), *Botticelli: Past and Present*, London: UCL Press, 2019, pp. 266–89.

Villa, Paula-Irene, 'Habe den Mut, Dich Deines Körpers zu bedienen! Thesen zur Körperarbeit in der Gegenwart zwischen Selbstermächtigung und Selbstunterwerfung' [Have the courage to use your body! Theses on body work in the present time between self-empowerment and self-subjugation], in Villa (ed.), *Schön normal: Manipulationen am Körper als Technologien des Selbst*, Bielefeld: transcript, 2008, pp. 245–72.

Villa, Paula-Irene, 'Frauen' [Women], in Hannah Fitsch et al. (eds.), *Der Welt eine neue Wirklichkeit geben: Feministische und queertheoretische Interventionen*, Bielefeld: transcript, 2022, pp. 251–63.

Voß, Heinz-Jürgen, 'Biologisches Geschlecht ist ein Produkt von Gesellschaft!' [Biological sex is a product of society!], *Soziologie Magazin*, no. 1 (2013): 87–91, www.europeana.eu/item/2048425/item_XU5TVVX25S6JIFXS3E G34L6MVMLXEIE3.

Wagner, Monika, 'Freiheitswunsch und Frauenbild: Veränderung der "Liberté" zwischen 1789 und 1830' [Desire for freedom and image of women: the transformation of 'Liberté' between 1789 and 1830], in Inge Stephan and Sigrid Weigel (eds.), *Die Marseillaise der Weiber: Frauen, die Französische Revolution und ihre Rezeption*, Hamburg/Berlin: Argument, 1989, pp. 7–36.

Wagner, Monika, *Das Material der Kunst: Eine andere Geschichte der Moderne* [The material of art: a different history of modernity], Munich: Beck, 2001.

Wagner-Hasel, Beate, 'Das Matriarchat und die Krise der Modernität' [The matriarchy and the crisis of modernity], *Feministische Studien*, vol. 9, issue 1 (1991): 80–95.

Wagner-Hasel, Beate, 'Amazonen – Ursprünge eines antiken Mythos' [Amazons – origins of an ancient myth], in Udo Franke-Penski and Heinz-Peter Preußer (eds.), *Amazonen – Kriegerische Frauen*, Würzburg: Königshausen & Neumann, 2010, pp. 19–34.

Walkowitz, Judith R., 'Dangerous Sexualities', in Geneviève Fraisse and Michelle Perrot (eds.), *History of Women in the West*, vol. IV: *Emerging Feminism from Revolution to World War*, Cambridge, MA: Belknap Press of Harvard University Press, 1993, pp. 369–98.

Warner, Marina, *Monuments and Maidens: The Allegory of the Female Form*, London: Vintage, 1985.

Warner, Marina, 'Altes Weib und alte Vettel: Allegorien der Laster' [Old woman and old hag: allegories of the vices], in Sigrid Schade et al. (eds.),

Allegorien und Geschlechterdifferenz, Cologne/Weimar/Vienna: Böhlau, 1994, pp. 51–63.

Warner, Marina, 'The Slipped Chiton', in Londa Schiebinger (ed.), *Feminism and the Body*, Oxford University Press, 2000, pp. 265–92.

Warnke, Martin, 'Politische Ikonographie' [Political iconography], in J. Arrouye and Andreas Beyer (eds.), *Die Lesbarkeit der Kunst: Zu Geistesgegenwart der Ikonologie*, Berlin: Verlag Klaus Wagenbach, 1992, pp. 23–8.

Weibel, Peter, 'Zur Geschichte der Künstlerfotografie, III. Künstlerfotografie in Österreich, 1951–1983, Abschnitt 2' [On the history of art photography, III. Art photography in Austria, 1951–1983, section 2], *Camera Austria*, no. 13 (1984): 46–58.

Welch, Georgia Paige, '"Up Against the Wall Miss America": Women's Liberation and Miss Black America in Atlantic City, 1968', *Feminist Formations*, vol. 27, no. 2 (summer 2015): 70–97.

Welsch, Sabine, *Ein Ausstieg aus dem Korsett: Reformkleidung um 1900* [Escaping the corset: reform clothing around 1900], exhibition catalogue, Mathildenhöhe Darmstadt, Darmstadt: Häusser, 1996.

Wenk, Silke, 'Der öffentliche weibliche Akt: eine Allegorie des Sozialstaates' [The public female nude: an allegory of the welfare state], in Ilsebill Barta et al. (eds.), *Frauen, Bilder, Männer, Mythen: Kunsthistorische Beiträge*, Berlin: Reimer, 1987, pp. 217–38.

Westmann, Stephan, *Frauensport und Frauenkörper: Sportärztliche Betrachtungen eines Frauenarztes* [Women's sport and women's bodies: views of a gynaecologist on sports medicine], Leipzig: Curt Kabitzsch, 1930.

Wierrer, Eugen, *Ueber die Eigenthümlichkeiten des weiblichen Körpers in Bezug auf seine sexuelle Sphäre* [On the peculiarities of the female body in relation to its sexual sphere], Würzburg: Becker, 1870.

Williams, Linda, 'A Provoking Agent: The Pornography and Performance Art of Annie Sprinkle', in Pamela Church Gibson and Roma Gibson (eds.), *Dirty Looks: Women, Pornography, Power*, London: BFI Publishing, 1993, pp. 176–92.

Wolff, Kerstin, 'Eine Bewegung muss sich bewegen können! Die Frauenbewegung und ihr Kleid' [A movement must be able to move! The women's movement and its dress], in Maren C. Härtel et al. (eds.), *Kleider in Bewegung: Frauenmode seit 1850*, catalogue of Historisches Museum Frankfurt am Main, Petersberg: Michael Imhof, 2020, pp. 78–83.

Wright, Alison E., 'The Hottentot Venus: An Alternative Iconography', *British Art Journal*, vol. 14, no. 1 (spring/summer 2013): 59–70.

Yalom, Marilyn, *A History of the Breast*, New York: Knopf, 1997.

Young, Iris Marion, 'Breasted Experience: The Look and the Feeling' [first published 1990], in Young, *On Female Body Experience: 'Throwing like a Girl' and Other Essays*, New York / Oxford: Oxford University Press, 2005, pp. 75–96.

Zeis, Eduard, *Handbuch der plastischen Chirurgie* [Handbook of plastic surgery], Berlin, 1838.

Zenaty, Gerhard, *Sigmund Freud lesen: Eine zeitgemäße Re-Lektüre* [Reading Sigmund Freud: a contemporary rereading], Bielefeld: transcript, 2022.

Zimmermann, Anja, '"Sorry for Having to Make You Suffer": Body, Spectator, and the Gaze in the Performances of Yves Klein, Gina Pane, and Orlan', *Discourse*, vol. 24, no. 3 (autumn 2002): 27–46.

Zimmermann, Anja, 'Wissen und Geschlecht: Ein visuelles Amalgam' [Knowledge and gender: a visual amalgam], *Frauen, Kunst, Wissenschaft*, issue 42 (December 2006; *Wissensstile – Geschlechterstile: Visualisierung, Erkenntnis, Geschlecht*, ed. Anja Zimmermann): 4–7.

Zimmermann, Anja, 'Medien und Metaphern des Schwarzweiß: Geschichte, Geschlecht und Bilderpolitik bei Kara Walker – mit einem kurzen Ausflug zu Cindy Sherman und Zwelethu Mthethwa' [Media and metaphors of black-and-white: history, gender and visual politics in the work of Kara Walker – with a short excursus to Cindy Sherman and Zwelethu Mthethwa], *Frauen, Kunst, Wissenschaft*, issue 43 (June 2007): 10–21.

Zimmermann, Anja, *Ästhetik der Objektivität: Genese und Funktion eines wissenschaftlichen und künstlerischen Stils im 19. Jahrhundert* [Aesthetics of objectivity: genesis and function of a scholarly and artistic style in the nineteenth century], Bielefeld: transcript, 2009.

Zimmermann, Anja, 'Misstrauen Sie der Kunstgeschichte! Transkulturelle Verhandlungen feministischer Ästhetik zwischen "Ost" und "West"' [Don't trust art history! Transcultural negotiations of feminist aesthetics between 'East' and 'West'], in Burcu Doğramacı and Marta Smolińska (eds.), *Re-Orientierung: Kontexte zeitgenössischer Kunst in der Türkei und unterwegs*, Berlin: Kadmos, 2017, pp. 81–98.

Zimmermann, Susan M., *Silicone Survivors: Women's Experiences with Breast Implants*, Philadelphia, PA: Temple University Press, 1998.

Zöllner, Frank, *Botticelli: Toskanischer Frühling* [Botticelli: Tuscan spring], Munich / New York: Prestel, 1998.

Zwierlein, Konrad Anton, *Die Ziege als beste und wohlfeilste Säugamme* [The nanny goat as the best and cheapest wet nurse], Stendal: Franzen & Große, 1816.

Index